That Bitch

Protect Yourself Against Women with Malicious Intent

by
Roy Sheppard
Mary T Cleary

centre

First published in 2007
by Centre Publishing,
PO Box 4168, Radstock, Bath
Somerset, BA3 4WX
England.
Tel: 00 +44 (0) 1761 414541
Fax: 00 +44 (0) 1761 412615
Email: info@ThatBitchBook.com
Web: www.ThatBitchBook.com

A catalogue record of this book is available from the British Library.

Paperback: ISBN 978-1-901534-10-8
Hardback: ISBN 978-1-901534-11-5

Cover photograph by Lev Dolgachov Visit: www.dolgachov.com
Book design and typesetting by Antony Parselle
Cover design by Roy Sheppard

Printed and bound in England by Biddles Ltd

Thank you department

The men and women who were consulted and interviewed for this book have requested anonymity. We have respected their wishes. All the stories and case studies in this book are true. However, some details have been amended to protect the identities of those involved. You all know who you are. Thank you for sharing your personal experiences. Let us all hope that by helping to bring these issues to a much wider audience, others can learn from what you have been forced to endure, at the hands of malicious and vindictive women.

Thank you to all the men who have contacted Amen since we began in 1997 and to all of the staff and volunteers who helped them.

After each draft of the book manuscript was completed, a team of intelligent, open-minded and articulate men and women volunteered to read through it for us. We are incredibly grateful for every one of your insights and comments. Thank you. Your contributions have been invaluable.

In particular, thank you to Peggy Williams, Sophie Kenos, Fiona David and Rosie Tomkins. Rosie was the first person to recognise this book is about healing. A special thanks to Dr. Moosajee Bhamjee. Thank you to Cara Davani and her husband Professor Dave Muller. And, as ever, thanks to Sallie and Geoff Burch for their encouragement and friendship.

Thank you also to Brian Collett, Henry Harington, Alistair Palmer, Curt Tuck and Ian Johnston for their editorial knowledge and judgement. And Joe Robertson. Joe's contribution went far beyond what anyone could reasonably ask from a volunteer. His wisdom, insight and support has been appreciated more than he could imagine. Additional thanks to Kevin Parr, David Cooper and bestselling author Allan Pease for their insights and advice.

Thank you to assistants Dawn Milsom and Carole Pring at Centre Publishing. And last but not least, a huge thank you to Mark *"Marcus Maximus"* Bendle for his technical expertise and for creating the website that accompanies this book.

Table of Contents

She Did *What*? Described as 'domestic terrorists', read these real life, shocking stories of what malicious women have done to innocent male and female victims in order to get what they wanted at the expense of others.

How Women Abuse. The tools of their tyrannical trade. How malicious women so skillfully and covertly inflict physical, emotional, financial and sexual abuse.

Two of a Kind. Meet Ms Truly Evil and Malice in Plunderland. Detailed case studies of two women who preyed on unsuspecting men. And what can be learned by analysing their behaviour and the common mistakes made by their male victims.

The Psychologies of Malice. Personality disorders, sociopathic and psychopathic behaviour. How to recognise the tell-tale signs, tactics and behaviour of these women who may be mad, bad or sad.

Chapter 5

Girlfriend, Wife or History? How some women manipulate men into marriage in such a way that he thinks it was his idea! Why men and women marry. What men must do before they ever 'pop the question'. The pro's and con's of marriage from a male perspective. Pre-nuptial and post-nuptial agreements. And what to do if she refuses to sign one.

Chapter 6

Divorce - The Final Frontier. Why women divorce. What to expect from a vindictive wife. What she is probably advised to do to win a higher settlement. What men must do. What men must NOT do. How to select a lawyer. For any man contemplating divorce, this chapter is must have information.

Chapter 7

Children as Weapons of Male Destruction. How malicious mothers learn to hate their former partners more than they love their children. And how family courts effectively collude with these women to deprive children of contact with their fathers. And why this is tantamount to child abuse.

Chapter 8

Protection Strategies. Coping strategies that work, and those that won't. Why she has picked on you. Assessing your options. How to gather proof to protect yourself against false allegations of physical or sexual abuse. How to recognise, deflect and disarm her covert fighting tactics.

Introduction

They say you should never judge a book by its cover. But did you? And what feelings did it evoke?

You must have wondered many times why so many lovely women end up with men who can only be described as utter bastards. And why so many nice guys marry women who can only be described as absolute bitches?

In simple terms; men and women with no conscience prey on those with too much conscience.

Being a 'nice person' is seen as a character weakness to be exploited. Of course, not all relationships start that way, but when they turn sour, a woman with no conscience seems to have a capacity for cruelty that most of her victims find difficult or impossible to cope with.

This book is about such women and its primary aim is to help 'nice' men and women recognise what is happening to them so they can extract themselves from the clutches of these women, who often punish when no crimes have been committed.

We are defining a bitch as a woman who is prepared to hurt innocent men, women and even children to get her own way. This ruthlessness takes the form of physical, emotional, psychological, sexual or financial abuse. As queens of manipulation and deceit, vindictive women will say or do *anything* to wage war on their chosen victims when they don't get what they want. Many are nothing short of domestic terrorists: Al Qaeda in high-heels and lipstick. These pampered predators, routinely pretend to love their prey.

Some of these women fight dirty, often using covert guerilla tactics to inflict maximum pain for maximum personal gain. Telling lies to the police or playing the victim when they are the aggressor are everyday tricks of their trade, and when they are found out, they instinctively find others to blame. Anybody will do. Nothing is ever *their* fault.

Society, and the law in particular, are conditioned to accept without question that men are always the aggressors and women the victims; even when they are not. It is still relatively straightforward for a nasty woman to destroy a man without having to prove any of her false accusations.

Obviously, some men possess these qualities too. So, in the interests of fairness, a book called *That Bastard: Protect Yourself Against Men with Malicious Intent* is a possible follow-up. All true stories welcome.

If a bitch is ever challenged by a woman who is prepared to stand up for herself, the challenger risks being hounded, humiliated and undermined relentlessly behind her back. When an aggressive or unhappy woman doesn't like what a reasonable man has said to her, her knee-jerk response is to label him a misogynist. Merely disagreeing with such a woman is routinely manipulated by her into an 'attack'. If he tells one person of her wrong-doing he is being 'hateful'. If he tells two or more she will accuse him of mounting a hate campaign against her.

The word misogynist is now used so often by the media and women who declare they are feminists, that it has become built into the vocabulary of society in general. Yet hordes of men-haters (misandrists) exist too. But how often do you hear this word being used against such women? Hardly ever.

During initial research among men and women and before writing began, the title of this book evoked momentary stunned silence. But then it was like a dam bursting as men and women shared countless anecdotes, urban myths, stories about women they knew, women married to friends or women to whom they had been married. We've lost count of the number of men we thought we knew who would add: *"I'm not sure I ever told you this. It was a long time ago. But I was married once before – she was crazy. "* Then they would recount horrendous stories of extreme and totally unfounded jealousy, irrational and violent behaviour, false allegations of abuse, manipulation and malice.

When asked who they would choose to call '*That Bitch*', most came up with at least one woman. This response seems to sum up what we heard from a lot of people:

> *I can think of someone easily. She's a client. She is vile. Horrible. She has no redeeming features about her whatsoever.*

How many can you think of?

When asked to think of men who could be put into the same category, most men and women actually struggled. One said: *"Even my ex-husband doesn't come close to these women!"*

Everyone seems to know at least one of the women this book is about. But confront a bitch and you run a high risk of becoming the target of her venom. Many potential victims take the view that it's probably better to keep a low profile and let her pick on someone else. As a society, therefore, we let them get away with it. Abusive, vindictive women are 'the elephant in the room'. Everyone knows its there, but no one is prepared to say so.

> *The world is a dangerous place to live, not because of the people who are evil, but because of the people who don't do anything about it.* Albert Einstein

Some manipulative behaviours are certainly shared by male and female abusers, although dealing with a woman, especially when you are a man, often requires a very different approach. A lot of men in particular need help. This book aims to provide that help.

This book is a journey. In the next few chapters we share many true, and often horrific stories of how innocent men, women and children are abused by malicious women. Then we focus on what the reader can do to minimise the chances of becoming involved with such women. This is followed by specific guidance on what to do to protect yourself against physical threats to your safety, false allegations which may or may not involve the police. Some of this information is specific to married men. In the last two chapters we explore ways to look forward into the future, and regain one's self-esteem and self-confidence to lead a happier and more fulfilling life without her.

> *When a man gives his opinion, he's a man. When a woman gives her opinion, she's a bitch.* Bette Davis

Bitches hurt people. They harm countless decent, hard-working, honest and genuinely innocent women, children and men; sometimes very badly, occasionally fatally, and they'll infect anyone who stands in their way.

Being a bitch has become an aspiration for many. So how do you learn about the intricacies of being a bitch? Easy. You can read countless articles in women's glossy magazines, newspapers and a growing number of books on the subject.

And if you're in Moscow, why not attend a night school class on bitchology run by the husband and wife team Vladimir and Yevgenia Rakovsky?

How many young women in particular now think it is acceptable to be rude and disrespectful, especially to men?

> *I'm tough. I'm ambitious. And I know what I want. If that makes me a bitch, okay.* Madonna

Some want to know how to *"Treat a man mean to keep him keen"*, while others are more interested in living the designer lifestyle, paid for by a man. They will do whatever is necessary to get what they want. She will trample over anyone. If that means making the most of her intellect or sex appeal, she will, for as long as she can.

Some women even admit to 'behaving like men' to get what they want. Although the actress Dame Edith Evans once said:

> *When a woman behaves like a man, why can't she behave like a **nice** man?*

How many of these wannabe bitches don't really want to behave badly? Are they perhaps more interested in ensuring they don't get hurt themselves? They may be constructing these bitch shields to cover up anxiety, insecurity, low self-esteem or a lack of genuine self-confidence. The aspirational bitch may think: *"I won't let anyone get close. That way I can't be hurt. Lashing out is my best defence. I will be respected – and feared."*

If you have been the victim of a nasty woman, you may recognise some, if not all, of the following:

- You didn't realise what was being done to you until it was too late and the damage had already been done.
- While licking your wounds, you look back and feel angry for not recognising what she was up to, and you ask yourself: *"How could I have been so stupid?*
- It is made worse when you then remember that your initial gut instinct told you something wasn't quite right about her.
- However, she seemed so incredibly friendly, charismatic, vivacious, sensuous and sexy; your instincts had to be wrong!
- She was brilliant at playing on your sympathy and pity by claiming to be the victim, when all along she was setting you up to be her next one.
- Was she a *'drain'* rather than a *'radiator'*? A drain is ultra-needy, someone who has the knack of making you feel down or worn out just by being in her company. You tend to be relieved when she leaves, or gets off the phone to you. She'll keep talking about herself and dumping on you, but you don't have the heart to tell her to stop. Everything is *'Poor me'*, *'Life is so unfair.'* A *radiator* is the opposite, always making you feel good about yourself. But be warned; some highly charismatic *radiators* are *drains* in disguise.
- If you tried to confront her, did she give you a guilt-trip for thinking such shameful things about her? Did you then beat yourself up a little more for thinking she could be as bad as you suspected?
- Have you ever been through weeks, months or even years of questioning your own sanity, after coming into contact with such a woman?
- Sometimes she attacks others quite visibly, but mostly she causes mayhem by using covert tactics; lying, cheating, deceiving and conniving.
- She is an expert at the put-down. She believes that putting-down others will somehow lift her up. She has no qualms

about doing so among friends, or other company, because she delights in making you and those around you squirm with embarrassment. Complain and she retorts: *"Don't be so silly. That's typical of you to over-react."* Or she maintains: *"I was only joking."*

- You go over and over in your mind exactly how she could possibly have interpreted the various things you said to her in all innocence, in the ways she did.
- Has she implied that for some spurious, unprovable reasons you are not fit to spend time with your own children?
- She is never wrong – about anything. Being right all the time is the only thing that matters to her.
- Yet she is the first to blame others for their shortcomings.
- She doesn't want a conversation, she wants an audience.
- She rarely, if ever, has a kind word to say about anyone. Hearing what she says about her friends begs the question: *"What does she say about me?"*
- She is always too busy to do anything for others.
- She breaks promises. You can't rely on her to do what she says. Often this is her way of exerting power in a relationship.
- She lives moment-to-moment and will say whatever she needs to say in that moment to get what she wants.
- She was highly judgmental and critical of others, often for no apparent reason.
- No matter how committed you were, no matter how much you did to help her, you never quite did enough.
- She rarely, if ever, complimented anyone, unless she wanted something in return.
- She expected you to be at her beck and call all the time. She always got her own way and did whatever was necessary to win.
- At the end was she one of the most cold-hearted people you have ever met? It was almost as though she had the capacity to flick the 'off' switch to her emotions, if she had any real ones to start with.
- When she got found out, she just moved on to her next unsuspecting target.

- Trying to reason with her was often a lesson in futility. It was a waste of your breath.
- Finally, the one thing that has kept you awake at night has been the question: *"Why did she pick on me?"*

Her targets are invariably unsuspecting 'nice' men and women, who are the least likely to confront, fight back or question her unreasonable behaviour.

If you can identify with any of the above, this book is definitely for you.

> *A good part - and definitely the most fun part of being a feminist is about frightening men.* Julie Burchill

Chapter 1

She Did **What?**

"Sugar and spice and all things nice – that's what little girls are made of."
Well, not all of them stay that way when they grow up. We have heard
countless stories of ruthless, cruel behaviour by the *'fairer, gentle sex'*.

False allegations against men are particularly poisonous, because
they hurt other women too, especially the genuine victims of domestic violence and rape, the most heinous of all violent crimes.

Consider rape accusations. Only 5 per cent of rape cases lead to
the conviction of the rapist. By definition this means that 95 per
cent of accused men go free. It is a travesty of justice when rapists
get away with their brutality, but what proportion of men accused
of rape were actually innocent all along? How many men are accused
of rape by women who agreed to have sex but simply regretted doing so later? Nobody can say, but those innocent men become the
victims, not their accusers. And how many of their false accusers are
prosecuted for their lies? Hardly any.

Take the case of the man who had been a licensed cab driver for 35 years. This man, a grandfather, worked nights near Glasgow taking home the drunk and the occasional disorderly character, the noisy, those who threw up inside his cab, and those who dropped cigarette butts that burnt holes in his upholstery.

At about 3am he picked up two women in their early twenties outside a well-known nightclub. They had had a great night out with their girlfriends. He dropped the first one outside her home and took the other to her home, a couple of miles away. The moment he stopped the cab she ripped open her blouse and bra and screamed at the top of her voice: *"Rape! Rape! I'm being raped!"* Two men heard her screams and rushed to her aid. They dragged the driver from his cab, punched and pinned him to the ground, while one of them called the police. They held him down until the police arrived.

The cab driver was taken in handcuffs to a police station. His cab was impounded while he was kept in custody for days being interviewed for hours on end. All the while he protested he had not touched the woman. Under police questioning he claimed that during the journey he had even tried to warn the women about some of the more unsavoury men who frequented that nightclub. He had picked them up in the past and knew what he was talking about. He also told them about his grand-children. The police didn't (or couldn't be seen to) believe him.

From that moment, nobody else seemed to believe him either. The cab company had prided itself in its marketing that it was the firm to trust. Its advertising even offered single women the 'safe way home'.

News spread. This man was now a rapist. He explained to a colleague that the idea you are innocent until proven guilty was a myth. It may apply to other crimes he said, but not when a man is accused of rape.

Out of the blue he was told that all charges had been dropped. The police would not be prosecuting him for rape, or any other crime. *"Why?"* he asked.

They had been told that the father of the first woman had

asked her what she knew. He persisted when she clammed up. Eventually she burst into tears and said: *"Dad, all she did was try to get out of paying the fare. What's wrong with that?"*

The cabbie has never driven his taxi since.

Warren Blackwell, a 36-year-old father of two, came off even worse. He was arrested, convicted and jailed for sexual assault and rape. He always maintained his innocence. His wife stood by him throughout. He served three years as a convicted rapist. Then in July 2006 he was released after a detailed investigation by the Criminal Cases Review Commission concluded he was innocent all along.

Who can imagine the horrors he had to endure because of the evil actions of the woman, whose identity was protected under British law while his name was published repeatedly in the national press? Even the woman's mother described her as *"A persistent liar, very manipulative and a bully."* It emerged that the woman had a history of making serious false allegations. To date she has not been prosecuted.

British law allows an accused man to be named in the media but guards the identity of a rape victim or supposed victim. When an outraged peer used parliamentary privilege to name this woman in the House of Lords, the woman, who had since changed her name, complained that he had violated her privacy.

How many other innocent men have had their lives wrecked because anonymous accusers make false allegations and get away with it?

And how many of these dishonest women make it even more difficult for genuine rape victims to secure convictions against their vicious attackers?

In early 2007 Emma Golightly was jailed for two years in Newcastle upon Tyne for conning men out of £250,000 ($500,000). She was described as a serial liar who created the perfect illusion of everything a man would want from a woman, specifically to extract cash from them. In an article in *The Mail on Sunday*, Stephen Keenan, her 24-year-old fiancé said: *"I couldn't believe my luck that someone with her background would be interested in an ordinary working man like me – I really thought I had hit the jackpot."*

She was not what she claimed. She created a web of lies to deceive various men. She said she had a highly paid job and was the daughter of a millionaire High Court judge. She said she was born in South Africa and educated in Dallas, and attended university at 16 because she was so intelligent. In reality, she lived in a shabby bedsit in a poor part of Newcastle with her mother, who she claimed was her stepmother because her mother had died of cancer. Golightly also had a child that she didn't mention. She told Keenan she had been married but her husband raped her at the age of 17, that she was pushed down some stairs and lost her twin babies.

To another man she claimed to be a millionaire but was suffering from terminal cancer and wanted to marry before she died.

One of her victims recounted that many of her stories related to highly sensitive, personal matters, which no decent man would ever insist she prove.

But like so many women of this type, she played the sympathy card almost perfectly. When Keenan attended court the day she was sentenced, he is reported as saying it was like attending a funeral. The difference was that the woman he had loved had not died – she had never existed.

Golightly broke the law and went to jail for it, but it is still possible to extract millions from men when you know how to use the law to your advantage.

> *Women complain about PMS, but I think of it as the only time of the month I can be myself.* Roseanne Barr

In 2007 one of the highest-profile divorces in the UK was between Heather Mills, allegedly a former call girl and Sir Paul McCartney, the British music icon. Who will ever know the truth about their relationship?

Men who grew up listening to *The Beatles* are prepared to accept that McCartney is a highly gifted *'good bloke'*. Could he possibly be the ogre Ms Mills has claimed he is in the tabloid press?

Ms Mills' father, who once served a prison sentence for fraud, has described his own daughter as a liar for making unsubstantiated allegations of sexual abuse against him in her autobiography. Ms Mills has also been criticised by the police for making too many unnecessary emergency phone calls. Did she make up the stories? And how economical with the truth has she been while using the legal system to extract as much money as possible from McCartney?

Morality and fairness has no place in matrimonial law, it seems.

Because of some of the astronomical financial settlements being handed out in the divorce courts, how many ordinary, honest, decent, young and ambitious men are concluding that marriage isn't worth the financial risk any more? After all, 57 per cent of British marriages now end in divorce.

No entrepreneurial man would invest in a business start-up in which the risk-reward ratio was so stacked against him. It's worth remembering that marriage is a business partnership according to the law, and when divorce breaks it in two, the partners must share all the wealth created while it was intact. Is it any wonder that more men are questioning the idea of making a commitment to a woman when he has potentially so much more to lose than she does?

The desire for children in a relationship is not always in synchronisation. A proportion of women ignore the man's feelings and make the decision to get pregnant without consultation.

Anecdotally, a high proportion of fathers admit they merely go along with the idea of having children when their partners persuade them. It's after the birth that they wake up to the wonders of parenting. But not always. Yet, by law a man must pay to support the mother and his offspring, even though he had no say in what happened.

> A now-divorced woman 'complained' that her new husband was less than pleased to hear the news that she was pregnant. His instant reaction was: *"You need to have an abortion."* She claimed it was an accident and went ahead with the pregnancy.

She ended the relationship soon after the child was born. The man was relieved that he was not pursued for child support. But she now had what she wanted; a child to love her unconditionally. The government effectively became the child's father, and paid for everything she needed, including somewhere to live.

A couple of years later the same woman became involved with another man and moved in with him. She was in her early thirties with a two-year-old and wanted another child 'before it was too late'. Time for another accident. She claimed her new partner also insisted on an abortion but she went ahead with the pregnancy all the same. Soon after this child was born, she also walked out on this partner. But this time she pursued him through the courts to force him into providing child support. Her overall income was topped up with payments from the British government.

Neither man had any say in becoming a father, and this woman selfishly satisfied her own urges at her partners' and the taxpayers' expense.

In the United States, Dr Sharon Irons was accused by Dr Richard O. Phillips of a *"calculated, profound, personal betrayal."* after an affair six years earlier. She allegedly yearned to be a mom. Her approach, if true, was inventive, to say the least. He claimed she secretly kept his sperm after oral sex, then used it to get pregnant. She issued a paternity lawsuit against him. He claimed she stole his sperm. The court ruled it was a gift!

Research conducted for the Marriage and Relationship Counselling Service (MRCS) in 2006 found women are more likely than men to perpetrate domestic violence. This report, based on a survey of 530 MRCS clients, found mutual violence accounts for 33 per cent of domestic cases, female-perpetrated violence 41 per cent, and male-perpetrated violence 26 per cent. Some women's organisations need to perpetuate the myth that all men are a threat to women, just to qualify for the vast sums of public money to fund their work. If they do not maintain the victim status of women, the cash will stop. By refusing to acknowledge the true extent of violence perpetrated on men by women, these organisations effectively deprive male victims of the help they need and deserve. They too, are abusing innocent men.

In the UK about 150 people are murdered every year by a partner or ex-partner. But how many are men who have been murdered by their wives, ex-wives or girlfriends? The statistics are surprising. When men and women are asked this question, the average answer is *"probably three or four"*. They aren't even close. The accurate answer is nearer 30. Still a minority, but 20% is not insignificant.

These women do not destroy the lives of just their victims.

> *"I am a mother. My heart is broken. My handsome son was the victim of domestic violence. His long-time girlfriend of seven years murdered him on July 7, 2002. He was aged 25 years. He had suffered severe violence at her hands prior to his death but was too ashamed to admit to it openly.*
>
> *At the Old Bailey in March 2003 she was sentenced to three and a half years in prison, having previously denied all knowledge of what happened and then claiming self-defence. When the police proved both claims as lies she pleaded diminished responsibility.*
>
> *She served 21 months for her crime and is now walking the streets without remorse knowing she beat the system."*

This lady's daughter, the victim's sister, wrote her side of the story in a UK *Cosmopolitan* article in November 2004.

She described how Sonia, the girlfriend, was something of a loner thanks to a difficult childhood. She seemed angry at the world in general and became guarded, prickly and agitated whenever she was challenged by a question, however innocent.

Because she was so insecure, distrusting and jealous, her brother, Peter took on the role of 'looking after her'. Despite his kindness and caring attitude she would snap at him, scream and constantly berate him over the most insignificant things. Once he arrived at the family home covered in cuts and bruises.

Sonia convinced herself that her boyfriend was seeing other women, even though he wasn't. She threatened to stab him if she discovered he was cheating on her. She made him feel sorry for her but he was not happy. The guilt became the glue that held them together.

Peter's father tried to warn him off by saying that such people never change. If she was causing him grief then, it would happen again and again. But he continued to defend her and make excuses for her behaviour.

All the while, the life seemed to drain out of him as he became increasingly frightened of her anger. The sister described how he became a shadow of his former self. He did try to leave her, so she then shredded his clothes.

In July 2002 she stabbed him through the heart with a 4.5 inch kitchen knife. She was arrested but released without charge, claiming the killing was self-defence. However, forensic evidence disproved that because of the angle of the wound. That's when she changed her plea to guilty of manslaughter on the grounds of diminished responsibility.

In court she was described as volatile with a jealous temperament and claimed to have attempted suicide twice since the stabbing. Doctors gave evidence that she was not responsible for her actions before she was found guilty and sentenced.

Without wanting to pump up the figures of women killing men further, here are two more factors to be added into the mix.

We received a call from a distraught male friend. He is intelligent, in his forties, successful, and divorced with three children he adores. He had met a woman via the internet and fallen in love. Initially, things were absolutely fantastic. They were both head-over-heels, even though everything happened more quickly than he would have liked. It was exciting and passionate. He got on famously with her children, and she loved being with his. An instant family of five children. So what was the problem?

His exact words: *"She is driving me crazy. One minute she's all over me, the next she's calling me every name you can think of – and I haven't done anything wrong. I have tried to reason with her. She goes from hot to cold to hot again. I have no idea where I am with her. One minute she wants us to move in together, the next minute she doesn't. She's really doing my head in."*

He continued for half an hour talking about her and how and why he was besotted with her, and what they were planning together. He was certainly under her spell. Then he added *"I felt quite sorry for her too. I've really tried to help her get over it. She'd been with a guy for a couple of years. It was tragic really. He committed suicide."*

He was quietly asked to listen very carefully to what he had just said. There was a loud silence. The penny had dropped.

Who will ever know for sure whether this woman made her former partner's life so miserable that the pain of living was worse than the pain of dying? This friend needed no further convincing. He realised something similar could happen to him. He forced himself to withdraw from the relationship. But the backlash was severe. She turned on him even more viciously than when they'd been 'in love'.

Another woman subjected her husband to such a sustained campaign of hatred, cruelty and psychological torture that he too committed suicide. Then she got everything – and enjoyed all the attention from well-wishers who felt 'so sorry' for her loss.

How many other innocent men have resorted to suicide to escape the clutches of a woman who has made their lives unbearable?

From the Fathers-4-Justice website in the United States (www.f4j.us) comes a tragic end to a story in which an angry mother and the US government unwittingly colluded against an ordinary, normal, average, hard-working guy. This was posted by one of his lawyers:

> *"As a divorce lawyer in Phoenix, Arizona, as a father, and as someone who cares about such things, I feel compelled to tell about a piece of news which brought tears to my eyes when I first heard it today while participating in an unrelated court hearing.*
>
> *I was the second of a series of four attorneys for Randall Couch, a Phoenix architectural consultant. In his long-ago divorce he had been poorly advised by his first attorney to stipulate sole custody to the wife, and to a peculiar stepped-increase child support arrangement. A few years later, his first lawyer, who had been his high school classmate, helped him work out*

a stipulated order in which he and his wife agreed to stop the child support because of the large percentage of time he had each week with his son. But, unbeknownst to Randy, that first lawyer didn't file the agreement with the court.

Years later (last year) the ex-wife decided to go after him by claiming that he owed a huge child support arrearage ($28,000), and alleging that the never filed agreement was void. He hired me as his second lawyer, and after a heavily contested trial a judge ruled against us and found that he owed the $28,000, plus his wife's attorney fees. I withdrew, and Randy hired his third attorney. Several months later he hired his fourth.

With $28,000 judgment in hand, the wife's lawyer seized all of Randy's money from bank accounts, garnished receivables from his architectural clients, had his car taken from him, and most recently, dragged him and his fourth lawyer into court for contempt proceedings.

Randy was ordered to pay $1,500 by noon today, or go to jail.

Last night Randy blew his brains out.

There's a little kid somewhere in Phoenix who will never again spend the majority of the week with his dad. There's an ex-wife who is never going to get the rest of her $28,000 pound of flesh. There's a wife's attorney and a judge in Phoenix who will have to live for the rest of their lives with the weight of this tragedy on their heads.

I was in a hearing before a commissioner this afternoon when I learned of the suicide. I'm not ashamed to say I cried. I've been through and survived some pretty gut-wrenching events in my life as a lawyer, especially over the past months, most especially last week. But nothing like this.

A good man has been sacrificed on the altar of the 'dead-beat dad' mentality. A little bit of all of us died with Randy."
Bob, Phoenix, AZ."

Obviously, not all male suicides are because of women, but statistically men in the UK are three times more likely to kill themselves than women. The government's National Suicide Strategy showed suicide as the biggest cause of death in men under age 35, and 65 per cent of them are fathers. Some of these suicides have been attributed to alleged hounding of even 'good' fathers by the now defunct Child Support Agency (CSA). This agency was set up to protect children but in pursuit of its government targets, some men were robbed by the state to pay money to women who were capable of supporting themselves.

The second point to add here is that if such a woman doesn't want to do something illegal herself, she'll convince someone else to do it for her.

Anthony Riggs, known as *Slowpoke* to his friends and colleagues because of his gentle demeanour, saw military action in Operation Desert Storm in the Persian Gulf in 1991. He fought for his country, but soon after returning he was gunned down and killed outside his own home. His 22 year-old wife, Toni Cato Riggs, appeared distraught. The police caught his killer; his wife's younger brother Michael.

This woman had persuaded her brother to murder her husband in return for half the $20,000 insurance pay-off. This is just one of many horrific examples of women who commit murder recorded by Patricia Pearson, a highly acclaimed feminist writer, in her controversial book, *When She Was Bad: How Women Get Away with Murder*. Pearson tells many thoroughly researched, publicly documented stories of women with malicious intent and articulates fascinating insights into why society, the courts and the media fall into the traps of what she describes as 'chivalry justice'. On the subject of female aggression and the multiple ways women tend to get away with it, this is a must-read book.

Here is a more recent British example. *The Daily Telegraph* reported on December 16, 2006, that 18-year-old Natalie Connor from Manchester was sentenced to life imprisonment after she developed such an obsessive hatred for a school classmate that she persuaded her father to pour petrol through her victim's letterbox at home. The father then set it alight. Within two minutes the hallway was ablaze, with temperatures of more than 1,000 degrees. The classmate, Lucy Cochrane, survived with horrific burns, but, tragically, both her parents were burnt to death.

Natalie Connor's behaviour fits a clearly understood profile that starts with an obsession that gets blown up out of all proportion. When she fails to get her own way, the woman begins a campaign of false allegations. At one point the police arrested Lucy Cochrane on what they later described as *"an entirely false allegation"*. It was when that failed, Connor dragooned family members into doing her dirty work for her.

'Scissor Sisters', Charlotte and Linda Mulhall are now serving long prison sentences in Dublin for chopping up their male victim into small pieces, cutting off his penis and dumping his body into a canal. The head of their mother's boyfriend and his penis are thought to have been buried somewhere in a park and have never found. Passing sentence, Mr Justice Carney said: *"This is the most grotesque of killings that has occurred within my professional lifetime."* Valerie Solanas, the late founder of SCUM (The Society for Cutting Up Men) would no doubt, be proud of these women.

Poison also seems the weapon of choice for many murderesses. Incredibly, they are not always discovered because these 'loving' women aren't considered as murder suspects by the police.

Clearly, men are not the only perpetrators of violence. But society doesn't want to acknowledge that women kill more children than men and that mothers are statistically more likely to abuse their children.

Men are statistically the *least* likely to abuse their children, but try convincing a family judge of that when a mother has falsely alleged that 'her' children (not 'their' children), are unsafe with the father even when he has no history of such behaviour.

> Even though she was capable of washing herself, one of her parents insisted on using a scrubbing brush to clean her genitals vigorously. They were dirty, she was told. She was 'cleaned' so thoroughly and so regularly that she would bleed because her skin became raw. The little girl was also cleaned inside with a rough flannel.

> The abuser was her mother. This mother was a cruel, cold-hearted, sadistic bitch, the commandant of her own private, domestic concentration camp. The rest of the family stood by as the torture of the girl was allowed to continue.

They may have disapproved, but learnt to look the other way. They did nothing to protect her. The sibling who said anything could be the next persecution victim. So beatings, humiliation, threats, put-downs and intense anger continued. Other physical and psychological abuse was a daily occurrence. When the girl was three, her mother gave her an LSD tablet 'for a laugh'.

For her mother, she could do nothing right. If she did as she was asked or told, her mother would change her mind to ensure that she failed.

As a teenager, this girl sought comfort from food. She became chubby. This started a whole new chapter in her life. She was made to feel ugly for being overweight and was told repeatedly by her mother that boys would never find her attractive. She was forced to 'exercise' in her underwear in front of the family.

In her teenage years she found a way to lose masses of weight, even though gorging on comfort foods continued. She learnt to purge herself daily, sometimes more often. Her bulimia served her purposes – she now had at least some control of her own life and the weight fell off. Unfortunately, the prolonged purging caused irreparable damage to her stomach and throat. Yet boys were attracted to her and mother was wrong again.

Perhaps the boys were keen on her for the wrong reasons though. As a passive, quiet and withdrawn girl, she 'accommodated' them more than she felt comfortable with, but they gave her the attention and intimacy she craved. Getting pregnant was not part of the plan, and when her mother found out, her reaction was predictably savage and vicious. Her *"darling little girl"* instantly became a *"disgusting slut"*. The girl's self-esteem by this time was all but destroyed. But surely, she reasoned, the unborn child would give her all the love she desired. She was forced into having an abortion.

Nevertheless, she was academically bright and won a place at a good university, where she could indulge her intellectual passions. She experimented with drugs and booze and for a time found solace and comfort among her gay sisters. Her mother was homophobic and described how ashamed she was of her 'dyke daughter'.

The girl's traumatised childhood led her to develop close relationships with some special friends, her 'protection squad'. Sadly, these friends lived inside her head, seven of them in all. Fortunately, most would leave quietly by the time she was 40. Her therapist called her condition MPD (multiple personality disorder), now better known as DID (dissociative identity disorder).

This woman met a kind man, who did his best to deal with her problems. They married, but it was tough for him. He wasn't a therapist, though he needed to be at times. Sex with the woman he loved was impossible due to the various personalities he knew lurked inside her; an aggressive lesbian who wanted nothing to do with any man, even a kind and loving one, and, even worse, a six-year-old girl.

The husband's lack of physical interest was seen as a wholesale rejection, an invalidation of the woman she was working so hard to become. After ten years, her pent-up rage exploded and the marriage collapsed. Was it just a coincidence that the six-year-old girl inside her had grown into an intensely angry rebellious teenager?

Now that she is a middle-aged woman, with young children of her own, she suffers the continuing torment of not knowing whether the mental problems she has been plagued with all her life are due to her mother's genetic make-up, (and what that could mean for her own children), or the LSD tablet that she is still convinced 'fried her brain'. A cruel confusion. One can only hope she has now found true, lasting happiness.

Damage caused by cruel mothers often gets passed like a baton in an inter-generational relay race.

In Poestlingberg, Austria, an horrific story emerged in October 2005. For seven years a divorced mother kept her three daughters locked up in almost complete darkness. As a lawyer, she successfully won residence and did everything she could to ensure her former husband, a local judge, could never see them. Despite his own detailed legal knowledge, the father repeatedly failed in court to win the right to see his girls. The local authorities allegedly received repeated complaints from neighbours but they were ignored. The mother outmanoeuvred everyone.

When the authorities eventually removed the girls and took them into care, they found indescribable filth at the house, excrement at least a metre deep and no running water. Floors and pipes had been corroded by rodent urine. The girls were six, 11 and 13 at the beginning of their ordeal. Even after prolonged specialist therapy, the development of these young women is described as *"truly catastrophic"*. Experts fear that the eldest is so traumatised that she will never recover. During their ordeal the girls learnt to communicate in their own language. In care they could not bear sunlight and huddled together under a kitchen table for protection.

Could these examples be dismissed as non-representative of the 'truer' picture, in which men are always the aggressors and women the victims, as perpetuated by so many feminist groups? No.

Warren Farrell Ph.D, the author of fascinating book *The Myth of Male Power* is the only man in the United States who has been elected three times to the board of directors of the National *Organization for Women* in New York City. He says *"I'm a 100% supporter of the portions of feminism that are empowering to women and a 100% opponent of the portions that hone victimhood as a fine art"*. Farrell believes *"All women's issues are to some degree men's issues and all men's issues are to some degree women's issues because when either sex wins unilaterally both sexes lose."* He warns *"In America and in most of the industrialized world, men are coming to be thought of by feminists in very much the same way that Jews were thought of by early Nazis. The comparison is overwhelmingly scary."*

Germaine Greer, the doyenne of feminism, wrote in *Marie Claire* in December 2006: *"Feminism has become the new F-word. Nobody wants to be caught using it. But it has always been like this – partly because the media have always presented feminism as an extreme, humourless, anti-men, anti-motherhood, pro-abortion minority movement. We've got very used to hearing women airing their grievances, prefacing them with 'I'm not a feminist, but ...'"*

How many women hide behind this cloak of feminism when the only thing they are really interested in is their own personal, short-term self-interest? And damn anyone, male or female, who gets in their way.

Greer went on: *"Feminism ... exists in questioning and challenging and in defence of all women who are being abused, whether bashed by their partners, humiliated by religion, wrongly accused of killing their babies, forced into prostitution, or persecuted and exploited in the workplace, whether it be a brothel or the civil service. Feminism exists to fight misogyny wherever it is found, and **especially in the hearts of women themselves.**"* (Bold text added)

What fair-minded human being, male or female, cannot wholeheartedly agree with that?

All abuse of women should stop. But so should all abuse of men. As Mary T Cleary, co-author of this book, often says: *"It's also a crime to beat a man."*

““ *A great many people think they are thinking when they are merely rearranging their prejudices.* ””
William James (1842-1910)

In the chapters that follow you will learn how malicious women find and target their victims, how they build and misuse trust to get what they want and in so many cases inflict harm when they don't succeed.

During our research, a male victim of malicious behaviour made this remark: *"It made me realise how lucky I am in a perverse way. I had only ever known nice, genuine, honest people up until that point. Most people I know are just not equipped to deal with this type of deplorable and despicable behaviour."*

Once these women are recognised for who and what they are, it may become easier for men and women to know how to stand up to them, when and how to report them to the relevant authorities, and how to say: *"No. Enough is enough."*

In the same spirit, may we offer you two options as you read the rest of this book. You can use your intelligence to be open-minded about what you read, and accept that the research and the examples given at least show that something is very wrong when we allow these extreme women to continue causing untold misery to hundreds of thousands of innocent men, women and children. The other option is to use your intellect to reinforce what you already think or believe.

> *The mind of a bigot is like the pupil of the eye. The more light you shine on it, the more it will contract.*
> Oliver Wendell Holmes

Chapter 2

How Women Abuse

" *Eve is reputed to be the world's first deceitful woman. But things could have been so much worse for Adam. She could have had a lawyer.* Roy Sheppard "

When anyone mentions domestic violence, we instantly think of battered women. People believe women are always the victims and the patriarchal model of feminist ideology perpetuates this view.

However, if women are not guilty of physical violence, despite mountains of evidence to the contrary, how does one explain the high numbers of co-habiting lesbian victims of domestic violence?

And what of the other victims of domestic violence – straight men and children? These casualties of physical and emotional attacks are discriminated against by governments in practically every 'civilised' country you can name.

Erin Pizzey, who set up the world's first shelter for battered women in Chiswick, London, has some startling statistics. A 1975 study of 100 women who visited the shelter found that 62 per cent who were being protected also participated in mutually violent relationships. Many of the women were more violent than their male partners. *"Time and again,"* said Pizzey, *"I've dealt with men who are physically attacked by women."*

Domestic violence is more complicated than the stereotyped scene of a victim and a perpetrator. Threats of physical, sexual, psychological, mental or emotional violence are started and finished by men and women equally. The belief that men are the main perpetrators is simply incorrect.

Yet innocent men are routinely removed from their homes by the police merely on the basis of false allegations against them by their wives or co-habiting partners. Men are not given opportunities to contest such allegations or insist that their accusers provide proof. These men may have no alternative accommodation and some are made homeless. Without a home they can't get a job, and without a job they can't meet financial obligations either to themselves or to their estranged children. In these circumstances, women who are prepared to tell lies wield enormous power against the men in their lives.

When such threats are directed at women they are regarded as serious crimes. When the same threats are directed at men, they are not. Even worse, men are often ridiculed, ignored or simply disbelieved by the police and social services.

In this climate most men don't report incidents in which they have suffered even serious abuse. If these men require hospital treatment, they protect their aggressor by claiming to have had an accident. It's remarkable how so many of these men seem to have fallen down the stairs or walked into a door!

This well-meaning cover-up behaviour is misplaced, particularly as it harms other men too. Domestic violence statistics are based on reported incidents and official figures show that more men attack women. The data will remain skewed until all men report women for violent behaviour against them.

Women are as aggressive as men; as the next few pages demonstrate conclusively. Anyone who claims anything different is lying, has an ulterior motive, or simply does not have accurate data to back up their claims.

In July 2005 the National Crime Council (NCC), in association with the Economic and Social Research Institute (ESRI), published the first large-scale study undertaken to give an overview of the nature, extent and impact of domestic abuse against women and men in intimate partner relationships in Ireland. Among the notable findings are:

• 29 per cent of women and 26 per cent of men suffer domestic abuse where severe and minor abuse are combined.
• 13 per cent of women and 13 per cent of men suffer physical abuse.
• 29 per cent of women (one in three) but only five per cent of men (one in 20) report abuse to the police.

This study broadly reflects the findings of three other two-sex studies carried out in Ireland, for ACCORD, the Marriage and Relationship Counselling Service (MRCS) and the Department of Health.

The MRCS report in 2001, based on a survey of 530 clients, found that mutual domestic violence accounts for 33 per cent of cases, female-perpetrated violence 41 per cent, and male-perpetrated violence 26 per cent.

Similarly, the ACCORD research in 2003, based on a survey of 1,500 clients, found women were perpetrators in 30 per cent of domestic violence cases, men were perpetrators in 23 per cent, and mutual violence accounted for 48 per cent. An interesting feature of this study, in which couples attended counselling, was that 84 per cent of women and 74 per cent of men agreed with their partner's response to this question, suggesting that the self-reported prevalence is reliable.

In 1997 Mary T Cleary set up Amen to help male victims of domestic violence. She reports that since then every two-sex study in Ireland and abroad has vindicated Amen's position that a significant number of men are victims of domestic abuse.

In the UK, adult patients attending the emergency department of Addenbrooke's Hospital, Cambridge, were interviewed in randomly allocated time blocks, using validated questions from an American study. Altogether 256 completed interviews were returned out of a possible 307. The incidence of domestic violence was 1.2 per cent. The lifetime prevalence of domestic violence was 22.4 per cent among men and 22.1 per cent among women.

Still in the UK, the BBC's *Here and Now* programme commissioned a poll undertaken by MORI, which interviewed a representative quota sample of 1,978 adults. These were the main findings:

- One in five, or 18 per cent, of men have been victims of domestic violence by a wife or female partner, as opposed to 13 per cent of women by a man.
- One in nine women admit using physical aggression against a husband or male partner, compared with one in ten men.
- 14 per cent of men say they have been slapped by a partner, compared with 9 per cent of women.
- 11 per cent of men have known a partner to threaten to throw something heavy at them, compared with 8 per cent of women.

In the United States doctors reported on domestic violence among male patients attending a hospital emergency department in Philadelphia over 13 weeks. They wanted to establish the prevalence of the violence committed by women against their men. And what did they find? The incidence was staggering.

Of 866 men interviewed 109 (12.6 per cent) had been the victims of domestic violence at the hands of a female intimate partner within the preceding year. The most common assaults were slapping, grabbing and shoving, applying to 60.6 per cent of victims. These were followed by choking, kicking, biting, and punching (48.6 per cent), and the throwing of objects (46.8 per cent). 37 per cent of cases involved a weapon.

Seven per cent of victims said they were forced to have sex, 19 per cent contacted the police, 14 per cent required medical attention, 11 per cent pressed charges or sought a restraining order, and 6 per cent had follow-up counselling.

The final calculation was that almost 13 per cent of the men in this sample population had had domestic violence visited on them by a female intimate partner within the previous year.

In Canada the National Statistics Office estimated in its 2004 social survey that 7 per cent of people had experienced spousal violence in the previous five years. The figures were 7 per cent for women victims and 6 per cent for men, representing an estimated 653,000 women and 546,000 men.

A slap, a punch, a push, scratching, a knee in the groin, being strangled, smothered in your sleep, being stabbed and being struck with an implement are all forms of overt aggression or physical abuse. Overt aggression is the easiest type to identify, mainly from the evidence it leaves, including cuts, abrasions, stab wounds and, in extreme cases, dead bodies. Overt aggressive behaviour is therefore the most likely form of abuse to be proven, in court or elsewhere. It is less easy to prove cases of covert aggression, the abusive behaviour that is more psychological or emotional.

Generally speaking, an abusive woman is inclined to use covert aggressive behaviour. Because covert aggression is harder to prove, a malicious woman who has mastered the skills required, gets away with it more often. The following stories are all true, although names and identifiable details have been altered to ensure anonymity.

Before you read these examples, here is an important insight. While researching this book we were initially concerned that nobody would want to tell us anything. The men, we thought, might be too embarrassed, or even afraid to talk to us, in case anything got back to the women involved. However, it's almost as if everyone we spoke to had an horrific or bemusing story of an experience or encounter with a malicious or wildly abusive woman. Many of the stories are anything but bemusing. Many are starkly factual case studies of men who have been helped by Amen. Appropriately, Mary Cleary relates the stories.

For many years I worked as a nurse in a hospital casualty department, where I met a variety of men who came in for treatment. Some of them had cuts, bruises, scratches, broken bones, even stab wounds, all of which they claimed were 'accidents'.

Something didn't ring true for me. As part of my job, I would travel with a paramedic team to homes where injuries had been reported. Gradually I built up a clear picture of how men were so often the victims of domestic violence, though nobody was prepared to accept that it was possible. Women are 'always' the victims. Feminist groups have rigorously reinforced this view in the media for decades, but I saw at first-hand that men are just as likely as women to suffer domestic violence and abuse.

Since 1997 when I and a small team of volunteers created Amen, we have collected and catalogued the stories of predominantly Irish men who were often too embarrassed to report constant abuse. We put together a 60-page booklet of letters telling their stories. It is painful reading. The heartache, frustration and the lack of support, care and understanding by the authorities seeps out of every page. The booklet also includes letters from women in despair, appreciating that they have a problem with their violence, which they seem incapable of controlling.

What we have learnt about domestic violence based on our gender-neutral approach is equally relevant in every other country in the world. But remedies can't happen without adequate funding, and most, if not all grants for domestic violence issues go to women's groups. In my view, that remains a travesty.

The vast majority of *recorded* domestic violence incidents are of men on women. Society, although aware of the male victim, treats him as a joke. He is a man in fear, a man in isolation, a man stigmatised as weak. Why? Because he does not conform to the stereotypical male image.

In law, a male victim faces two obstacles. First, he must prove he is a victim, and second, he must ensure that his children are protected and do not become the new victims. Men often remain in an abusive relationship to protect their children, and most of them choose silence. Frequently this silence is encouraged by factors such as fear of ridicule and the realisation that the woman is unlikely to be evicted. Even when a man has proved that he is the victim, it seems that his only course of action is to leave the home. He is then separated from his children and he often has difficulty in obtaining regular and meaningful contact with them. Thus he is treated as the perpetrator rather than the victim.

That is not the only injustice. Modern medicine is aware of certain conditions that may cause people to be violent but we expect such sufferers to seek help or medical treatment. Men are told to take responsibility for their violence and abuse and no excuses are accepted. Yet when a female is violent, society provides a list of excuses. Take your pick from post-natal depression, stress, PMT, eating disorders, personality disorders, menopause, addictions, childhood traumas, provocation and self-defence. Although most men will be sensitive to these problems, they should not have to endure violence as a consequence.

Parenthood is viewed in an unequal way too. When a woman is violent and abusive in a relationship, she is not necessarily assumed to be a bad mother. If a man is violent towards his partner, it is automatically assumed that he is an unfit parent. The law almost always presumes that the children are better off with their mother. The only options for men seem to be either to put up with the abuse, or to leave the home. The law gives them no real protection.

If a male victim seeks help, society should offer the same protection and support to him and his children as is given to female victims. Women should be judged by the same standards as men, and women who are violent should be held accountable for their actions.

In her book, *Who Stole Feminism?*, Christina Hoff-Sommers, an American professor of philosophy, has a chapter on domestic violence, entitled *Noble Lies.* She writes: *"In examining research on battery, one sees that respected medical periodicals uncritically indulge the feminists in their inflammatory tendencies. It is hard to avoid the impression that the medical journals have dropped their usual standards when reporting findings of the battery studies. It is pretty clear that studies of this poor calibre on some other subject of medical interest and importance would either not be reported or be reported with many caveats."*

A GP from Tipperary in Ireland commented: *"From the outside these appear to be model families, but for many men life behind closed doors is hell on earth."*

For many years we have been fed this prejudiced diet portraying men as the perpetrators and women as the victims, and we have swallowed it whole and without question. So long as the issue is polarised by sexual politics into this simplistic and incorrect scenario, effective and balanced solutions are unlikely to result. Marie Murray, a clinical psychologist, says: *"In a society that has yet to acknowledge that women can be and are perpetrators of abuse, how can men be expected to have the courage to speak out? Their experience has been unrecognised, unobserved, unattended to and unarticulated. What we have often believed were truths were really politically convenient social inventions."*

Since setting up Amen we have been contacted by many research students from various disciplines, including social science. This is heartening as we feel these are the people who will make the difference. Often they say their views have been coloured by the prejudices of lecturers and managers, whose minds are caught in the straitjacket of political correctness and ingrained bias. One such student, after meeting some of the abused men, said: *"My eyes are being opened and I have already begun to question the status quo. Earlier this year I was busy helping a woman get a barring order against her husband when I received a call from the school principal telling me the husband was the stable parent in the family."*

In almost every case the men at our meetings are happy to talk to anyone who will listen. It is, for most, the first time they have been given a safe forum to speak and be heard. Some professionals in this field know that men are being abused daily in their homes. To date it has not been politically correct to record this fact and give it due attention.

Let me share some of the comments I have heard from male victims of physical abuse:

> She said: *"You realise I could kill you and get away with it.' She slept with a knife under the pillow."*

> *"I am 80 years old this coming Christmas. I am blind. I obtained a protection order against her. She laughed at it and the beatings have increased."*

> *My little darling is 4ft 11in, I am 6ft 2in. The police suggested I go home and sort her out myself."*

"As I put away the shopping she stabbed me in the back with a 7 inch knife. I was put on life support. It was several days before my family knew whether I would survive."

"I'm a doctor. Who do I talk to? Who is going to believe me?"

"My hair has been pulled out in tufts. I am not allowed to wash before going to work in the morning. She is obsessively jealous, even though it is she who is having the affairs."

"I am 84 years old. My wife is 75. The violence has gone on for 40 years and has become progressively worse."

"She beat me and the children. I took out protection on the children. She promptly got an interim barring order against me. The police removed me from my home. For God's sake I was the victim! Who will protect my children now?"

> *Heaven has no rage, like love to hatred turned,*
> *Nor Hell a fury like a woman scorned.*
> William Congreve, *The Mourning Bride* (1697)

This quote became widely known as *"Hell hath no fury like a woman scorned."* The point is that she has only to *feel* scorned. Even if what actually happened to her was minor or insignificant, her revenge may be savage and unremitting. Her justification may be nonsensical to anyone else, but not to her. I have listened to many heart-rending stories. This was told to me:

> *"I remember when the first knife was thrown at me. It stuck into the fridge. When one of the neighbours asked what had happened to the fridge, my wife's reply was, 'I fired a knife at him and un-fortunately it missed.' The neighbours sensed what was going on but they never said anything. I felt very afraid after that.*
>
> *A few years after the birth of our three children, my wife became abusive. She started to abuse me verbally. It then turned*

to pushing and slapping. She didn't care that the children were around. I didn't have to do anything, neither did the children. It would depend on her mood.

She used to elbow me in the face at night. I moved into the spare room and locked myself in. I felt that everything was closing in on me, but at least I was safe. I asked her to see a doctor, but she would never go. I suggested it to her family and they thought I was mad. But she was different when we went out. She was Jekyll and Hyde. To her own friends she was fine, but to mine she was totally different. If we went out for the night and a woman spoke to me, that would set her off. She would cause a row, no matter where I was or who was around. It was humiliating.

She would try to provoke me to hit her by saying the children weren't mine, or by grabbing me, cutting telephone cables or filling the lawnmower with water. She would harm herself and tell the police I had beaten her. One Christmas she even left with the kids. When I went to the police they told me that my wife and children were away for their own protection. She had told them I was abusing her and the children.

I believe it was because the children talked to me more than their mother. I had more time for them. They confided in me. She slapped them several times. I wasn't aware of this at first because the children were too scared to tell me. She was beating them in places that wouldn't show.

I was afraid to let anyone know what was happening because as a man I'd be classed as a coward. I thought other men would laugh. I couldn't hit back. I wasn't brought up like that. I hoped it would go away. But it never did. Sometimes I thought she'd changed. Then suddenly it would happen again. Life was hell.

There were lots of silences. If you asked a question it would not be answered. I couldn't have a conversation with her. Our physical relationship also stopped. There was no sex. She taunted me saying, 'You're no good anyway.'

The abuse made me feel worthless and useless. I couldn't leave the children because I knew what she was capable of doing. And I had nowhere else to go. I never considered suicide, but I have been so low that I can understand why people do it. The thought of the children stopped me. We knew that we had to get through it together.

The first person I spoke to was a priest. The children told him how they were beaten. One of them had been beaten so much that she bled. Unknown to me, my youngest daughter had reported everything to the school. When I approached the teacher she said she couldn't make a complaint. I'm sure that if she had said her father was beating her they would have done something. I felt very embarrassed and broke down in front of the priest, but it gave me great relief that at last I had told someone.

Things were getting very bad. In May my youngest daughter overheard my wife and my mother-in-law talking about 'getting rid' of me. When my daughter told me I was afraid to sleep at night. Around that time my wife was also starting to threaten me with scissors. She lifted them as if to say, 'I'm going to stick these in you.'

In June I could just sense that something was going to happen. I almost felt that I would be shot. I went to a social worker and explained the whole situation. But she laughed at me. She said that if the situation was that bad then I should just leave home.

I went to the police. They were more sympathetic but also told me to pack my bags and leave. I told them I couldn't leave the kids and they said the same as the social worker, that my wife wouldn't harm them. I then went to a solicitor and I asked him about getting a barring order, because I feared for my life and for what might happen to the children. His answer was that men don't get barring orders. He told me I was wasting time and money.

The turning point came on July 10. It was about 8:50 on a lovely summer's evening. I thought that I was in the house on my own. I was putting away the shopping and suddenly I felt a thump in the back. I turned around to find my wife standing, smiling. Then I heard the words, 'That's the last fucking shopping you'll ever do.' I felt soaking wet. I couldn't believe that this *blood was running out of me. My shirt had changed colour. I put my hand up and felt a knife in my back. I had to get out of that house if I was going to have a chance to live. I banged on my neighbour's door, screaming. She called the emergency services. I fell down in the garden.*

There was blood everywhere. I remember thinking 'I'm dying and I'll never see my children again'. I remember lights flashing and crowds gathering. I felt people slapping my face and calling my name. I was driven by police escort to the hospital. My daughters were screaming. I was taken straight into theatre. I remember telling the doctor I could see no colour. Everything was yellow. I think at that stage I was dying. They performed the operation that night and later I had part of my lung removed. I was also put on a life support machine. I spent five weeks in hospital. When I was in hospital the police arrived and asked me if I wanted to press charges against my wife. I said "yes".

When I was discharged my wife was still living in the house. She was arrested on the night of the stabbing at 9:30pm and was released at 10:45pm. The children left the home and stayed with my family.

For me to get into my own home I had to seek a barring order. I was brought from hospital to the court and even after the stabbing, the judge was reluctant to grant me one. He was more concerned about where my wife was going to sleep that night than what was going to happen to me. I eventually got a three-year barring order and court proceedings were issued. The charge was originally attempted murder. It was then reduced to grievous bodily harm and when it finally came to court it was actual bodily harm. She received a nine-month suspended sentence, which is a complete joke. I believe I would have got about nine years inside for the same assault on a woman.

If I had ever hit back, I'd have been thrown out of my home. No hesitation. I'd have been arrested and would have served a sentence.

The day after the trial I couldn't believe what I was reading in the papers. They portrayed me as a violent man. I couldn't go out anywhere. I received nasty phone calls and was called a 'wife-beater'.

My wife now lives 400 yards away, although she's never tried to contact me. If we see each other we pass like strangers. I suffer from terrible flashbacks and panic attacks. I am scared of what might happen if I don't get the barring order renewed. I fear my wife will try again to kill me.

I still have violent pains in my chest, and the area where the operation was performed is numb. I find it very hard to breathe sometimes. What has happened has stopped me from getting a job.

My advice to other men in this situation is that they must talk to someone. I attend counselling, which has helped.

I feel angry against my wife for what she did to me. I feel angry towards the system and I feel very angry towards how the media wrongly portrayed me as a violent man. It is strange but I never wanted her to go to jail. I just wanted justice. I would have liked her to receive a longer suspended sentence with medical help. But she was never recommended any.

I would like my name cleared even if it means taking my case to the European courts. I feel it is important people realise that women can be just as violent as men.

I am happier now. I have my home. I have my children. I can go home and not be afraid. Iust recently I see a change in myself. I now want to live my life. I remember a surgeon saying to me, 'You shouldn't be alive.' I now realise I had a second chance and I want to build a new life and hope that tomorrow is a better day."

The next example contains a significant element of sexual as well as emotional and physical abuse:

"I didn't realise at the time, but my wife was having an affair. She had told me repeatedly that I was sexually inadequate, which didn't really help me want to make love with her. She would routinely ridicule the size of my manhood, my inability to perform when it suited her. I went to see a therapist at her insistence. This in itself destroyed my already severely dented self-esteem.

My lack of expertise and my inability to give her pleasure was thrown at me every few days. She said repeatedly, 'If you knew what my lesbian lovers did, it might make you at least tolerable in bed.' I was made to feel that she wanted an exercise machine, not a lover.

I distinctly remember one time she just sat up in bed with her arms folded. I must have hallucinated. In front of my eyes she transformed herself into a 'queen' cobra, as opposed to a 'king' cobra – my queen cobra was slightly smaller but far more venomous. It was as though she was only a moment away from making a strike. As her husband, it was my job to get into bed with her.

Things had been bad for a long time. Nothing I did was enough. Everything was my fault. No matter what I said it would be twisted into something that would astound me. How could she possibly interpret what I had said to mean that? She was always spoiling for a fight.

One time she punched me while I was lying in the bath. She insisted that she watch me going to the toilet. I never let her. When that didn't work she verbally abused me for not flushing the toilet numerous times during a 'sitting'.

She started going out a lot. At first, I didn't figure out why. I was just so relieved to have some peace and quiet.

But she started coming home late and full of hate. When she'd been drinking, she was worse. Her favourite trick was to stand over me while I slept and yell abuse at me only inches away from my ear. I cannot adequately describe how terrifying it was to be woken up in that way. Once I went crazy. I was out of control. I attacked her and kicked her legs repeatedly. It caused multiple bruises. She told me she had reported me to the police and said they photographed the bruises. She never provided proof of this, but used it repeatedly as a threat against me if I ever refused to do what she told me. My life was a misery.

One night she threatened to stab me in my sleep. I didn't dare fall asleep. I was so terrified. I knew she could have done it.

The next day, I had to leave work because I was so tired. I double locked the front door when I got home. I fell into a deep sleep. The next thing I knew I was woken by two police officers in my bedroom. They cautioned me for barring my wife from her matrimonial home. She'd called my office earlier and was told I had gone home. She then took time off work to come home to taunt me. When she couldn't get in she went to the police who smashed down the door. I'd heard nothing.

It's been over 15 years since that happened. I still wish I'd insisted the police officers looked in her handbag. She had started carrying a kitchen knife 'for her own protection'. At the time she was taking a particular diet pill that has since been banned in the UK. Apparently the drug had a side effect - it induced psychotic behaviour.

I didn't have the courage to walk away or file for divorce. Even though she was having an affair, eventually she decided we were going to be divorced. For a quieter life I was prepared to accept my 'unreasonable behaviour' as the cause of the marriage breakdown. My lawyer told me it didn't make any difference, even though she was the unreasonable one. It seemed so wrong, but I went ahead with it, even though I knew she would then use it to 'prove' how unreasonable I was and how hurt she was.

It turns out she got pregnant during the divorce proceedings by her boyfriend, who quickly dumped her. She then had an abortion. I was staggered to discover that she then applied to the Catholic Church for the marriage to be annulled on the grounds that I refused to have children with her. So, even though she had had an abortion and the Church was told this by a lay preacher acting on my behalf, they gave her the annulment! How could that happen?"

This is a story of particularly nasty non-physical violence:

At the height of the troubles in Northern Ireland, a young undercover soldier working for the security services risked his life every day. His job was extremely dangerous and the pressure was intense. His wife was his oasis of calm, the sweet girl he could return to. He treated her like a princess but the pressure was too much for her. She constantly lived under the fear of being yet another army wife who might one day receive a call telling her that her husband had been killed in action.

Their marriage fell apart and she left him. After the divorce she became bitter – and turned on him in a somewhat vicious way.

One day she phoned him to say that for some vague, inexplicable reason she had been in West Belfast, a particularly dangerous place to be at the time. She claimed she had left her diary in a pub, although this has never been proven. In that diary was her husband's name, his rank and detailed information about his selection for SAS training. It included his full home address in Aldershot. She added *"I have been told by the army to call you and tell you that you need to check your car for booby trap bombs every time you get into it. I wanted you to know. They also said that you need to sell the house."* He did.

Another soldier made this statement:

"I have been married for 15 years. Her abuse was physical, verbal, mental, emotional and psychological. Physical abuse includes the following: a broken rib from a punch, three other broken ribs, a back injury with nerve damage, which occurred when I was pulled out of bed by the hair during my sleep, a fractured finger from an impact blow as my hand was on the kitchen worktop, multiple bruising on many occasions, tufts of my hair pulled out again and again.

I have been kicked, punched, kneed in the groin, pushed and pulled around. This is a partial account of some of the abuse I have endured.

I received a particularly bad beating from my wife. She used various tools – pliers, screwdrivers, snips and others. I suffered extensive bruising to my arms, legs, buttocks, back and legs. Most of the attacks took place to the rear of my body. I crouched in a defensive position and used my arms to protect my head, so most of the bruising was to my arms and back. I did not use any physical means to defend myself. I did not retaliate. I simply waited for the beating to stop. A day or so later I had my injuries recorded by the family doctor, a female. Her attitude was one of bemusement, indifference and hostility. She insisted on telling me about the female victims of domestic abuse she encounters, as if it was my fault. She certainly did nothing to encourage me to report further incidents.

I appealed to a female social worker for help. She suggested I should pack my bags and leave even though I have three young children. My life would not be worth living without my children. They mean everything to me. I did not take that option. This woman gave me no support whatsoever. In fact, she was positively hostile. I went to the district court to apply for a protection and safety order. At the front desk the clerk was both surprised and amused at my plight. In the interview room the next clerk was a little more sympathetic, if somewhat disbelieving. The clerk who called my name to appear in court forcefully suggested that I was the respondent and my wife, the applicant when in fact it was the other way around. He said men were 'always the respondents'. He had a very aggressive attitude towards me from start to finish.

I was wearing a short-sleeved shirt and the bruising to my arms was clearly visible. This did not register with any of them. At this point I was feeling isolated and very nervous as I had never been in court before. I was the victim and was treated badly by all to whom I turned for help.

The judge gave me a protection order. My wife laughed at this and said, 'I'll fix you', and promptly applied for a protection and safety order against me. There was not a mark on her. She was verbally very abusive to me, said I was a 'fucking idiot, not a real man, she could have any man she wanted and suggested that perhaps I was not the father of my two boys'. According to my wife I was useless, no good, full of shit, thick, an arsehole, no one else would have me etc. etc. etc.

I have medical evidence of the injuries described in this account. I encountered disbelief, amusement and unwillingness from others, merely to justify my wife's behaviour.

> *On occasions I have, at my wife's insistence, left the family home. Then she accused me of desertion.*
>
> *I was denied access to my children. Then again at her behest I returned to my home. When I returned she said I was a wonderful husband, a good father, and she couldn't live without me, until she felt safe to return to her violent behaviour. I have put up with this abuse for years in order to be with my children."*

We have encountered numerous examples of women attacking husbands in the military, confident in the knowledge that no one would believe a soldier could be a victim of domestic violence. Based on this anecdotal evidence we are convinced this is a widespread problem for members of the defence forces around the world.

One man described how he would come home from work in fear, not knowing what to expect this time. One day he came in through the kitchen door at the back of the house, when suddenly a teapot full of hot tea smashed against the kitchen wall next to where he stood covering him with tea and debris. He said: *"Somehow I'd upset her again, even though I had absolutely no idea how. I hadn't even had time to say, 'Hello, dear'!"*

The same woman was having an extra-marital affair. The first he knew about it was on Valentine's Day when a huge bouquet arrived for her with an intimate note. She'd persuaded her lover to send the flowers so that she didn't have to tell her husband about the affair. After the subsequent divorce she now has four children – two from her ex-husband, and two more from two different fathers. She lives off a complex alimony income stream and is also subsidised by the state.

This man tells of a cocktail of abuses:

> *"If there are other men out there like me, all I can say is God help them, if they went through what I did. When we got married I had a good job. My wife changed when we married. I had to take my four-month-old daughter to work with me as my wife did not want her. She would vanish for days. Every job I got, I lost because of the amount of time I had to take off to*

look after the children. I was abused more and more as the years went on. I was scalded, scratched, kicked and lots more.

When I was at work during the day she would leave our five children on their own all day long. I gave in to her moods. She scalded two of the children and they spent a long time in hospital with burns on their legs and backs.

On many occasions I went to the social welfare for help, but because I was a man I could get no help. Eventually I stopped asking. I did not bother any more. Had I been a woman I would have received money and anything I wanted. Social workers do not want to know the lone man parent. They treat the man as an outcast and will not give him any help. A man will always suffer in silence and will not look for help.

My wife had affair after affair, and because of this I was given a legal separation. I was left to bring up the children, the youngest being three months old, all on my own. I got no help from anyone and nobody cared either because I was a male. I had to sell all my belongings. I reached suicide point but the children held me back from this, as I love them so much."

Another man had this experience of physical and insidious emotional abuse:

"I have been a victim of domestic abuse and I am now being abused through the children. On one occasion I was hospitalised when my wife hit me on the head from behind with an iron. I suffered concussion. Up until the summer I lived with my wife and four children aged from four to 11, but since then my wife has moved out to live with a married man in a rented house about three miles away, taking our children with her.

At one time when my children came to me they were always at the gate waiting for her for at least a half an hour before she was due to collect them. My youngest son told me that the first to the car got £1, the second a bar of chocolate, the third a nice sweet and the last a yucky sweet. As part of the access arrangement we were to meet in a nearby town. She changed the children's watches and the clocks in the house and told them, 'There you are, your Daddy doesn't care for you. He doesn't even bother to come and collect you.' Off she would go. I would then have to go searching for them, very often unsuccessfully. The access time would be over if or when I caught up with them."

A tale of unexpected violence was told to me by this sad man:

"It began, I suppose, about five years ago. I was happily married, I would say, for 13 years. I had never experienced any violence, apart from one isolated incident in which she abused me in public two years into our relationship. Up to that point neither of us had known violence in our families. We married two years after that incident. Neither of us drank, and we didn't smoke, so I felt I was unique because virtually everything I have ever heard said that violence comes from drink, or because it was begotten of other violence. We hadn't experienced any of this.

However, what did come to pass was a shock when I returned home after being away for a few days. I walked through the door and my wife announced to me that she wanted a separation and she wanted me to leave the house. I had six weeks to leave. She wouldn't give me a reason. She just said, 'I don't love you any more. You've got to go.' I begged her to give me a reason, but she wouldn't.

Eventually I was forced into taking legal counsel because of the amount of letters that were hitting me every day, threatening me with exclusion, being thrown out of the house etc. So I did go and I spoke to a number of solicitors and they asked me about my life. I explained my circumstances to them and they said, 'You have a problem. It's your best friend.' I couldn't believe this. I had been going to this best friend with all my troubles.

I was devastated. I had known him before I was married. I was going downhill fast at this stage. Up to that point there was no violence at all apart from the isolated public incident where she grabbed me by the hair, flung me to the floor and kicked me in the testicles. The trouble really began when I said to her, 'You're having an affair with my best friend. You know this is crazy. We can solve this.' That very night she started to taunt me. She said he was better in bed than I was. All sorts of things like that – nasty horrible things. I would be pushed in the hallway. She was trying to provoke me to hit her back. I wouldn't do it, I knew better.

If I hit out, she was going to have me put out of the house. I just knew that was the game. The taunting continued. She moved out of our bed. She moved into one of the other rooms in the house. It is very difficult for me to talk about this.

One night my wife was quite friendly and said to me, 'Do you want a cup of tea?' She hadn't spoken to me in something like three weeks at this stage. I said, 'Yes, thank you.' She came into the room with the cup of tea and threw it in my face. Then she laughed at me. I was working long hours at the time, trying to keep the house together. She would play the radio all night long, she would try to keep me awake, she would knock on the door, she would taunt me. She then started to accuse me of the most horrendous things and said she would use them against me, that I had to get out of the house, or never see my children again.

I tried everything to talk to her. I said she could have the house, the car, anything. I just wanted to be allowed to see my children. She said she didn't need to negotiate with me. She was going to get it all anyway. Why did she need to negotiate with me? I went to my lawyers and asked them, 'What would I get out of this, what are my chances of being able to see my children?' And they said, 'No chance. You'd be lucky to get a few hours a month.' I was really, really, really down at this stage."

Prolonged physical abuse is not uncommon. Here is one husband's story:

"My wife has been beating me for years now but for the sake of the child and my home I have said nothing, and because of the embarrassment of people laughing at me. I am big and she is small. Nobody would believe that when she was pregnant she stabbed me with a knife, but for the sake of the child I let it go.

I don't want to lose my child but she tells me that the judge will not believe me and he always takes the woman's side.

My wife had an affair. She is still with him and she stays out until 4am or even 8am. She is gone three and four nights a week. I asked her to come home early but she said that she was under a curfew to nobody. In the morning my son asks me, 'Is Mammy home yet?' It is so sad to hear him say that. We would be better off on our own. I always took my child to Mass, but now she won't let him go with me.

When my son was eight to ten months old I was feeding him in the sitting room when Joan came in and said she did not know why I was so fond of him as he was not even mine. I felt sick but I told her I did not care, that I loved him and I would mind him.

Last Monday night when I came home from work I asked her to get her dogs out of the house. She hit me across the back with the brush and said that I would be gone before the dogs. I told a police officer about it and he was very nice and understanding about it. He told me to go to a doctor about it, so in the morning I went to the doctor and he sent me to hospital. This is a sad life."

Another unhappy man was driven to drastic action:

"One day she told me that she didn't want me any more. I would have to leave. I refused. I came home and found all my stuff in the driveway. I was presented with an interim barring order on the grounds of mental cruelty. I've never heard of such a thing before and was in shock that she could get this order without me knowing. I had to leave when the police arrived. As you can imagine, I was absolutely shattered.

I got a room for myself and tried to start again. But it wasn't easy. I was constantly harassed by my wife for money. With this and the extra cost of my rent I ended up borrowing heavily and got into debt. One night I couldn't take any more and I attempted suicide. I didn't plan to be found but, by a freak chance I was discovered. I had taken 49 sleeping tablets and woke up in intensive care. I was devastated that I was alive. The only one who came to see me was my father and he gave out to me for being the cause of shame on the family.

Nine months later my wife asked me to come home. I was glad to be back in my own home again. When I told her how much debt I was in she exploded. After a long time I managed to sort out the debt. I had nothing left. I sleep in one room and she sleeps in another. I have been hit with just about everything in the house, kicked and called everything under the sun. Bank accounts have been cleaned out on different occasions and life has been pure hell. She forged my signature to get money.

I decided recently that I had had enough. I simply cannot take any more of this abuse. Now that my children are away at college I have asked my wife for a separation. I'm starting a new life. I'm not going to be a victim any more. I found strength that I didn't know I had. I now intend to lead my life as a decent person and never let anyone humiliate me again. We all have an inner strength that sometimes takes a long time to find."

This man had to leave but will not divorce:

"Serious problems for the relationship started almost immediately after we got married. My wife was given to regular outbursts of violent temper tantrums, rages and irrational behaviour, which usually resulted in physical violence against me – punching, scratching, hitting with anything in reach, threatening with knives and kettles of boiling water and smashing up the house.

She threatened to harm herself, commit suicide or kill me while I was asleep. Although her behaviour started before the children were born, their arrival did not deter her in any way. She did not make the slightest effort to moderate her behaviour for the sake of the children. This continued throughout the marriage, gradually getting worse and more serious. I am certain that both my children, in particular my 13-year-old son, have suffered greatly from their mother's aggression. They missed lessons and days at school as a result of her behaviour, which included keeping us all awake at night with her shouting and tantrums. I sought help from marriage guidance counsellors on four occasions. In every case my wife stopped the sessions after only two or three visits. She claimed that it was all my fault and there was nothing wrong with her behaviour.

Even though I have suffered physical injuries, which have been painful and persistent, what has been even more harmful has been the emotionally draining effect of her behaviour with her constant threats, more often than not followed by actual violence. This simply wore me out physically, mentally and emotionally to the point where I needed treatment for severe depression and anxiety. I had hospital tests for severe abdominal pains, which were diagnosed as irritable bowel syndrome brought on by stress. Since 1994 I have been on medication for this condition and am now going for stress counselling.

Throughout the years I put up with her behaviour, partly because as a Christian I am opposed to divorce and, largely, because I thought it better for the children. However, notwithstanding these views, which I still hold, I eventually found it impossible to carry on, so I left my home for the first time and stayed away for 18 months. The threats and abuse continued throughout this time with persistent telephone calls during the day and throughout the night, sometimes as many as 35 calls in one day. She also took to turning up without invitation and without warning. At times during her many telephone calls I would try to reason with her for the sake of the children. She created problems and interfered with my contact with my children.

My concern for the children eventually drove me back to her in the spring to try, once again, to make a go of the marriage. Predictably, it was a disaster. Her rage has continued unabated and in September I was forced to leave again. This time I made up my mind that it was permanent. At present, I am living with my parents. I need a place for my children and myself."

The memories hurt and linger for this husband:

"I still feel pangs of shame when I think of it, nearly 20 years *later. After months of sustained verbal abuse and threats of physical attacks, I had had enough. She was angry with me, yet again and for no specific reason. This time, she went to the fridge, took a can of Coke, opened it and then in the sitting room poured this freezing cold drink over my head. I just stood there motionless as she emptied the can over me. I then snapped and went to slap her across the face. She raised her hand to protect herself. My open palm caught and bent one of her fingers back. A bone was fractured. But she refused to get treatment. I couldn't figure out why. It didn't make sense. But it did to her.*

Two months later when the fracture had healed itself, she admitted herself to hospital, where they re-broke and re-set it. Now she was able to tell everyone that I had 'hospitalised' her!"

Countless men tell the same story. They were slapped, punched and kicked repeatedly by their wives or girlfriends. In some cases it went on for months or years. The 'punchline' (no pun intended) is often the same. He will say: *"One day I had enough – and I slapped her back. I didn't do it very hard, just enough to say: "That's it – no more."* But the moment he did it, he realised what a HUGE mistake he had made.

She would then tell all her friends and family that he had assaulted her. Some reported their husbands or boyfriends to the police.

> *When they told me that by the year 2100 women would rule the world, my reply was "Still?"*
> Sir Winston Churchill

Chapter 3

Two of a Kind

Ms Truly Evil

He is a highly respected, fifty-something Professor of Political Science at a leading American university, a remarkably intelligent and learned man who has published leading-edge papers. He is divorced with one child. She was 32, charismatic, attractive and intelligent. She came on to him. And this is how he recalls the whole experience:

> *"When I met her she was so friendly, so helpful, so attractive, so everything. I couldn't believe my luck. It was as if all my Christmases had been rolled into one I fell head-over-heels in love or perhaps it was the illusion she created. We were together for more than a year.*
>
> *To this day, I can't believe I got taken in so much. I still feel so angry and stupid. I know I'm not – I'm a professor for goodness' sake! She shook the very foundations of what I believed about*

others. I also came to realise that I had led quite a sheltered life. I had only known nice, generous, kind and loving people. My ex-wife and I still have a warm and friendly relationship.

If I'm honest, looking back I was always suspicious of her, but I couldn't put my finger on precisely why. So I ignored it at first. As the relationship continued, more and more pointers showed up. Call it ego, but I thought I could deal with her. I failed. It all went so horribly wrong.

I hate to say this but I can only describe her as truly evil. She is the only person, and certainly the only woman, for whom I have ever wished bad things. Thinking such thoughts has also made me feel bad about myself. Her memory lingers like a foul smell.

At least I had enough sense to bring the relationship to an end. Truly, I have no regrets. Indeed, I count my blessings because I believe deeply she would have ruined me financially as well as psychologically if we'd stayed together.

She was very attractive. And I was very attracted to her. When she walked into a room she turned heads. She really wanted to be a model and could have been the Chanel type, a very cold-looking woman. She was not a 'girl-next-door'. Beautiful yes, sexy no. She said sex wasn't important to her because she claimed she'd been abused when she was younger. I later discovered she bed-hopped with an army of guys while we were together.

Soon after we met she was looking for somewhere to live. She sounded spontaneous at the time, but now I suspect it was part of a plan. I invited her to move in. She didn't pay rent.

In a social setting you'd find her incredibly charming. Colleagues constantly told me how lucky I was to have her as a girlfriend. They described her as a "fantastic woman, interesting, charismatic and lively". Yet she treated some people appallingly. In restaurants she was always complaining to waiters that the food was sub-standard. And she put down so many people, in an attempt to lift herself up.

When asked, she always gave men her phone number and/or her e-mail address. It was such a shoddy thing to do, and she did it all the time. When I challenged her she said I was being silly. I now realise I was merely her 'route to market'.

Publicly she presented herself as terribly loving and committed to me, but in private she was totally different. Smashing things on the floor was the norm for her. She threw bottles of wine across the room when she didn't get what she demanded. I discovered she was stealing from me. The money she took were in small amounts, trivial in themselves, but she also took things from my filing cabinets, including official documents such as my will.

Sometimes I'd catch her out when she lied but she always had a plausible answer.

I've never met anybody so mean in my entire life. For example, I gave her carefully chosen and relatively expensive Christmas gifts. She once gave me a pirated Barry Manilow CD! On another occasion she gave me a box of chocolates when she knew I don't eat candy. One of her many male friends had a clothes shop. She gave me one of his old-stock neckties. She would never buy a glass of wine or a coffee. I wasn't special – she treated everybody the same.

She always claimed she had no money, of course, so I paid for everything. One day, by pure mistake, I opened a letter from her bank. She had $50,000 in her account!

Somehow she got a first-class honours degree. But she wasn't interested in intellectual activities. It seems she had befriended her tutor and he gave her student essays, which she then copied and handed back to him. Subsequently, he gave her top marks. This, of all the things she did, enrages me. I have devoted my life to education and the importance of qualifications. To me it is utterly scandalous that she did this. As for the tutor in question, words fail me.

On reflection, I can see she used me as a vehicle for her career and wanted me to help her to skip a few rungs on the corporate ladder by finding her a better job than she was qualified for. But I refused. In any case, she was totally unemployable. She will never work as part of a team because she's so self-obsessed.

She has discovered her personal strengths in life – using and lying to men to underwrite her chosen lifestyle. It was quite clear that she saw herself as a very desirable 'unit of consumption'. She had positioned herself in the marketplace as somebody on whom money should be lavished, somebody to be polished and cleaned like a high-performance and high-maintenance car. She no longer had the slightest intention of getting a job. Her whole life strategy was to be given money and to live off men.

When it didn't work, she probably did some strategic analysis and concluded: Why work? Who needs a mortgage? Why should I be forced to take in a lodger? I could easily become one myself and live in a large expensive house instead. Sex isn't important to me, so I could offer that as 'payment'.

I have an excellent lifestyle. I'm quite well-off and presentable, but not one woman I had met had ever, in any way, tried to take advantage of me materially. Until I met her.

She'd ask when I was going away for my next lecture. "Would I be travelling on the day or going the night before?" "Oh, poor you, having to be away." she'd say. I realise now that she was setting up other men to see in my absence.

I could guarantee that when I was away her cell phone would be switched off. The next day I would ask her why I couldn't get through. She always had an answer. She was either in the bath or the radio was on and she didn't hear the phone. At the time I always gave her the benefit of the doubt. I know now she was almost always with someone else.

I still can't figure out, even years later, how anyone could do what she did, not just to me but to other men and women who she claimed were her 'best' friends. She was so charming – on the surface. She was so nasty on the inside and had absolutely no conscience.

The worst thing is that I ignored my gut instinct as I had a sense that she was too good to be true. And I paid the price. To this day I feel sick to the stomach when I recall the loving things she used to say to me and what I discovered she was doing behind my back. I was so captivated, hypnotised and in love with her, or so I thought. She wove such a web of deceit. She could look you straight in the face and say that the sun sets in the east.

This woman was such a convincing liar that I suspected she had a mental illness. If you lie so convincingly, you have to operate with several personalities. I researched her character traits on the internet and discovered narcissistic personality disorder. She fitted the descriptions perfectly.

She lived a lie, but she had no concept of when she was lying and when she wasn't. Some stab scarring down one side of her body was among her deceits. She claimed to me that someone had tried to murder her, but she was left-handed and the scars were all down her right side. I'm convinced she did the stabbing herself. She also attempted suicide in my house. I found her in the bath fully clothed. I'm not sure, but I think she did that for the attention.

*She was so incredibly manipulative and loved to stir it up and play one man off against another. She **always** played the victim. I've come to learn at my cost that when she behaved like a victim you could be fairly sure it would be your turn next.*

She thought she was so fantastic and believed she was perfect at everything she did. Her world was structured around her, she always had to be the centre of attention and she always wanted things. The more she was given the more she wanted. It was "Take, take, take".

After six months she appeared devoted to me and we were having a fantastic time, or so it seemed. But here's a confession. She used to keep a diary and she left it lying on the bed one day, maybe deliberately. I've never admitted this to anyone, and I felt incredibly guilty and even ashamed of myself for doing it. I read her diary. Within three days of moving into my home she was seeing another man who lived downtown.

After three weeks she was describing me as an "asshole". That was when she wanted me to be a guarantor so that she could buy an apartment. When I refused she reacted badly, accusing me of not trusting her.

She also wrote: "The most difficult thing I find is faking my orgasms." Indeed, everything about her turned out to be fake.

She claimed she had no self-esteem and swallowed holistic anti-depressant pills by the handful. She already had a nose job. I'm guessing it will be a tit job next.

Her relationship with her mother was tempestuous. When the girl was growing up they had violent rows. She also claimed she was sexually abused by her stepfather when she was young. I'm sure her mother abused her too. I am convinced she will end up like her mother, who left her husband when her daughter was three and ran off with her psychiatrist! While bringing up a daughter she discovered she was no longer the centre of attention and was responsible for someone else. The mother attempted suicide a couple of times, allegedly had more than 30 affairs, and slept with more than 50 men. Her mother is now a sad, bitter woman in her early fifties whose looks have faded. She lives alone in a one-bedroom apartment in Chicago.

If my ex-girlfriend ever decides to have a child, she will have to go from being a little girl to being a mother, and she probably won't be able to cope with that. In spite of everything, I fear for her future.

She was jealous of my children, and she physically attacked me when I told her I'd had an innocent drink with a woman I'd known for years. I put my arms up in self-defence and she dug her fingers into my arms so deeply that she drew blood in many places. To this day I have scars on my forearms as a constant reminder of what she did. It was horrific, although at the time you just accept the unacceptable. I went for treatment but lied about how it happened. I said an out-of-control drunken woman in a bar had attacked me. At least, my treatment was recorded. And that's a good thing.

She had few friends of her own. Her female 'friends' were all plain or downright ugly women. Nobody was going to distract attention from her.

As beautiful as she was on the outside, you could almost see the transformation as she walked out of the door in the morning. At these and other times I saw through the façade to glimpse an ugly, cruel, really nasty piece of work.

None of my own friends could stand her. She was never polite unless she thought they were important and wouldn't make the slightest effort to engage with them. One close friend said the only time she was ever truly happy was when she was surrounded by four or five guys giving her attention.

He warned me: 'Her job is to live off you. Psychologically, it must be very demanding for her. She's working when she's with you. She has to pay a great deal of attention to what she says and does at those times. But she can relax more when she's with others.'

That friend later observed that I had had a lucky escape. I could have lost half my house and all my friends. If we'd had a child, the consequences don't bear thinking about.

I was damned angry with myself, and all these years later I still am. I had never met anyone like this in my whole life, someone who meticulously manipulates men as her job.

As practically a size zero, she hardly ate anything and was always cold. The heating in my house was always flat out. So she was also bad for the environment – she was certainly bad for mine!

I realise I was a target because I am basically a nice guy. Her next victim was also an older man and exactly the same type. She used me as a stepping stone to meet him and has been with him for the past few years. So long as she gets her own way and he keeps spending money on her, she'll be happy.

However, within a week of moving in with him she was having sex with somebody else. I know this for sure because it was me. I think she'll destroy him. There are lots of mugs in the world – let her pick on them. I should be able to laugh it off. But I can't. I was a mug.

I came from a poor background. I have worked hard to get where I am, building up a modicum of wealth. I now realise just how fragile and how vulnerable you can be when there is a financially predatory woman on the prowl. She is the archetypal gold-digger."

These are the lessons he learnt from knowing her:

- Trust your intuition and develop the confidence to act on it.
- Don't give people the benefit of the doubt.
- If you see flaws in a relationship at the very beginning, don't think those flaws will resolve themselves.

- Don't believe you can change her behaviour – you can't.
- Beauty is only skin deep.

Malice in Plunderland

She is a striking blonde with piercing blue eyes. A sexy, charming and dishonest forty-something. Nobody actually knows her. You just see an incredibly friendly, vivacious and upbeat woman. Over the years she has perfected the illusion of looking happy.

Her boyfriend lent her about £40,000 during the time they were together – but the loans were never secured. She avoided committing the debts to writing and also used him as her personal ATM machine.

During the relationship, as part of her way of evoking sympathy and pity, she shared with him her disastrous financial situation. She claimed at all times that she was the victim of circumstances. Her business was a financial mess. She was up to her neck in debt. Bailiffs regularly confronted her staff with demands for unpaid debts. She was hardly ever there to meet them herself. Attending yoga and keep-fit classes were a higher priority.

He devoted himself to sorting out her legal and financial matters, which were hampered by a less than cooperative brother who had effectively tied her up in legal knots.

Within three months her legal issues were settled by bringing together her bank, the Inland Revenue (who were owed about £80,000 in back taxes and had successfully recovered additional unpaid tax by taking her to court numerous times) and various lawyers representing different members of her family. He received a congratulatory note from her lawyer stating that the complex negotiations would have fallen apart without his efforts. When the deal was concluded, his girlfriend was £350,000 better off. For months afterwards, as he re-built her business and revenues started to climb, he was regularly asked to help her out with salary shortfalls and various large expenses. Men are 'fixers' and being in love, he was eager to help. She moved in and lived rent free. She drove his second vehicle, again at no charge.

But it all went wrong for him. He discovered that while he looked after her young daughter, she was seeing another man. When he finally asked her to leave, she had already moved in with a different man - also rent free.

Only days before she left, she had been involved in a road crash that caused £3,500 of damage to his car. Against advice from friends he still allowed her to use the replacement hire car. Imagine his disbelief when he received two parking tickets she had acquired. Because the hire car was in his name, he was liable for paying them! She promised to pay, but didn't.

She left without taking any of her possessions or those of her daughter. Repeatedly he asked her to collect them, but his requests were ignored. Yet the moment he went abroad on business, she showed up at his home with the police in an attempt to force entry, even though she had been informed in writing that everything had been removed and had been put into storage awaiting her collection. She allegedly lied to the police to convince them to attend.

She spread false allegations about him to her family and mutual friends. Her alleged affair was covered up by false accusations she made that he was the unfaithful one. She ensured that all their friends were charmed with 'loving' text messages that implied that he was the villain, even though he was not. At no time did she share any information with those people about her huge debt to him and even larger debts to others.

Her lies were many and various. She claimed he had behaved fraudulently. She falsely accused him of causing *"severe emotional trauma"* to her daughter. She also claimed she had been 'threatened' by him. In reality, the only thing that threatened her was the truth. He delivered the truth, so in her mind, he was the threat.

If the truth was too unpalatable she fabricated what she wanted to believe. She lived in her own fairytale world. It emerged later that she also owed her parents £25,000, and even her brother had repeatedly threatened to bankrupt her for the £105,000 she owed him. There were many other court actions and judgments against her. When the boyfriend was finally forced to appoint a lawyer to recover the money she owed him, the lawyer's first comment was: *"Ah, I've sued her before."*

When no money was returned and more promises broken, the former boyfriend was forced to issue bankruptcy proceedings against her. Only days before a scheduled bankruptcy court hearing she finally agreed to repay the money. But even then she and her lawyers tried to wriggle out of paying the full amount. She was forced to settle in full. He says of the experience;

> *"What makes me feel so sick is the realisation that during all the time we were together, she lied to me. Then after we split she lied about me.*
>
> *She felt the world owed her whatever she wanted. When she suspected I had had enough of her broken promises and refusal to accept full responsibility for her finances, she then made a point of telling me that she was available to me sexually whenever I wanted. I can see now that this was simply a ploy to keep me hooked.*
>
> *It also makes me feel sick that she would be prepared to do such a thing and makes me question everything else she said and did. She used me any way she could. I also noticed near the end that she would say anything she could think of in the moment, if it meant getting what she wanted. In my view, she had no morals.*
>
> *I can now see how she trapped me. Initially she invited me to a number of social occasions which I couldn't attend because I had prior commitments. Eventually I was able to accept one of her invitations. When I showed up, she told me her friends had cancelled. She came back to my place without too much encouragement.*
>
> *We slept together that night, but there was no sex. In fact, she withheld sex for about a month. That was tough as she was a sensuous woman. I recall her saying at one point that she was so turned on by me, but was so 'committed' to our relationship she didn't want to spoil it by having sex. She even said "I am seriously thinking about asking an ex-boyfriend to have sex with me to curb my sexual appetite for you! How weird is that?" And I fell for it.*
>
> *She was constantly receiving text messages on her phone. I was suspicious for quite a while and on one occasion I made a comment about how secretive she was. I have to admire her nerve. In a grand gesture she handed over the phone but at the*

last moment said: "If I show you this, it's obvious you don't trust me." I didn't get to see the sender's name.

I now know that everything was a lie, but I didn't at the time. By sheer coincidence I met a single man socially at a dinner party. I was just getting over this trauma and got talking. I mentioned I'd just come out of a bad relationship. It turned out she had targeted him too. But he spotted her intentions immediately when she insisted she meet him at his home (to check that he was as wealthy as she'd heard). She also made a point of going to see him play hockey one day. I then remembered early in our relationship she'd said she was going to see a 'friend' play hockey. He told me "She wasn't a friend - I'd just met her. I made sure one of the women there told her that I was a confirmed bachelor. She got the hint and was gone."

This made me feel even more foolish about how gullible I'd been. Perversely I felt better about it when I told another a friend recently about what had happened. He shared the story of a colleague who divorced his wife. It cost him a lot of money. Then he met and fell in love with another woman. A few months later he moved in with her. He then used the £100,000 he received after he had to sell the matrimonial house, to pay off his new girlfriend's entire mortgage. She then ended the relationship. And refused to repay him the money! Thankfully I got my money back, but this seems to happen a lot.

My advice to any man is NEVER lend money to a woman who is in financial difficulties without drawing up a legally binding loan agreement that details exactly what she must repay, including interest, if the relationship ever ends."

How do intelligent men allow themselves to get involved with such women in the first place? What do these women do to ensnare their victims and what are they prepared to do in order to get what they want? The psychologies of malice are explored in the next chapter.

Chapter 4
The Psychologies of Malice

The case studies in previous chapters detail a range of psychological or behavioural disorders. Some of these women may be mentally ill, whilst others have learned sets of behaviours that work for them but cause untold misery for the men, women and children in their lives. Knowing at least something about these different conditions could help you to understand a little more about how a difficult woman in your life may operate, or alert you to possible problems from those you have yet to meet. Men, it must be said, also suffer from the same psychological conditions.

It would be impossible in the space available to define accurately all the symptoms of all mental or emotional disorders, so the following are very simplistic descriptions, intended to offer only a basic understanding. These definitions are insufficient to base a clinical diagnosis.

It is most likely that you are dealing with a woman who does not have a specific disorder, but possesses a dominant personality which may have been learned in childhood. If she was brought up in a household where a parent seemed to get their way by being a bully, she may have realised this was the way to get more of what she wanted. Possibly, she has become domineering as a means of protecting herself from being bullied by others. Her targets may not be bullies, but her self-protection instinct may be so deeply rooted that she doesn't distinguish between people who are threats and those who are not. She may choose partners who are mild-mannered and non-confrontational and who increase the likelihood that she can maintain the dominant position within the relationship, thus improving her chances of protecting herself. She may be any variation of the following: a normal 'strong', independent woman; she may exhibit some domineering traits or; she could be an extreme 'control freak'.

Most normal people occasionally experience at least some of the following symptoms. However, when an individual exhibits 'clusters' of these behaviour traits on a very regular basis, they may be suffering from a combination of any one of these emotional disorders.

The intention here is to help you recognise patterns of behaviour so that you can become more aware of what is happening and so you can better cope with your situation. It is not intended as a way to 'pigeon-hole' someone.

Narcissistic personality disorder (NPD)

This condition was named after the mythical Greek youth Narcissus, who fell in love with his own reflection. The disorder was named in 1971 by Heinz Kohut in *The Analysis of Self*. Symptoms exhibited by those with the condition include:

- An extreme and grandiose sense of their own importance.
- An assumption of very high levels of their own talent, success, good looks, power and beauty, even when these qualities are absent or would not be recognised by people they know.
- An insistence on excessive and constant admiration.
- A belief that they have a high degree of 'entitlement'. Because they believe they are special, they demand special treatment.
- Selfish, self-serving and arrogant tendencies.

- A readiness to take advantage of others in any ways they see fit.
- An inability to feel empathy for others. They often find it difficult to love others. Love for themselves will always come first.
- A conviction that others envy them.
- High maintenance.

Borderline personality disorder (BPD)

How many of the following behaviours apply to your abusive wife or girlfriend?

- At the beginning of the relationship it is now obvious that she was on her best behaviour. She seemed to be your perfect partner, but have you found that the more she has relaxed into the relationship with you, especially if you married her, the more of the real woman has been revealed? In the safe environment of the marital home, is she now letting out years, or even decades, of anger that she has had to suppress until now?
- Are you now the focus of these intense, even violent, rages that seem to leap out of nowhere? And do these alternate with periods when she acts perfectly normally and is so loving towards you?
- Are you walking on eggshells most of the time, knowing that, no matter what you say or do, it will get twisted and used against you? Are you blamed or criticised for just about everything that's wrong in the relationship, even when the criticism doesn't make much sense?
- Do you find yourself concealing what you really think or feel because you're afraid of her possible reaction, and it just doesn't seem worth the confrontation, a horrible fight or hurt feelings that will inevitably follow? Has this become so automatic that you have a hard time even understanding what you think or feel any more?
- Does this woman who you care about appear to see you as either all good or all bad, with nothing in between? Do you

find yourself wishing she would act the way she once did, when she seemed to love you and everything was wonderful?

- Do you feel she is *Dr Jekyll* and *Mr Hyde*? Is she a loving, caring woman one moment, and someone so vicious that you barely recognise her the next? Do you wonder which one is real? Do you hope it's a phase that one day will go away but shows no signs of going?
- Do you feel you're on an emotional roller coaster with high highs, when things are incredible and fantastic, and very low lows, consisting of feelings of despair, depression and grief for the relationship you thought you had?
- Are you afraid to ask for things in the relationship because you will be told you're too demanding or there is something wrong with you? Are you repeatedly told your needs are wrong or unimportant?
- Do you feel nothing you do is ever right, or when you do manage to do what she wants she suddenly presents new expectations? The rules keep changing and, no matter what you do, you can't win. Do you feel helpless and trapped every time this happens?
- Are you constantly accused of doing things you didn't do and saying things you didn't say? Do you feel misunderstood a great deal of the time, and when you try to explain she doesn't believe you or want to listen?
- Are you constantly put-down, yet when you try to leave the relationship she tries to prevent you in a variety of ways? She tries declarations of love, promises to change, or implicit or explicit threats such as *"You'll never see the children again"* or *"Nobody but me will ever want or love you."*
- Do you have evidence of being lied to? Does she violently deny lying and deflect any conversation away from the topic when you raise it, or does she seem to manufacture accusations to 'prove' you are the liar? Do you feel you're being manipulated or controlled?
- Do you regularly wonder whether you're losing your grip on reality because she is always putting you down, or denying your right to a point of view? Does she tend to act normally

in front of others, so that nobody would believe it if you revealed what was going on between you?
- Does she insist that you don't have contact with family or friends?
- If she drinks or takes mood-altering drugs, does her behaviour become more erratic and obnoxious?
- Is it next to impossible to plan anything, such as a social engagement, because of her moodiness, impulsiveness or unpredictability? Sometimes you find yourself having to make excuses for her.
- How often have you tried to convince yourself that this is normal behaviour?

Perhaps you've read this list and thought: *"Oh, my God, I had no idea that other people go through exactly the same thing."* If you did, you might like to know this has a name - borderline personality disorder (BPD).

BPD was once thought to 'border' on schizophrenia, although it is now regarded as more closely related to mood disorders such as depression or Bipolar (see below). The cause of BPD is still unknown. Sufferers experience dramatic mood swings where one moment their partner is fantastic, to the next when they are the object of their hatred. Some sufferers also have a history of eating disorders such as anorexia and bulimia. Threats to commit suicide are sometimes carried out. Extreme fears of abandonment may stem from childhood trauma, yet their irrational intense behaviour often encourages the very rejection they fear the most.

Bipolar disorder

This relatively common disorder, also known as manic depression, affects about 2.5 per cent of the population and runs in families. Those with bipolar disorder switch between deep depressions, when they are barely able to function, to euphoric, manic highs.

It's a treatable condition, but a significant proportion of sufferers choose not to take their medication because they actually like the highs - the increased energy, the creativity, the fast focused thinking and even spending sprees, all without feeling the need to sleep.

The highest highs swing to the lowest lows. When the lows arrive, spells in hospital are often needed to protect bipolar sufferers against self-harm and suicide. Many turn to the excessive use of recreational drugs and alcohol, causing mayhem for their partners and children.

Schizophrenia

The symptoms are clear, but correct diagnosis is complex and lengthy. Sufferers experience visual and auditory hallucinations; seeing and hearing things that don't exist. Some have delusions that they are being persecuted and are ultra-suspicious of everyone. They sometimes feel someone is out to get them. They hear 'personal messages' via radio and TV broadcasts. They may imagine they are someone famous. Their speech may be disorganised, rambling or nonsensical at times while they talk to invisible people. They often refuse to accept there is anything wrong with them and refuse to see a doctor or psychiatrist.

DID (dissociative identity disorder)

This was formerly referred to as MPD, or multiple personality disorder. Sufferers evolve additional personalities called 'alters' as a means of self-protection after a personal trauma such as rape or sustained childhood abuse. These alters can be aggressive if they perceive you as a threat.

The condition is controversial. Some doctors still question whether it is a real condition. Anyone in a relationship with a woman suffering from DID will tell you the condition is very real, and incredibly unsettling.

The sufferer can switch between her personalities at any moment. She may see a totally different person when she looks in the mirror.

Actress Sally Field won an Emmy for her remarkable portrayal of *Sybil*, in a TV movie of the same name, about a woman who suffered from this condition.

When you are wrapped up in yourself - you make for a very small package. Anon.

Munchhausen's syndrome and Munchhausen's by proxy

A woman suffering from Munchhausen's syndrome will exaggerate or fabricate the symptoms of illnesses to attract attention to herself and elicit sympathy from family and friends. Munchhausen's by proxy is the condition in which somebody caring for a child, usually a mother, convinces doctors that the child has specific illnesses that she has deliberately induced or made up. She may falsify physical symptoms by suffocation or poisoning to make the child vomit. Mothers who spend most of their time with children have the opportunity to harm them in this way. The mother benefits from sympathy and being seen to be a loving, dedicated, highly compassionate parent. Even when she isn't.

It is thought that up to nine per cent of children with mothers who suffer from Munchhausen's by proxy die as a result of their mother's behaviour. The condition is very difficult to prove, but there are telltale indications, including a higher incidence of illness or 'accidents' while in the sufferer's sole care. A child may have many different illnesses within a short time and may not respond to treatment, or may develop side-effects to medication that should not have been administered. If the child recovers, the problems return. It has been known for a mother to harm a child deliberately in order to pull a failing marriage back together.

There are many more personality disorders and variations but these seem to be the most widely experienced by unsuspecting men, women and children.

Some of the women described below have 'unfixable' pathological problems. Even if they wanted to change, some can't.

> *Did you hear about the woman who stabbed her husband thirty seven times? I admire her restraint.*
> Roseanne Barr

Sociopaths and psychopaths

A sociopath is defined as an individual who knows the difference between right and wrong but is afflicted with a personality disorder marked by antisocial behaviour. Sociopaths are rarely physically violent but are often unscrupulously cruel and ruthless with their victims.

Male and female sociopaths are estimated to account for about 4 per cent of the adult population. About 70 per cent of sociopaths grow up without a father. As an increasing proportion of divorced fathers are being denied contact with their children while mothers are being given the primary care role by family courts, expect the number of sociopaths to increase in the next few decades. UK teenagers have been described as the worst behaved in Europe.

An estimated 1 per cent of the population are psychopaths. These are men or women with an antisocial personality disorder that manifests itself in aggressive, criminal or immoral behaviour.

Sociopaths and psychopaths both lack conscience, empathy, guilt and remorse. They don't care about anybody else and sometimes they don't care about themselves either, or what happens to them.

Most diseases and disorders harm the person suffering from them, but these conditions are perverse in that the innocent bystanders, family members, partners and colleagues invariably suffer even more through coming into contact with them.

Most people with these disorders refuse point blank to accept that there is anything wrong with them. Denial is one of the symptoms of a sociopathic or psychopathic disorder. Refusing to accept any treatment or cure is another symptom. They don't want to be treated because they either feel so great about being who they are, or dismiss their condition as somebody else's problem. They are like the reckless driver who claims never to have had an accident but who has seen many. It won't occur to these drivers that they were almost certainly the cause of the accidents!

Don't confuse sociopaths and psychopaths with neurotics. Quite simply, neurotic men and women tend to turn in on themselves emotionally or physically and are more likely to harm themselves, while sociopaths and psychopaths tend to harm others physically or psychologically.

Now that we've looked at the different personality disorders you may be dealing with, let's consider some of the traits and tactics you could encounter; deliberate deception, clever manipulation, convincing and plausible stories and even jaw-dropping lies.

Always remember the chances are that this is all being done by someone who is probably not only highly intelligent, but who also has convinced herself that she has truth, justice and fairness on her side, and that it's only right and proper that you should suffer.

It is fairly safe to say that if you have seen more than a few of the characteristics outlined in this chapter, you are advised to tread carefully with such a woman. You will not win against her, so don't even try. Confrontation is not recommended. A low-key approach that helps her to decide to move on is often your best option.

Appearances can be deceptive

Sociopaths are notoriously difficult to spot because most of them are incredibly adept at hiding their true self and their motives. Since childhood the female sociopath may have developed complex and often subconscious methods to deceive her targets. On the surface she appears excessively friendly and charming. In fact, an early warning sign is that you suspect she is too good to be true. She probably is.

Occasionally she may let the mask slip. In isolation these behaviour traits are unreliable indicators, but if you witness a number of them, a queen of manipulation may be operating on you.

She is an aggressor and she picks fights with opponents who have been duped into believing she is a friend or a lover. Once she befriends her victims, she relies on their reasonableness to forgive her transgressions. However, most of her actions are hidden, because she has learnt to fight with invisible weapons and wields them with the deadliness and accuracy of a samurai warrior. Invariably, you don't see anything until the fight is over and she has won.

She is capable of being furious if she is ignored or is not given what she wants. She has mastered the art of expressing an opinion so forcibly and convincingly that it takes on the appearance of being a fact.

Her regular tantrums involve swearing, shouting, intimidation and threatens. She will wear people down until, for a quieter life, they agree with her. Interestingly, what she threatens to inflict on others is what she would find most damaging and hurtful to herself. Equally interestingly, she feels criticism and humiliation intensely, even if none is intended or given, and she will fight ferociously to defend what she sees as an attack, whether or not there is one.

Sometimes she will create a threat in her mind merely to defend and excuse what she knows to be her own dreadful behaviour.

She will expect you to keep quiet about her conduct towards you, assuming you will feel shame or embarrassment because you tolerate it. If you collude by maintaining your silence, it perpetuates her behaviour. She needs her victims to stay quiet about her. Beware of allowing yourself to get sucked into this game. She'll take delight in knocking you down a peg or two - for your own good, of course!

This attitude demonstrates a lack of concern for other people's wishes, welfare and rights, and she matter-of-factly shows a blatant disregard for society's rules, regulations and laws. A petty but common example of this is her blasé attitude towards parking her car. Parking restrictions simply don't apply to her and parking tickets are stuffed in the glove compartment to be forgotten and left unpaid.

Parking fines are not the only unpaid bills that mount up. When the bailiffs call she spins her sob story and plays the victim. Yet the moment they have been persuaded to leave she feels nothing more than contempt for those to whom she owes money. Her definition of a personal loan is often more like a donation; so don't expect to see your cash again. Don't ever open a joint bank account with her. She defaults on formal loans, and will almost certainly have a poor credit rating. She may even have stacks of County Court Judgments (CCJs) against her.

She routinely fails to honour other promises and commitments. The consequences of her behaviour are always somebody else's problem, not hers. She is never to blame for anything and is highly likely to be one of life's complainers. Because she's out to control, she manipulates and punishes at will. She is the witness, the judge, the lawyer, the jury, the executioner - but never the accused.

She may believe that antisocial behaviour is justified because of her 'difficult' circumstances, even though she may have contributed to them. She will break the rules without a second thought, if the end justifies the means.

She believes she is entitled to everything she desires. With an overdeveloped sense of self, working for what she wants is an inconvenience. Hard work is for everybody else. She wants the fast buck and the short-cut to success. Becoming a social parasite is quicker than toiling for anything. And when she pulls it off, she can then congratulate herself on cheating, conning or defrauding others who may be more intelligent or successful than she is.

Her every whim must be accommodated. Humility is alien to her. She is self-centred, opinionated and over-confident, and expects to be pampered and treated as superior.

She has possibly dabbled at shoplifting to feed her sense of entitlement for whatever she wants and for the 'buzz'. So obsessed with what she wants, she will ignore or neglect her children while claiming the opposite. She plays the martyr and expects constant attention. Her demanding behaviour almost guarantees it.

If she is divorced, she may have grown to hate her ex-husband more than she loves her children. She abuses the children by depriving them of access to their father, because she's punishing him for not delivering what she wanted in a husband. She refuses to consider that she played any role in the marriage break-up.

> *There's nothing wrong with a woman welcoming a man's advances - so long as they are in cash.* Zsa Zsa Gabor

She expects her man to do what she wants to prove his 'commitment' to her, and will try to control all aspects of her victim's life. She insists on choosing his friends, making him account for every moment of his day, making decisions for him, telling him what he can and cannot wear. She may even insist on watching her victims go to the bathroom.

Some women are genuinely unaware of the emotional pain and suffering they cause, but others know exactly what they are doing. They derive pleasure from putting others down and humiliating friends, colleagues, lovers and ex-partners. For some, revenge consumes their lives.

If there are any times when you start to suspect that you are being used, she is equally skilled at making you feel bad for thinking such thoughts. Mind you, she will probably never tell you explicitly that you are wrong, except perhaps if you confront her. She may feign shock and surprise that you could possibly think such unkind thoughts.

Unreliability goes hand-in-hand with her desire to control. Things always seem to crop up at the last minute making it *'impossible'* to do what she promised. She is often brilliant at providing rational excuses rather than reasons for her behaviour. She makes promises about a bright future but they are always promises of 'jam tomorrow'.

You find, too, that these women are stimulation junkies known for sexual promiscuity, gambling and taking illegal recreational drugs. If something gives the sociopath an adrenaline rush or makes her feel good, even in the short term, she'll probably give it a try or become addicted to it. This could lead to high-risk behaviour, with a reckless disregard for her own safety and that of others. She rarely thinks about the possible or probable consequences of her actions.

> *A successful man is one who makes more money than his wife can spend. A successful woman is one who can find such a man.* Lana Turner

These women want to create the illusion of intimacy quickly and are prepared to take short-cuts. They are full-on and their friendliness positively gushes. They often smile too much, but with their teeth, not their eyes. The woman will say all the right things and appear keen to be seen to make plans with you, but it's a ploy to gain your affection quickly and hook you in.

She will seem very loving and capable of intimacy and will pretend to care. However the intimacy, depth and commitment are illusions. They merely enable her to collect what she wants. Her true colours show only when all other tactics fail.

She's quite happy to steal her best friend's boyfriend. It's a great way to prove she has what it takes to be desirable, and simultaneously to prove the shallowness of the man and the delusion of her friend.

The picture is emerging of a woman who must get what she desires at all costs and must always be right. Sometimes she will deliberately claim to misunderstand something to justify doing what she wants, even though she knows it is against your wishes. She may cause problems just to attract attention to herself, because she likes to feel important.

Creating self-doubt in her victims' minds is an integral part of her approach. She plays on their reasonableness to give her the benefit of any doubts they may have. She knows that reasonable people don't like to think badly of others and will often beat themselves up for thinking uncharitable thoughts. She always sounds so convincing. Her approach is intended to make you question whether you were correct in your thoughts about her. It slows you down. It's meant to.

The sociopath seeks positions of authority for herself to ensure that she is never challenged. If you meet someone who you suspect fits this profile and discover she has a position of authority; maybe she's a police officer or a judge, don't fall into the trap of accepting her behaviour because of that authority. Don't assume she is trustworthy and should have the benefit of the doubt. Be more on your guard, not less.

Alternatively, she may target and associate with high-status and wealthy people. This gives her prestige or financial gain through 'gold-digging', conning or both.

It gets worse. Because she has no conscience, remorse, guilt or shame, she will use others mercilessly, ruthlessly and callously to get what she wants. If this involves bullying or humiliation, so be it. Her lack of feeling offers her enormous freedom to say or do whatever she wishes to whom she chooses. What is more, she gets away with it, and this is, to her at least, 'proof' that her victims are weak and gullible. In her eyes, they get what they deserve.

Another word of caution. Her victims are rarely aware of what is happening to them. It's rather like the instructions for boiling a frog. You put the frog in a pan of cold water, where it will sit comfortably. You turn on a slow heat and the frog will continue to sit there as the heat increases slowly and imperceptibly. That is, until the water gets too hot, but by then it's too late. One boiled frog.

Men have even been known to commit suicide because of her.

She lives for the moment and is incapable of delaying gratification or controlling her impulses. What she wants, she wants **now**. She conveniently forgets anything good you have done for her in the past, and despite making grand gestures about the future she does not plan. Her way of life is hand-to-mouth.

Martha Stout, author of *The Sociopath Next Door* says, "The most *universal behaviour of unscrupulous people is not directed, as one might imagine, at our fearfulness. It is, perversely, an appeal to our sympathy."*

This is a key point. If you take only one message from this book, make it this one. She is probably brilliant at eliciting pity and knows precisely how to do it.

She may have learned these skills from a young age. Treated like a little princess by her father, she learns to wrap him (and others) around her finger. By learning to get her own way, she perfects the illusion of appearing fragile. She is anything but....

She also appears so wonderful, sweet and demure, as if butter wouldn't melt in her mouth. Of course, she is a chameleon, capable of becoming exactly who her victim needs her to be.

She is meticulously turned out, expertly masking her inner personality cracks with flawless make-up, perfect hair and an extensive wardrobe, often paid for by past boyfriends. She may have learnt to cover up who she really is by appearing confident and self-assured. Yet underneath this confident and highly manicured exterior may lie an insecure, inadequate and ultra-needy woman.

How dysfunctional is the rest of her family? If she looks like the only sane one, she may be the only one who has managed to cover it up!

The disguise is so good that nobody would ever suspect that she could do anything unscrupulous. Beware the woman who flatters without offering sincere compliments. Flattery has been described as *'counterfeit charm'* and is usually a little over the top. She's probably setting you up to make demands on you or to manipulate you in some other way.

She holds grudges too. Her revenge and retribution can be savage and harsh. Surprise is her weapon. Expect the worst, then double it.

This woman doesn't think twice about destroying the reputations, health and well-being or the livelihood of others if they represent obstacles to getting what she wants. She's the sort who will force you to get down on bended knee to beg forgiveness and then take delight in saying *"No"*. She makes you feel bad to *'keep you on your toes'*.

Such women will not be happy until they have ripped the very heart and soul out of their victim. Even then, there is no guarantee they will be any happier.

Sadly, most men ignore what their gut instinct is trying to tell them about her, because they think she wants them.

How she chooses her target

The sociopath has a remarkable ability to spot weaknesses in people, and use them to get her way to improve her position, and increase her power over them. She counts on most people being trusting and forgiving. When (not if) she cheats on you, she banks on you forgiving her.

> *Smart girls know how to play tennis, piano and dumb.*
> Lynne Redgrave

She prefers the path of least resistance, her victims are the most easily deceived, manipulated and entrapped with fake charm and charisma.

What is it that attracts you to these personality types, and what is your attraction to them? Are you drawn to women with issues'? And to what extent might you be contributing to your situation?

Do you like trying to 'fix' people? Are you a 'people-pleaser'? Are you a good samaritan? Are you addicted to intense relationships? Do you have a history of being in co-dependent relationships? The classic example of this is the person married to an alcoholic who cleans up and looks after them so well that there seems no need for the alcoholic to stop drinking. Perversely, the 'carer' needs their partner to continue drinking to maintain their identity within that relationship. Perhaps you have stayed in relationships where you were unhappy but kept thinking, *'Maybe she will change.'* Some of these women cannot change. Are you someone who has a habit of thinking too much, or are you a bit neurotic at times? Or maybe you're just too *'nice'* for your own good?

Sociopathic women go for these personality types in preference to any other men or women. They sometimes string them along, claiming they want to be helped. The so-called carer tries so hard to help but keeps failing to please. The blunt truth is that the sociopath doesn't want anything to change or improve. If the circumstances did improve, she'd lose her power over you. In fact, creating failure is fantastic for the sociopath because it helps the carer to feel bad about their abilities. It's part of the sociopathic scam.

Sometimes the carer unwittingly achieves the objective they had supposedly agreed, only to find the sociopath turns on him. Why? By solving the problem, the carer proves the sociopath is inadequate for not being able to sort it out for herself.

Liar, liar

The sociopathic woman can and does lie through her teeth. In fact, if lying was an Olympic sport, sociopaths would win all the medals. And if not, they'd say they did!

A sociopath is almost incapable of not lying; lying to others; lying about others; lying about herself and even lying to herself. Lying is her core skill. She will sound extremely convincing and her inability to feel or express real emotions helps with this. Most normal people experience some degree of guilt about lying, but not her.

She is quick-thinking and flexible and has an outstandingly good memory (a necessary trait for any accomplished liar). Along with the lying and deception, she is secretive and insists on password-protecting her computers and phones from prying eyes because she knows how much she has to hide.

She will lie to you by saying whatever is the most appropriate thing at that moment to rescue her from a situation. She may flatly deny any wrongdoing. You may have unquestionable evidence to the contrary, but she will look you straight in the eye and, without flinching or batting an eyelid, lie superbly.

Lying by omission may be one of her specialities too. She doesn't tell you the full story, omitting important facts rather than saying something that enables you to prove she is lying. If she is ever challenged about anything she has said that doesn't seem to ring true, her initial responses could be particularly vague. She expects what she says to be taken at face value and believed. If a vague response is not accepted, she may then feign memory loss or skilfully change the subject to deflect the conversation away from what you're trying to discuss. If that doesn't work, she will probably resort to attacking you verbally to push you into defending yourself against her false allegation. She already knows it's false but it's a distraction tactic.

After this she may actually claim she had been mistaken. Her victim, however, will rarely bring up the topic again, because he is so relieved to have won his argument.

Particularly poisonous and vindictive women have resorted to total fabrications and outrageous allegations that could destroy a reputation to get their own back on a man who has simply refused to give her what she wants.

Some sociopaths are known to use false names to hide their identity. Her life story could well be pure fantasy. Many of these lies are deliberately made difficult to prove or challenge. If, for example, she lies about being raped by a stepfather (who may or may not have even existed), you will appear insensitive if you ask her to prove it. If it helps her to gain sympathy, she'll say anything.

If you have any doubts about what she tells you, ask for more detail. Ask for specifics. Precisely *when* did something happen, who was involved, how *old* was she, where was she living at the time? Then remember what she said. If necessary write everything down in your journal (see Chapter 8). Ask yourself whether she became more guarded or secretive. Use an interviewing technique by creating silence to see how she fills it. Does she change the subject?

She routinely refuses to accept what she has done, and will simply ignore specific information because it's not convenient for her to know. If she *did* accept the truth, she would not then be able to justify her behaviour.

These sociopathic, lying women often formulate complex rationales for what they do based on relatively minor indiscretions by others, which she exaggerates out of all proportion. Thus they can conduct a sleight-of-hand trick on their own brain to support and justify feelings of deep anger and bitterness.

What is generally referred to as 'flakiness' indicates typical traits of sociopathic behaviour. Some, although not all, are related to a poor attitude towards work. She exhibits a low level of conscientiousness, she may have a record of poor timekeeping, or she takes lots of days off. She isn't a finisher and constantly craves change. She may switch jobs regularly and she may use fake credentials to land a higher-paid job than she is qualified for.

Relationships

It is difficult for her to make and keep friends. She may have a string of short, intense relationships that are no more than liaisons. She will never be drawn on how many men she has slept with. She will accuse a man of having an affair, when the likelihood is that she is the one committing adultery or infidelity, possibly with more than one lover at any time. She may end relationships for the most spurious of reasons.

She may boast lots of male friends. She usually has fewer female friends. Other women are more likely to see through her, and she knows this. Men, however, are more easily deceived and they give her more attention; so men are her focus. What girlfriends she claims to have will almost always be less attractive than she is. She also chooses to spend time with losers to make her feel better about herself. She is a fair-weather friend. Often attracted to someone who is sensible and responsible, she realises these are qualities she lacks in herself.

Her fighting tactics

She will tie you up in emotional knots. The expert manipulator can perform this trickery so well that, no matter what you do, you cannot possibly do the right thing for her. She may set you impossible tasks and move the goal posts if there is a possibility that you will succeed.

She will keep you guessing. One moment she is loving and affectionate, the next she is abusive, angry and out of control. This erratic behaviour makes it impossible for the victim to know where he stands.

Watch for her skill at making non-threatening threats. These are innocent sounding remarks that seem to hurt. The sort of comment that if she was challenged on, she could offer a plausible explanation and then add *"No I didn't mean that, how stupid of you to think such a thing"*. Ouch, she did it again! She will push her partner as far as she can to exert maximum control. If she feels she has gone too far, she will try to salvage the situation by becoming intensely loving. This causes further confusion and increases any self-doubt you had. Every time she gets you to back down, she wins. Watch for her 'advance and retreat seduction'. She gives affection and withdraws it. It's a power thing.

She is capable of appearing intensely angry at someone's minor misdemeanours to distract attention away from her own more serious bad behaviour. This destabilises her victims and it's often part of her 'show'.

The silent treatment is another of her weapons. It's unnerving and cruel and an effective strategy that she has used many times to cripple her opponents. Encouraging colleagues and 'friends' to join her in punishing you is also a favoured strategy. It's non-aggressive aggression.

If she isn't getting what she wants, the sociopath uses her charm and persuasion skills to enlist others to do her dirty work for her. She will seek out the people closest to you, and try to get them on her side - or at least make you think she's done so. She'll recruit your close family, even your parents. She will choose to interpret innocent behaviour as a threat.

She needs to be seen as a victim so that she has a twisted, valid reason for her revenge and her outrageous behaviour. Furthermore, she actually *wants* a crisis. If things are working well, she may feel the need to disrupt everything and everyone.

Don't become complacent. She knows from experience that revenge is a dish best served cold and one day she will get her own back. Specific strategies and practical ideas to help you cope with her covert fighting are dealt with in Chapters 8 and 9.

Being found out

Eventually she may be found out, but even with incontrovertible evidence of her guilt, she will lie brazenly to convince you that you are wrong. You will be awe-struck at her audacity. She may machine-gun you verbally, believing that attack is the best form of defence. Much of the time it works for her because she always appears so convincing.

> *In future, I'm going to find a women I hate - then just give her a house.* Lewis Grizzard

A well-used ploy is to interrupt whatever you say. Psychologically she doesn't want to hear the truth and will therefore talk over you to delete it from her mind.

Another favourite trick is to dismiss the wrongdoing by trying to convince you that it was trivial. By this she means it is your fault for over-reacting. It's a tactic to make you redirect your thinking and forget about what she has been accused of.

All the while, a little voice in your head may say: *"What if I **am** wrong about her? Perhaps I **am** over-reacting."* Oh, she's good at this!

You'd think that being found out would put a stop to her behaviour. Not at all. She simply doesn't learn from her experiences. She *can't* stop. There will be no change in her behaviour even if she is ever punished; by you or by the law.

She will latch on to something - just about anything - you said or did (perhaps a very long time ago) to justify the vitriolic hatred and abuse she hands out. No matter what she does, she will say or do whatever she can think of to justify it. Often this appears to be a way of getting others to be convinced. In reality, she's trying to convince herself.

When all else fails, she can turn on the tears and claim to be a victim of whatever she can think of.

When to let her go

Everybody screws up at least some of the time. Learning to trust an individual takes time, especially if your trust has ever been abused. Therefore, you need to learn this lesson: never allow yourself to trust someone based on what you are told, only on her actual behaviour.

Secondly, as in rounders or baseball, it could be a case of three strikes and you're out. If she breaks promises or lies to you three times, give serious consideration to getting her out of your life.

In reality, doing this is rarely that simple. She may make it extremely clear that you are unworthy of her, but she may also make it very difficult for you to walk away from her. If you decide to end the relationship, do not engage in prolonged discussions about why you have reached your decision. She may try to argue with you to prove you wrong. It's a fight, and you are her adversary. She will say anything to convince you that you are being unreasonable, unkind or cruel, or that your grievances are petty or insignificant. It's a ploy to keep you.

She may insist that there is a future for the relationship. If you resist, she may force herself on you. Some are obsessive. However, rejected women of this type will sometimes decide: *"If I can't have him, I'll destroy him by making his life a misery."* To give you a flavour of what we mean, watch the movies *Fatal Attraction* and *Play Misty for Me*.

Why did she do it?

Some of these women are in a kind of relay race that lasts longer than their own lifetime. They pass on a baton of hatred, abuse and pain received from others, who in turn probably received it from a previous generation.

There is a strong possibility that the sociopathic woman was neglected as a child. If a woman has been harmed or abused in her early life, at a time when she had no power, she may misuse her power as an adult by devoting herself to 'getting back' at everyone, because she feels society has let her down badly. A spell of juvenile delinquency is sometimes a small indicator that she had used her growing power to rebel against authority.

If you have ever come into contact with a sociopath, eventually you will be forced to accept that you have been used and abused by her. Yet the legacy of her deceit, dishonesty and ruthlessness can last far longer than her actions. Victims will devote hours, weeks, months, even years, lying awake at night trying to work out just why she did what she did. When they fail to come up with a rational explanation, as they invariably do, they turn their thinking against themselves, beating themselves up for being so stupid and naïve.

Asking yourself questions such as *"Why didn't I see this coming? Why didn't I listen to my gut instinct?"* won't actually help you, so don't bother. She's not worth any more of your energy. It's over.

The short answer to why she treated you the way she did is that she is not logical. She simply made a decision to do it to you and probably to others. It is a futile waste of your time and energy to think there was any logic in her actions.

Whenever you find yourself slipping back into thinking more about what she did to you, as difficult as it may be, tell your mind (preferably not out loud!) to stop doing this and think about more useful stuff.

When she is caught lying or cheating, she expects you to forgive her *'just one more time'*. She will stay with you for as long as she thinks she can continue to get away with her behaviour. But the moment she realises she has been rumbled she'll probably leave. Then it's a case of 'Next!'

She will never change. She doesn't want to, even if she tells you otherwise. It is highly unlikely that she will ever be the reliable and honest person you are looking for or deserve.

She may have been a victim who suffered abuse or abandonment in the past. She only claims to be abused today. The hurt lingers and spreads. She is not a victim. She merely wants to be *thought* of as one so that people feel sorry for her. But no one will ever feel sorry enough. A self-defined victim can never be happy. Yet she refuses to accept any alternatives to playing the victim role. She has boxed herself into a corner. This is her identity which she believes she must maintain. If she can't remain as a victim, she loses her superiority over her chosen victims. She would then become a nobody. It's a deception; to herself and others.

If she defines herself as a victim, by definition she has to find a 'victimiser'. If there isn't one - YOU get the job.

She may have experienced severe abuse in her past, but similarly, her behaviour today is creating long-term innocent victims in order to feed her compulsive desires to punish and control. Her abuse is carefully orchestrated to trigger a reaction in her target. As part of her behaviour, she will deliberately create problems and step back to watch everyone deal with the ensuing chaos. When you are seen to respond angrily, this becomes her 'proof' that you are the unreasonable one! This reaction is the basis of her cries of abuse. She conveniently ignores or violently denies what she starts.

She somehow manages to twist your enjoyment for something innocent by interpreting it as a way of punishing her or making her feel sad or upset.

She perfects the appearance that she has to 'defend' herself against you, when there is nothing to defend. You are not abusing her. As far as she is concerned, *you* are the person who needs therapy. It's NEVER her, although she may insist on attending counselling sessions to 'prove' her need for help against you, and to convey the appearance that she is willing to '*support you*' to overcome your problem.

When you are not an abuser, you will be made to feel that you are.

It has been said that abusive women steal *'peace of mind'* from their victims. She poisons your personal and professional relationships with others by spreading convincing lies and deliberate half-truths. Their combined effects are deeply damaging and undeserved. She is assassinating you. She is spreading cancer of your character.

If you are accused of being abusive and you know you have not been; this is the beginning of the end. You WILL be made to suffer more and more as her desperation to maintain control over you intensifies.

One thing is certain. You'll never have a dull relationship with any of the women described in this chapter. However, becoming emotionally attached to such a woman is a recipe for disaster, as the next three chapters will show.

Just make sure you never marry, or have children with one of them.

> *However tough and hard and independent you may be, there are times when you have to have help.*
> Lord Tebbit.

Chapter 5

Girlfriend, Wife or History?

> *American women expect to find in their husbands a perfection that English women only hope to find in their butlers.*
> W Somerset Maugham

Marrying the wrong woman continues to be financially ruinous for a large number of unsuspecting men. Having a lasting, meaningful, mutually respectful and loving relationship with a sociopathic woman is practically impossible. Yet she needs a relationship. And almost any relationship will do, so long as she gets what she wants from it.

In the previous chapter we described a variety of personality types you would be best avoiding, however enticing some of them can appear. In this chapter we explore ways to protect yourself against potentially dangerous women and make it less likely you will end up marrying someone who could harm you emotionally or financially. Even if you are not in the market for marriage just yet, we describe the shocking tactics some unscrupulous women use to manipulate eligible bachelors into getting married. You will learn how to recognise what she is up to, and take the necessary counter-measures. Now that 57 per cent of marriages end in divorce and 70 per cent of those divorces are initiated by women, it has never been so important to choose your wife wisely.

Imagine this. You are a single 'nice guy' in your late twenties or early thirties. You have a good job and have finally paid off your university debts. You have a girlfriend, two years younger than you. You've been seeing each other for just over a year. It's an exclusive, monogamous, serious relationship. You are kind, attentive and generous. Things are OK between you but not fantastic.

When you started dating, you paid every time in the restaurant. You were happy to be chivalrous, but it quickly became the norm. She never offers to pay for anything because she's so 'careful' with her money. Even at *Starbucks* she always goes to 'find seats' rather than paying for her *skinny machiatto*. You made a joke of it once by telling her how much it cost - but she didn't have any change on her.

Most of the time she's good company. She ticks a lot of boxes, she's a good-looking woman, the perfect size and shape for you, and she always wants sex. In fact, she sometimes wants sex more than you, and that's saying something. When you're going out, she al-ways takes hours to get ready. Everything has to be perfect; clothes, hair and make-up. And on more than one occasion she's insisted you change because *"You're not going out looking like that."*

Be honest, it's worth waiting for her because when you walk into a bar or restaurant, she gets noticed by all the other guys. So in that respect she's something of a trophy too. And that makes you feel good.

In recent months, however, she has started to make more and more demands on you and your time. Once her friends cancelled a planned night out. You had fixed up a boys' night out to coincide with it but because she was now at a loose end, she expected you to cancel your arrangements. When you explained that it would mean letting people down, she accused you of not caring about her and complained she would now be home on her own *"because of you"*. In fact, you get the blame for quite a lot of things. There was that time when she over-reacted because you talked in a vaguely complimentary way about an ex-girlfriend with whom you are still friendly. But you've learnt not to argue - it's just not worth the hassle.

She runs hot and cold. One minute she's all over you like a rash, the next she is distant and sometimes won't even talk to you because of the most petty things. Giving in to her is easier.

A couple of friends have commented that she is quite domineering and has you under her thumb. You find yourself explaining that she is lovely in so many other ways. Your brother has some young children and she's wonderful with them. She'd make a fantastic mother, possibly as a mother to your children. She gets on well with your sister and makes a point of joining you to visit your parents. Yet all the while you have a nagging suspicion that she wants too much from you. Once she threatened to end the relationship because you made an off-the-cuff remark about not being ready to marry yet.

You think you love her but ...

She doesn't like your apartment. Out of the blue she said that if you got married one day you'd have to sell it to buy a house. She also wants to start a family *"before it's too late."*

Then last night she said: "*We need to talk. I think I might be pregnant.*" This is definitely not something you would have chosen. What if she is? What would you do? Would you encourage her to terminate the pregnancy? Or would you find that abhorrent for religious or ethical reasons? Would you marry her? How sure are you that it isn't a ploy to force you into marriage and starting a family because she's ready for it? After all, she *would* make a wonderful mother.

In this scenario, *what* you decide is less important than *why* you reach your decision.

Why some men marry

Generalisations are always extremely dangerous. Even so, here are a few reasons men have given for deciding to get married:

• Firstly, there's love. Both are so deeply in love. They were made for each other, true soul mates and best friends. They have found lasting happiness and will remain together for the rest of their long lives.

- 'Nice guys', especially, often marry out of a sense of duty. A significant number of these men faced with the above situation would go ahead and make an honest woman of her, even though, in reality, the woman wasn't as careful about her birth control as she might have been.

- Women who are looking to get married often realise that men usually tie the knot between the ages of 26 and 33. When the man stops studying and starts earning money he may realise it's time for the next phase of his life.

- Most graduates leave university or college with large debts, which take time to pay off. Marrying while in debt is not usually the way a man operates. However, a woman in debt may want to get married more.

- He loves his girlfriend. As she is so keen to get married, many men become GAGs - Go Along Guys. A man like this will propose to show how committed he is to the relationship.

- If his male friends are starting to get married, he may think he had better do it too. If not, he could be left on his own.

- It may never have been a priority but he may feel he 'should' be thinking about marriage.

- He may think that he's starting to feel a little too old for the singles bars he has frequented for a number of years - another sign that it's time for that next phase of life.

- When a man starts to lose his hair, he often sees it as the first sign that he'd better think about settling down before he becomes too unappealing to women. If the hair loss coincides with packing on a bit of weight, his fear of being left on his own sharpens his mind further.

- How old he feels and how old others make him feel will also have an impact on his openness to the idea of marriage.

- Perhaps she wants to marry him, so she proposes. He is grateful or flattered that someone wants him.

- Or he is incredibly needy, neurotic and desperate for a wife. He can't function without her - and she's the one who has to be convinced.

Why some women marry

Millions of kind, loving and well-meaning parents tuck their little girls up in bed at night and feed them a daily diet of fairy stories featuring beautiful young girls who meet handsome princes, fall in love, marry and live happily ever after.

Some of these parents even put stickers on their bumpers or inside their vehicles proclaiming to the world: *"Little Princess On Board"*. How many of these same parents are unwittingly creating unrealistic expectations for their daughters in years to come? How many of these innocent little girls start to believe they are princesses? And how many learn, subconsciously perhaps, to expect to be treated like royalty by everyone, especially men - because that's what Daddy did?

Marriage is therefore an aspiration for many women from a young age. They are in love with the ideal of what marriage *should* be, and the notion of having a party in their honour on a day when they will look as beautiful as they're ever going to.

> Over a coffee, a woman in her mid-thirties tells her girl-friend how her boyfriend of three months is turning out to be a bit boring. The sex is OK but nothing special. She is thinking about dumping him. Yet only a couple of weeks later the same woman gushes to her friend that this guy has proposed marriage to her - and she's accepted because she is *so* in love and *"You must come to the wedding"* and *"It's all go-ing to be so-o-o wonderful"*. The woman couldn't understand why her friend couldn't get as excited about it as she was. The poor guy. He doesn't know what is likely to hit him.

> *"Jennifer became pregnant, and Todd agreed to marry her. After Todd spent over $25,000 on the wedding and honeymoon, Jennifer became convinced that Todd had slept with a stripper at his bachelor's party. To retaliate, Jennifer aborted the baby."*
> *The Man's Guide to the Art of Divorce* by Michael Young

Choosing to marry for love, most women are also genetically pro-grammed to want children. Some are more determined than others, especially if they reach an age when their girlfriends are marrying in droves. A woman may start to feel that if she doesn't find a man soon, it might be too late to have children. Women from their late twenties and into their early and mid-thirties become increasingly aware of how loud their biological baby clock is ticking.

The urgency is encapsulated in this story by a single mother: *"I wanted a child. I didn't have a boyfriend or a husband. So I had a one-night stand to get pregnant. It worked. I told the guy on the phone. He didn't take it well, although he was a bit happier and relieved when I told him quite honestly that he did not have to pay for anything - ever. I got what I wanted. I was happy. She's now six and I'm still happy. It was a good decision for me."*

Not all men are that 'lucky'. Author, Mark H. Rudov expresses it this way:

> *Imagine that every one of your sperm cells holds a fountain pen in its hand. The moment one of them unites with an egg, it signs the state's contract. The woman decides whether or not to enforce it. Should she do so, it will endure at least 18 years.*

A woman's urge to reproduce is entirely natural and can be overwhelming for a high proportion of normal, well-adjusted, 'nice' women. However, that desire to have babies exists among nasty women too.

Just because a woman is ready to get married at a particular age, she may wrongly assume men of the same age also want to. Most women want to settle down and start a family at a younger age than men. Men can have children at practically any age.

The woman will often be able to choose to give up working for a wage if her man is earning. Therefore, a man's earning potential is often a big factor when a woman selects a man for marriage. When she's married her financial needs are catered for in law. The institution of marriage helps to shelter her from life's risks.

Realise that women don't usually marry a man for who he is. They're more interested in his potential. She wants to turn him into a better man. If a man fails to live up to those expectations she sometimes feels outraged that he has made her look bad because she was wrong about him. Of course, he had no say in the terms and conditions she laid down for the relationship!

When a religious woman is looking for a husband, she is likely to pick a man with the same beliefs. The older, unmarried woman or the older, previously married woman will go for the previously married man. She has sufficient proof that he is the marrying type.

If a woman cannot find a husband, she and other females sometimes see her as 'not validated as a woman'. If nobody is prepared to ask her to be his wife, she may choose to interpret that to mean she is not 'good enough' as a woman. She may be regarded as an outsider by her female friends, who have been 'chosen' and are therefore worthy of being wives.

> *Intimacy is a man listening to her feelings while she is listening to his hopes and dreams. Intimacy for a man is when his wife helps him wash the car.* Jay Carter

Commitment

When a woman decides not to marry she is applauded for her independence, free spirit and refusal to conform to societal and familial pressures. When a man decides not to marry it's because he must have issues about commitment. Women's magazines repeatedly run articles about men and their refusal to commit to a relationship. The implication is that these men are in some way 'bad'. It's simple. Women want something from their man that he is not prepared to give up easily.

It seems there are far more free-spirited women and commitment-phobic men in the UK than ever before because in 2005 there was a 10 per cent decline in the number of marriages. The figure was down from 313,550 in 2004 to 244,710 in 2005. This is the lowest number of weddings in one year since 1896. Is this a coincidence, or the start of a more widespread refusal by men to assume too high a proportion of the risks involved in getting married? The UK Government Actuary's Department has predicted that the number of people who marry will fall by a further 10% in the next 25 years. While the number of co-habiting couples will double from over two million to 3.8 million in the same period.

When it comes to getting married, a man often believes deeply that he has more to lose than the woman. The risks are no longer shared equally. If he isn't prepared to marry his girlfriend, even though he may be in love with her, it's because he doesn't trust her and the legal system enough. He has been forced to conclude that current marriage laws are too onerous and he has seen and heard of so many women who take their husbands to the cleaners, using the divorce settlement as a way of punishing them, rather than for the true purpose - spousal or child support.

If you're thinking about co-habiting with your girlfriend instead, changes to the law in England could mean that if you break up you may have to share assets and make payments to your 'ex' - as if you were married.

Could it be that the women receiving vast divorce settlements in British courts are the biggest reason for the drop in the number of marriages? There have been some phenomenal examples.

Ray Parlour, the England and Arsenal soccer player, was forced by a judge to hand over two mortgage-free houses worth more than £1 million, a £250,000 lump sum and a third of his annual earnings for four years - approximately £440,000 a year - to his ex-wife. Her lawyers managed to convince the judge that she had played a significant role in assisting his career as a footballer.

The Chelsea football club owner and Russian billionaire Roman Abramovich was divorced by his wife Irina after his affair with a young model. According to *The Sunday Times* Rich List 2007, the divorce settlement was approximately £155 million ($310 million).

John Charman achieved stellar business success. He was married for 29 years and is thought to have stayed for the children's sake. When his wife filed for divorce he said: *"I made a fair and reasonable offer to my wife of £20 million, which would be impossible for any reasonable person to spend in their lifetime."* If he had ended the marriage years sooner, perhaps he would not have been hit with a divorce settlement for £48 million ($96 million), 37 per cent of value of the business that he grew without her direct involvement.

In an article in *The Sunday Times Magazine* of October 9, 2005, the financier Allan Miller claimed he was a victim of what he described as *"legally sanctioned burglary"* when his wife of just 1,013 days was awarded a house worth £2.3 million and a £2.7 million lump sum, making a settlement that works out at £4,935.83 per day. The court calculated this would give her an annual tax-free income of £98,000. Her former husband said her e-mail address remained *Must-do-lunch-Melissa@...* There were no children. It was reported that, she lived in a one-bedroom rented apartment before she married.

In the appeal court Lord Justice Thorpe stated her marriage gave her *"a legitimate entitlement to a long-term future on a higher plane of affluence"*. In the same article the lawyer Raymond 'Jaws' Tooth said:

> *"It's a gold-digger's charter ... Any attractive woman will now say, 'Why should I work, when I can go down to Tramp, find a likely candidate, and seduce him?' She'll annoy him sufficiently that he'll probably go off with someone else. But then she'll be able to say he was responsible for the marital breakdown, and will obtain enough to live the rest of her life in luxury. Is that the state to which the law has descended?"*

James Turner, QC, put it more bluntly: "

> *"If you're a well-off man, or are likely to achieve wealth in the future, you'd be absolutely bonkers to get married from a financial point of view ... Many lawyers think the pendulum has gone from one side - being too pro-husband - to swinging wildly the other way. It's a disincentive for a man to get married ... a disincentive to work hard."*

His view is almost certainly shared by Charles Ashton, a corporate lawyer who was earning £450,000 a year. Following his divorce it has been reported that he has to pay his ex-wife about half of everything he will ever earn in the future.

And what man has not felt sorry for Sir Paul McCartney, who has been forced to endure savage media assassination by his former wife Heather Mills?

Not all men are bitter about marriage. With irony, this man expressed his views on the beauty of marriage by penning this internet chat room comment:

> *"If you can find a woman to be your companion who is not treacherous, a deceitful little actress, a sly whore or a manipulative nag or a shrieking hag, then you are among the lucky few. Congratulations."*

As so many other wealthy men have discovered, no matter how much they are forced to pay, no woman has yet been heard to say: *"No, that's too much. Take some back. You earned it. I didn't."*

Based on all the intense media coverage surrounding these cases and others, how many more women married to wealthy men are now giving serious consideration to the idea that they could get a divorce and still lead their luxury lifestyle?

There are the incentives of exotic holidays, expensive designer clothes, dining out at the trendiest restaurants, driving the latest sports cars and the freedom to enjoy the pleasures of younger, more virile boyfriends, all paid for by the ex-husband. How many rich married men are all too aware of their exposure to these risks? How many of these at-risk men are overtly bullied into doing everything their wife demands of them under the threat of a financially ruinous divorce? And how many cunning wives prefer the more covert approach, biding their time while preparing to jump ship when it's more convenient, possibly when their children are older?

What effect do these media stories have on young, highly ambitious and eligible bachelors who may aspire to become successful or wealthy? A man may find himself thinking that, if he works hard, gets to the top of his chosen career or builds up a business from scratch, his wife may be allowed, even encouraged, in years to come to take most of the fruits of his labours. He says to himself: *"What if I am as successful as I plan to be? My wife could take everything."*

In *Mugged by a toxic wife*, India Knight, a female columnist in *The Sunday Times* reflected on these women *"...the new breed of toxic wife has no shame, and therefore no need for any kind of occupation. She just spends her husband's money and, er, that's it. And if he should twig, as more and more men in this category seem to be doing, poor things, and realise that his domestic situation isn't quite as he'd envisaged it, she will smile sweetly and take him for every penny he's got.... Realise that their behaviour is not a million miles away from prostitution, except that with a prostitute you know what you are paying for."*

What man, therefore, wouldn't be forced to conclude that getting married is simply too risky these days?

The harsh realities of marriage in the 21st century

As part of a man's risk assessment when considering marriage he is increasingly aware that:

- If you cheat on your wife she gets at least half your assets. If she cheats on you, she still gets half your assets.
- A woman often quits working to bring up the family she wants, while the man may be forced to work in a job he hates just to support them. Women have this choice. Most men don't.

Women to avoid

Before you take the plunge into the potentially dangerous waters of marriage, ask yourself why you want to be married.

If you have a history of relationships with women who treat you badly, you need to think very carefully about why you are prepared to accept the unacceptable. Nobody has the right to make other people feel bad about themselves.

If you tend to fall for the same type of woman. In the first place, avoid that type of woman!

Avoid the following types of women. They are inspired by an amusing article by Matthew Fitzgerald:

1. *Miss Anne Thrope.* She is angry at everything and everyone. She will turn against you sooner or later. Get out before she does.
2. *Miss Anne Drist.* She hates men, in the way misogynists hate women. Avoid her. Her hatred may be directed at all men, probably following a bad experience with just one man, pos-

sibly when she was a child. Sad or even tragic as that may have been, avoid her. She has the capacity to make your life hell.

3. *Miss Take*. Her middle name is 'Gold-digger'. She expects you to pay for everything. What she wants she gets. If she doesn't get it from you, she'll push and push you into submission. If that fails, she'll move on to another willing man. That is, until he figures out what she's up to and stops lavishing money on her. *Miss Take* has possibly sold a number of engagement rings for 'sentimental reasons'!

4. *Miss Mimi*. Everything is about her. The Mae West quote comes to mind: *"Enough about me. What do you think of me?"*

5. *Miss Mirage*. She appears to be perfect, everything a man could possibly want in a woman. It's a mirage, a carefully constructed ideal of what she thinks he wants. She keeps up the act until she has trapped him.

6. *Princess Lay'er*. Sex is her lure. She uses either the promise of sex or the continuation of sex to get what she wants. Withdrawing sexual favours is a powerful means of controlling a man. If a woman *ever* uses sex as a weapon, don't marry her. She may appear to be sexually captivated by you until it no longer serves her purposes. Or she may have insatiable sexual appetites and make constant demands on you, or multiple partners, and any failure to perform could be greeted with humiliation and ridicule.

An attractive woman with a voracious sexual appetite may be something men dream of. But be careful what you ask for. A woman who wants a lot of sex certainly appeals to a man's ego. *"Hey, she wants me,"* he tells himself. But she might not. Some offer themselves to be liked, while others just want to control a man. And she may have a desperate need to feel desired. If she has a voracious appetite for sex, it could be an addiction, so she isn't necessarily into you. She just needs sex. If you are stressed, over-worked, or don't have sufficient time for sex, your libido could dip dramatically, albeit temporarily. However, a woman who requires daily sex is likely to interpret your behaviour as 'proof' that you don't find her desirable any more. This may be enough for her to justify getting sex elsewhere - immediately.

Princess Lay'er leads us to the subject of infidelity. The idea may be difficult for a younger guy to accept but a woman with a high libido is more likely to increase her need for sex as she gets older and into her forties. For a man, the opposite is sometimes true. This is not always the case, but you need to be aware that in later life when your energy levels are not what they were, and your job becomes more time-consuming and demanding as you work hard to support a growing family, you may not be as interested in sex as you are today. But if her interest remains strong, there is an increased possibility that she will seek a younger man, or men, to satisfy her sexually. A leading UK divorce barrister says that at least 60 per cent of the women who see her to explore divorce options admit they are having at least one extra-marital affair, possibly more. This has become far more common in recent years.

Susan Shapiro Barash, professor of critical thinking and gender studies at Marymount Manhattan College, found that 90 per cent of women interviewed in one of her extensive investigations claimed not to experience any guilt when cheating on their husbands.

A constantly partying, hard-drinking, glamorous, always 'up for it' sexual animal may be a dream girlfriend, but would she make a good, reliable wife and mother? If, incidentally, you're a similar type, would you make a good husband and father?

"	Question:	*"Have you ever paid for sex?"*
	Answer:	*"Only emotionally"* Lee Hurst

Learn to see past the looks she may so painstakingly construct to appear as attractive and as desirable as possible. Is her packaging of make-up and designer clothes meant to hide or distract you from noticing serious flaws in her personality?

What about her attitude to life in general and you in particular? How similar are your beliefs? What qualities are important to you - honesty, loyalty, reliability, trust, your relationship with money or fidelity? Find out what she is less than proud of. Find out in which ways she has be-haved badly. Does she constantly focus on what she doesn't have? How does she treat you and others? Does she make unreasonable demands of you some or all the time? Is she low, medium or high-maintenance?

Does she seek, even in the most subtle way, attention from other men? Is she a kind person? Does she have genuine compassion?

Accept that she is likely to become her mother as she gets older! Is what you feel for her really true love? Is that heart flutter down to her or the effects of a double espresso? Or is it just a carefully crafted illusion of love by a manipulative or self-serving woman? It can be very difficult to tell. But not impossible.

Use the following approaches to find out what she is really like:

- How does she behave when you are not prepared to give in to her demands or refuse to provide her with something she wants? If you refuse her in a polite, reasonable manner but she tends to react with a tantrum, she could be trouble one day.
- In what circumstances does she criticise you, complain about you or get angry and irritated by you?
- Does she know any people you know, dislike or distrust? If so, and without telling her what you think of somebody, ask: *"What do you think of X?"* Then pay particular attention to the way she responds rather than the specific words she chooses. Pay a lot of attention at this moment. If she responds instantly, without a nano-second's pause, that she likes them a lot, you could have a problem. Her values could be diametrically opposed to yours. If she hesitates even for a split second before answering, she is weighing up what she thinks of this person and is figuring out how to respond. If she is an honest, non-malicious woman she will not want to say anything bad about them, but at the same time will not want to lie to you, or offend someone who is potentially your best friend. So, without saying anything, you can often discover at a fairly deep level how she thinks, what she feels about someone and how she deals with this potential minefield. If you dislike someone and she dislikes him too but is not prepared to bad-mouth him, that's a good sign. However, if she likes someone you distrust because of past conduct, you could have a problem. If she is quick to bad-mouth someone, it tells you a great deal about the way she treats others. It begs the questions: Who else does

she bad-mouth? And how soon will she bad-mouth you?

- Alternatively, you might like to try the above test if she has been drinking, She will probably be a little less careful about what she says about others. This is a variation of *'Drink in, truth out'*.
- On the subject of alcohol, how does her personality change when she's tipsy? Some seemingly demure women turn nasty, physically violent and 'gobby' when under the influence. In the interests of fairness, are you the same?
- What are the circumstances in which she turns against you?
- How does she treat waiters, waitresses, shop assistants and lower-level or junior colleagues? Does she treat them with basic courtesy and respect, or like something unwanted on the bottom of her shoe?
- How does she deal with stress? Does she snap or lash out verbally at those around her? Worse still, does she lash out physically? Assuming you have done nothing nasty to warrant such an outburst, any woman who punches or slaps you is behaving unreasonably. In an ideal world, zero tolerance would apply. Bear in mind that if a man did that to a woman he could be arrested. It is no different.
- Ask her friends what it is they most like about her. And why?
- Casually ask these friends how she could be a nicer person.

Predictors of Divorce

These formulae predict future divorce. They are accurate 97 per cent of the time.

$$w(t+1)=a+r1*w(t)+ihw[h(t)]$$
$$h(t+1)=b+r2*h(t)+iwh[w(t)]$$

Professor James Murray from the University of Washington in Seattle is a mathematician who developed these formulae based on a 10 year study of 700 couples and worked closely with the psychologist, Doctor John Gottman at the same university. It's a remarkable study about attitude and behaviour in intimate relationships.

To develop the formulae, they used the *The Love Lab*, a scientific version of TV's *Big Brother* house. It's set on the waterfront of Seattle near the University Campus. Volunteer couples live there during the experiments, and include some newly weds, others who have been married for many years, as well as some gay couples. The experiments are conducted one couple at a time. Each participant is wired up to a variety of monitors so their pulse, sweat and stress levels can be measured. They are then put through a series of experiments that include being given contentious issues to discuss such as sex, money or bringing up children. Trained observers monitor their ability to communicate with one another; what they say and how they respond. They want to see how people deal with the situation. What tone of voice do they use, how do they maintain affection for the other? Critically, they want to observe how each participant attempts to repair the situation. Some behaviours score positive points, others score negative ones. The combined results are added into the algebraic formulae above - and this is used to predict how likely they are to divorce. To gain a full understanding of what these formulae include, you'll have to read their book.

In *The Seven Principles of Making Marriage Work*, Dr Gottman and co-author Nan Silver describe the differences that make a difference as *The 4 Horsemen of the Apocalypse*; the four key factors that contribute to the ultimate destruction of a marriage or intimate relationship. They are:

- Criticism
- Contempt
- Defensiveness
- Stonewalling

They make a clear distinction between a complaint and a criticism. If something is specific like, *"I'm really annoyed that you didn't put out the bin last night."* That's a complaint. *"Why don't you ever do as you say?" I hate having to put the bin out when it's your turn. You just don't care and you don't respect me."* are criticisms that contribute to a character assassination. Adding the phrase *"What IS wrong with you?"* is a nail in the coffin of any relationship.

On its own, criticism doesn't always kill a relationship. However, its power is directly linked to the other horsemen.

Some people take great pleasure in putting others down.

Usually it's a sign of insecurity and low self-esteem on the part of the person who exhibits the contempt. Probably the best example of contempt is sarcasm. Anybody who uses sarcasm will damage a relationship. Adding the words *"I was only joking."* doesn't make it any better, or funny. Sneering, mocking and name calling are all forms of contempt. But the biggest giveaway of contempt is rolling your eyes. Eye rolling demonstrates contempt. If she (or you) rolls her eyes over what others say or do, it's a relationship killer.

If you are verbally or emotionally attacked by your girlfriend or wife, its easy to see why someone would become defensive. Unfortunately, when people become defensive it doesn't achieve the desired effect because the attacker sees that as a sign that they are winning, and then escalates it to ensure they win the argument by totally crushing their opponent.

When disagreements escalate, eventually someone will stop listening. They'll tune out. Dr Gottman estimate that 85 per cent of the time men are the biggest culprits here. This is when the man retreats to his cave to have a sulk.

Stonewallers look away, they don't engage. They appear to not give a damn. But it's usually a coping mechanism for a man. The emotional pain can be so intense, they become 'flooded' by it. They can't cope. Women on the other hand tend to be much better at managing their emotions. It's a biological fact that men are more easily overwhelmed by marital conflict than their wives. But when a man 'retreats' in this way he inadvertently inflames her rage because she then feels she is being ignored. At that point, she can easily justify becoming even more hurtful.

So, look at your relationship with the woman you are thinking of marrying and ask yourself *"How do we currently resolve conflict?"* Using these factors, look at your relationship with the girlfriend you are thinking of marrying. Are you already galloping towards disaster based on this research, before you've even reached the starting gate? If so, and if nothing is done to remedy it, you increase the probability that your marriage would fail.

Listen to your gut instinct. It is trying to protect you, so do not ignore it. Time and again we have heard men say they had their suspicions but failed to act on them and learnt to regret it.

Man traps

To her, the objective is clear. She wants to be married. Even if that involves 'helping' a man choose to marry her. She may decide to trap a man into marriage if she feels she has to, because no one has yet asked to marry her by playing fair. As she grows older, she may become increasingly aware of her 'sell-by date'. Desperate times may require desperate measures.

Yet most eligible bachelors have *no* idea to what lengths some women will go to get a man. Some of their tactics are aimed at weeding out men who don't want to marry, and speed up the time it takes to get a man up the aisle, so that she can start having babies.

Girls who just want to have fun, are often quite easy-going about dating men. If they want to drink too much, they will. If they want casual sex, they will get it. In fact, single women call most if not all the shots in their lives. A single guy may hope he gets laid when he's getting ready to go out for a night. But a woman already knows. If she decides to, she is far more likely to succeed than a man. A man is so often portrayed as having all the power. It's a myth.

She can chat up men or date different guys every night if she wants to. A woman on the lookout for a potential husband behaves very differently. How many women have you dated who have done any or all of the following?

- She doesn't talk to men first. The man must always initiate the conversation and then pursue her. She'll wait. If you haven't got the courage to talk to her, she will conclude that you're *'obviously a loser'!*
- She pauses before agreeing to a date. It's intended to make the man feel nervous and uncomfortable. As if it isn't difficult enough to risk rejection, as it is!
- She won't go Dutch or pay for anything on the first few dates. She's being politely unreasonable to see whether you will put up with her. If you pass this test, you can pay to see her some more.
- Some women will deliberately order the most expensive item on the menu (and tell you) to see how you react (or don't).
- She always brings the date to an end first, so that you want to see her again.

- When you do manage to get her on the phone, she makes a point of ending phone calls first.
- There's definitely no sex on dates one, two or three. She acts low-key to build up your desire for her.
- She instantly stops dating you if you don't buy her romantic gifts for her birthday or Valentine's Day.
- She may play you off against other men to coerce you into making a commitment to her, tapping into a fear that you could lose her. Although this is a dangerous strategy, some women use it to test their man.
- She may try the *'Being mean to keep you keen'* ploy. She treats you badly to see how you respond, and to assess her ability to walk all over you in the future.
- She refuses all weekend date requests received after Wednesday.
- She may turn off her cellphone on a Sunday afternoon so you can't reach her. This is often a deliberate attempt to destabilise you as you try, and fail to find her. It's to make you think she's with someone else, so you work harder to keep her.

She definitely doesn't want you to think early on that she's too available or too keen. This could, by definition, mean that she is desperate or imply that nobody else wants her. This, in turn, could be a turn-off to you because she asks herself: *"What man would want a woman that nobody else wants?"* Therefore she may try to convince you she's indifferent towards you, or appear unattainable. It's another way of baiting the hook to make you try harder to get her. This is why she rarely, if ever, returns your phone calls. Even if you leave a voicemail message asking her to call you back she won't because she wants you to believe she is busy and in such demand by other men. This is intended to turn pursuing her into a challenge. If she's a challenge, you won't let her go because you invested so much effort in winning her in the first place. She figures that if men like challenges she will become a challenge!

Then, of course, after many months of dating you may hear the *"I think I might be pregnant"* ploy. This is sometimes meant to test you too. Genuine accidents do happen, of course. Calmly ask her how she feels about it. When, (not if) she asks you how it makes you feel, tell her that you want children only when they are planned. If she pushes you into telling her what she should do about it if she was pregnant, don't be drawn. This is the trap. Politely and considerately say you are prepared to sit down with her to discuss it properly if or when a pregnancy test proves positive.

This is why you must always use a condom when having sex with a single woman who may want children when you don't. Many a man has believed a calculating woman who told him she was using contraception when she wasn't. If a woman decides to get pregnant and have a baby without your agreement, and if she decides to take you to court, you will almost certainly be forced to pay for her decision for the next 18 years. It simply won't wash if you wail: *"But, Your Honour, she told me she was on the Pill."*

Women who are serious or desperate to find a husband invariably learn about a particular book that boasts more than a million copies sold. It has been described as an approach to manipulate an unsuspecting man into committing himself to a marriage that he thinks was all his own idea. The authors claim that if you follow their 'rules' the reader can rest assured that her husband will treat her like a queen - even when he's angry with her. Because he invested so much time and effort trying to get her in the first place.

Their book starts from the assumption that a woman's decision to get married is a noble one. The authors repeatedly claim that when women have followed their recommendations, their approach has led to countless happy marriages. What they don't share is how many marriages they have helped to start that resulted in misery for everyone, including any children produced by such duplicitous and deceitful scheming. Nor do they say whether such an outcome would be in the best interests of any man who is duped by a woman so desperate to get married that she would resort to this type of behaviour.

The authors also claim the book is about treating herself as a woman with respect and dignity and ensuring that men do the same. They fail to discuss how manipulative and deceitful this form of legal entrapment is. They claim it isn't immoral.

If your girlfriend is in possession of this book, look out. You are possibly what the authors describe as 'live prey'! She may adopt the following tactics:

- She will never show that getting married is foremost on her mind, even though it is.
- She always acts as if everything is great, even if it isn't.
- She wants to leave him hungry for more.
- She will remain emotionally cool.
- And will never ask the man where he's been or who he's been seeing. This helps her perpetuate the appearance of not being too bothered.
- She is encouraged not to show she is jealous or insecure.
- She won't tell you anything she'll regret.
- She will act as if she is independent so that you don't feel she is expecting you to take care of her, even though that may be her objective.
- She won't agree to see you more than twice a week.
- She insists you have to rearrange your schedule around her.
- She won't live with you or leave her things at your place.
- She wants to condition the man to feel that if you want to see her seven days a week, you must marry her.

The authors seem to think it is good when a man gets upset because it means he cares about her, and if a man is not angry, he's indifferent, and if he's indifferent, he'll leave. They believe the way a man is trained to behave during the courtship phase is usually the way he will behave after the woman has married him. They also define men as *'the adversary'* and state that men have the *"power to hurt you"*.

The book says: *"If you're a genuinely nice person, you will probably feel cruel when you do The Rules. You may think you are making men suffer, but in reality you are actually doing them a favour."* To them, playing games is not bad.

They beseech readers not to tell their therapist about the book. The therapist may just believe that such an approach is a manipulative, deceitful and dishonest way to trap a man into marriage. Surely not!

They advocate tucking the book away in a top drawer. Roughly translated, this means they recommend she hides it!

It's true that strong, independent women have a certain appeal to many men. Many of the women we are discussing here manage to perfect the illusion of being strong and independent. But here's another important point - if your girlfriend really wants to get married and is keen to start a family, and you are adamant that you do not, you must tell her and, if necessary, end the relationship. Let her find someone else. Do not string her along. She is as entitled to have a family as you are not to have one if that is your choice.

> "When deciding who to trust, bear in mind that the combination of consistently bad or egregiously inadequate behaviour with frequent plays for your pity is as close to a warning mark on a conscienceless person's forehead as you will ever be given. A person whose behaviour includes both of these features is not necessarily a mass murderer, or even violent at all, but is still probably not someone you should choose as a friend, take on as your business partner, ask to take care of your children, or marry." Martha Stout PhD. from The Sociopath Next Door

The business of marriage

Every business partnership involves risk. Marriage is a partnership. And like a business, the institution of marriage is governed by punitive and far-reaching laws. It is the job of the directors or partners of a business to protect and safeguard its future. A business has a separate legal identity, and so does marriage. Each partner should assume equal responsibility for its well-being and future success. When a business partnership fails, as part of the winding-up process all the partners share equal liability. They may be made bankrupt and lose all their assets, including their homes.

However, when a marriage fails, in almost all cases the male partner pays for everything. It is irrelevant how the wife has behaved towards the husband during the marriage.

Due diligence

With so many marriages now ending in divorce, a marriage partnership is an extremely risky venture. And if this partnership creates a number of little 'subsidiaries', that is, children, and it breaks up, the man will almost certainly be forced by law to pay 'dividends' for every child for up to 18 years. Or even up to the age of 23 if they are in full-time education.

In the business world some investors are prepared to take a bet on a business proposition. They may see the potential for a decent return on their investment and may go ahead without asking too many questions. They may or may not fully understand the risks they are taking. They may win, or they may lose their shirts. Failure could wipe some of them out, while others just put it down to a bad experience. When it comes to romantic or intimate relationships, love is not a reliable indicator of future success or happiness - for either partner.

Again, in a business context, before successful entrepreneurs or wise investors put time or money into a new or existing business they will almost certainly conduct *'due diligence'*. In other words, they check out the business. They check out the people involved in that business, their backgrounds, skills, strengths, honesty, integrity and any weaknesses that could jeopardise the success of that business. They ask around. They verify any information they are given about the business. They don't give people the benefit of the doubt. The bigger the business risks, the more forensic the due diligence will be. To protect themselves and their financial investment they assess all these risks before they get too involved. It saves time, heartache and, potentially, a great deal of money.

So why not use a similar approach for our relationships? Is it so ludicrous? Not really.

To minimise your risks, what do you need to know about your future marital partner? That depends on a number of factors, but it starts at the level of your commitment to the relationship. If you do not see the relationship as long-term, many of the questions in the Appendix at the back of his book will not be that relevant to you.

You need to understand how comfortable you are about the risks you are prepared to take. If your relationship is casual, you probably wouldn't want to bother with the checklist at all. Even so, if you are both embarking on a sexual fling, it is almost certainly worth knowing whether you or your partner is likely to give the other a nasty rash - or worse.

For entrepreneurs, assuming a higher risk in exchange for a higher potential return may be acceptable. They may be prepared to lose a lot if they are likely to gain more. If, however, you are seriously contemplating marrying a particular woman, most of the questions in the Appendix will be highly relevant to you.

This detailed checklist is not foolproof. Nor is it scientific. It has been drawn up to help you gain more factual and values-based information about your future partner. At the very least, you will gain a better idea of what you need to know about her and therefore what you are getting into. It is our view that if this checklist stops just one bad marriage from taking place, it will have been worthwhile.

Use the checklist to help you make a better-informed decision about your future spouse. A free download of the most comprehensive and up-to-date version of the due diligence checklist without any reference to this book, laid out and complete with spaces to write answers, will be sent to readers who request it. Send an e-mail to DD@ThatBitchBook.com

If you decide not to download the checklist but prefer to ask her the questions, don't ask them all in quick succession. It takes time to acquire this information. You have a right to make a better-informed decision to marry. But your girlfriend won't respond well to being tested, even though she might not think twice about testing you. It's also a good idea to get a friend to ask her a few of the questions too.

If you feel uncomfortable about talking to your partner about these issues because you are concerned about her reaction, that in itself is a danger sign.

Both parties need to go into a marriage equipped with the most relevant information. Offer to answer all the questions for her too. This is reasonable. She may refuse to take part in what she dismisses as a load of nonsense, or she may say: *"If you loved me, you wouldn't force me to do this."* These may be ploys to make you feel guilty. Be afraid and give serious thought to how committed she is to the relationship, or what she may be hiding from you. Part of the due diligence process in business requires *'full disclosure'*, meaning total honesty. The download checklist includes spaces for each of you to sign and date the form. Is this all a bit over the top? Possibly. But you have a duty to yourself to minimise making a bad marriage choice.

In theory at least, this becomes a legally binding document, although enforcing it may prove impossible. However, it provides at least some commitment on her part to tell you the truth about herself. By signing the due diligence document, your partner is making claims that could be seen as fraudulent if you later discover she was lying. You may be able to use it as evidence against her. But it must be stressed - you cannot rely on this. Obviously, if you make statements that turn out to be false, she may have the same rights!

Assuming you have both completed the checklist and you feel that marrying her is still a great idea, you are ready to tackle the next issue; pre-nuptial agreements.

Pre-nups

A pre-nuptial agreement is a legal contract laying down who has the rights to what assets the man and woman own, and will continue to own should a marriage fail. In some legal jurisdictions pre-nuptial agreements are worthless, but in others they are becoming increasingly commonplace. In Britain, the law is likely to change on this issue and even if they are not binding, may carry considerable weight in the future.

Pre-nups are particularly useful for high-net-worth people with inheritances or significant investment portfolios, owners of businesses or those who are planning to remarry and may have children from previous relationships. A professionally prepared pre-nup can go a long way towards protecting the financial future of those children. Think of it as a form of insurance. If the man's assets are greater than the woman's, it's normal for the man to pay both sets of legal fees when drafting the pre-nups.

If you don't have a mutually agreed pre-nup, the State will decide who gets what, and this is not in the best interests of most men.

It has to be said that a pre-nuptial or post-nuptial agreement is never guaranteed to offer you full protection and more divorce lawyers are encouraging their clients to challenge pre-nups. During a divorce they have little to lose from doing so and, potentially, a lot to gain. It is a commonly used strategy to destabilise and frighten a spouse. However, regardless of their legal validity, it's still worth asking your fiancée to sign one before you go ahead with a wedding.

If she refuses on principle, it is a bad sign. Be even more wary if your bride-to-be refuses when you have more assets than she does. She may try to justify refusal in any way she can think of. She could, for example, claim it is proof that you don't trust her. Explain that it's the system you don't trust, not her. However, if she truly loved you, she would want to protect you as much as you would want to be protected. By refusing to sign a legally binding contract she is already putting her needs ahead of yours.

If your instinct tells you she's being self-serving and interested only in her own wellbeing, listen to your instinct. Show deep hurt and sadness because she has forced you to end your engagement.

Be prepared to walk away from the relationship. Do not agree, under any circumstances, to allow yourself to feel guilty or to be bullied into backing down. Do not listen to anything she may say that is intended to change your mind. If she will not agree to sign a fair, mutually agreed pre-nuptial contract, do not marry her. Unless, of course, you don't mind the increased risks of a potentially ruinous divorce!

Creating a pre-nup

For a pre-nuptial agreement to be binding, it is essential that each party is represented by a different lawyer. Both of you must be seen to be offered independent legal advice so that you both fully understand the legal and financial implications of signing such a document. Paying legal fees for drafting such a document is a tiny price to pay to test the robustness of your relationship. Indeed, a pre-nup prepared without the involvement of a specialist lawyer could be invalidated by a judge. It could also be invalidated if one of the parties doesn't have legal representation. So do it properly.

The pre-nup has to be seen as fair. Both of you must give full disclosure of all assets and understand that during a marriage you also become jointly responsible for all debts. Full disclosure therefore includes all debts too. If it is found at a later date that either party has hidden assets or debts, it could make the pre-nuptial agreement void. The individual who has hidden assets could lose them entirely in a divorce settlement.

The document must not impose poverty or extreme hardship on the other party. Nor must it be frivolous in any way. It must state clearly who owns what before the marriage, and what are deemed joint marital assets. In other words, what are his, hers and ours. A lawyer will advise you on other factors to consider.

When drafting such an agreement, be the one who creates the first draft.

As a starting point go to www.ThatBitchBook.com/prenup.htm for a list of links to free template pre-nuptial agreements. Put together your own version based on what you read, then take it to your chosen lawyer to improve on it.

Once the pre-nup is in place, and after you marry, your personal assets must never be mixed up with marital assets. For example, if you have a lump sum, don't use it as a down payment for a house. Any monies that you use to purchase a property or any other assets should come out of joint income. Make this clear before you marry. If your money has to be used for such a purchase, prepare a separate legally binding loan agreement to the marriage 'pot'. Even include details of how much interest would be payable on the loan if the marriage ends. Of course, you would also need to pay the mortgage from a joint account.

Whatever you agree within the pre-nup, you have to honour the terms. If you don't, a judge could throw it out at a time when you most need it.

If a judge can be persuaded that it was signed under duress it could also be invalidated. Therefore, prepare and sign it at least a month before your wedding to show that it wasn't thrust upon your partner at the last minute. Once you have both agreed its contents, you might consider video-taping the signing to prove that neither party entered into it involuntarily.

Before you pop the question get a second opinion, then a third. Ask your friends what they think of her. Be gently insistent that they tell you what they really think. A twice-divorced man shared the following: *"After each of my divorces I was shocked at how many times I was told, 'We knew this wasn't going to work. I never liked her anyway. I never trusted her. She only wanted you because you had money. She was a bit odd, wasn't she?' It would really have been more helpful to hear all this before I had to go through these terrible experiences."*

So if you know a man who is planning to marry someone who you suspect is a 'bad one', give serious consideration about telling him what you think. You could be doing him an enormous favour. Everybody seems to know with frightening accuracy when a marriage is going to fail, except 'the happy couple'. Stella McCartney is reported to have tried to tell her father Sir Paul McCartney not to marry Heather Mills. He didn't listen.

Remember, feeling that you should get married isn't a good enough reason. Nor is it good enough that you believe your girlfriend thinks it's time to wed.

Post-nups for marrieds

If you're already married, you may want to consider creating a post-nuptial agreement, which is basically the same as a pre-nup. You might be asking yourself why a wife would ever agree to a post-nuptial agreement? Actually, she may be more inclined to do so if she is given a financial incentive, as a way of *'thanking her for her fairness'*. This could be a lump sum, a piece of expensive jewellery or a new car. Everyone has a price! If she refuses point-blank to even consider a post-nuptial agreement, this is a loud warning bell of future trouble.

If, after all of this, you still intend to marry, may we jointly wish you all the very best of luck. Have a long and happy life together. But if things haven't worked out so well for you in the marriage stakes, you need to read the next chapter to learn what she may have planned for you when it comes to the divorce.

" *Married. I've been. Now I just rent.* Frank Sinatra "

Chapter 6

Divorce - The Final Frontier

" You don't know a woman until you've met her in court.
Woody Allen *"*

Important warning

As we have stated earlier, it is critically important to seek independent, qualified and specialist legal advice before making decisions to protect yourself against a vindictive woman. This is even more important during a divorce or a relationship break-up. Divorce laws differ around the world, so the information in this chapter is intended purely for guidance and to highlight areas you may need to be more aware of. Always consult a specialist divorce lawyer before you act.

The aim of this chapter is to help a man protect himself against a wife who has committed sustained, nasty, abusive and malicious behaviour in the marriage. Her abuse could certainly escalate if or when divorce proceedings begin.

" Mark Twain once wrote on the subject of divorce
In love, you pay as you leave. "

What you need to realise about divorce

Divorce rates are soaring in just about every so-called civilised country. In the UK, there are about 150,000 divorces every year; 1.8 million in the past decade. There are nearly one million divorces a year in the United States. If you're married already or are about to get married, you are far more likely to become divorced than win even a small *National Lottery* prize.

Marrying and then divorcing a nasty woman hurts. And in more ways than the non-divorced man can begin to imagine. The vast majority of divorced women walk away with the most valuable marital assets. Vindictive women can do it with a ruthless passion that is impossible for most men to understand. On top of that, the legal system is preferential to women. In up to 95 per cent of cases, residence of children is awarded to the mother, even when the father may be the better parent. The next chapter, *Children as Weapons of Male Destruction*, explores those specific issues in more detail. For now, realise the following:

- Once married, you have a one in two chance of having to go through a divorce.
- Imagining your marriage will improve without you doing anything about it is a mistake.
- *You* are not a failure because your *relationship* failed.
- Whoever 'transgresses' through extra-marital affairs or physical or emotional abuse, both parties played a role in it, whether that role was active or passive.
- An amicable divorce is extremely rare in abusive relationships. It can get very nasty indeed. Emotionally and psychologically it can be overwhelming, draining, frustrating, time-consuming, and of course, expensive. When children are involved it is all far worse.
- Don't be surprised if your wife decides to behave maliciously during the divorce, encouraged by friends, members of her family or her legal advisers.
- Stories abound of women who had strings of affairs during

their marriage but were still awarded punitive damages against their good husbands.

- It is irrelevant that you have been a good husband. In fact, being fair and honourable could end up costing you even more.
- What kind of man you are doesn't matter. You will be punished as if you were a bad husband.
- Divorce for a man is always a damage limitation exercise. If you are dealing with a scorned, vindictive woman, a speedy exit is important.
- There's a lot you can do to ensure you lose less.

While reading this chapter, you may think we are being needlessly alarmist. Perhaps in your circumstances it will never happen. However, you have a duty to yourself and your children, if you have any, to become fully aware of the risks you face should things go from bad to worse in your marriage. You may need an exit strategy.

Numerous men who read earlier drafts of this chapter found themselves '*defending*' their wives as they read about the extreme behaviour of the women we are writing about. We are describing **worst case scenarios** here. Therefore this information is NOT about your partner. Although one day it could be!

> *My husband and I had our best sex during our divorce. It was like cheating on our lawyers.* Priscilla Lopez

But is divorce the only option?

Carefully consider whether divorce is your best option. If you can sort things out between you, stay married. It can be much cheaper. But you must also realise that a temporary patching-up of your marriage could cost you even more in the future. The longer you are married, the more a court could order you to pay your ex-wife. Therefore you need to ask yourself these searching questions:

- On a scale of 0 to 10 how happy are you in your marriage? Be really honest.
- Imagine asking her: "*If you had the choice to marry me again*

right now and we weren't married, would you?" If you suspect
the answer would be *"no"*, why stay married?

- How miserable is she making you?
- What would make you happier in your life?
- How much does your wife want to have a happy marriage
  with you?
- How much do you want to have a happy marriage with your
  wife?
- If you did not have financial or family obligations would you
  stay married to her?
- Are you trying to stay together purely for the children's sake?

Many men, through a sense of loyalty, stay in unhappy marriages
for the children, but this loyalty is based on a dangerous assumption. Why believe that staying together is inherently better for your
children? If you truly love your children, they might be far better off
if you and your wife separated or divorced. In many cases, though,
staying together is not really only about the children - it's more to
do with having nowhere to live. So accept this; if your wife decides
to divorce you, it is extremely likely that you will have nowhere to
live anyway, and you may have little or no say in the future of your
children either. Deciding to divorce your wife may therefore provide
you with more options about their futures.

Get real. If she is making your life a misery, why stay? Would you
rather be unhappy together or unhappy apart? Don't misunderstand
us - do not embark on divorce just because you're unhappy. Some
of your unhappiness may have nothing to do with your marriage. It
could be your age, job, energy levels, or even a mid-life crisis. Seek
legal advice before you make a decision to divorce. It's what a high
proportion of women do.

You can't make a half-decision to divorce. You must make tough
decisions and stick to them. As part of your assessment you will need
to calculate your living costs if you decide on divorce. You must remain calm and focused. You have to learn to set aside your emotions,
difficult or seemingly impossible as that may be. If you allow yourself
to be distracted by anything, it will almost certainly cost you more
than it needs to.

> *Ah yes, divorce, from the Latin word meaning to rip out a man's genitals through his wallet.* Robin Williams

You must also understand fully how divorce works. Divorce requires a clear head. Your wife may step up her abusive behaviour and do everything she can think of to maximise your pain and emotional exhaustion. It's a common strategy. Be aware of this whenever anything happens that pushes your buttons.

Perversely, women are renowned for their emotional sensitivity, while men are thought of as being logical and analytical. When it comes to divorce, women are frequently experts at being incredibly strategic, logical and analytical, while men fall apart trying to handle the problems using their under-developed emotions and discard their logic. When it comes to divorce, abusive women seem to have the capacity to flick the emotional switch to the 'off' position and behave in ways that defy belief.

It's true, of course, that many women are treated badly by their husbands. Married men have affairs. But so do married women. Men betray their partners. And so do women. Some men abandon their families. And so do some women.

The point is that when a marriage collapses it affects both parties. When children are involved, it hits them too.

The divorce process

Ask even a divorced man to explain the divorce process, the legal aspects of asset distribution and the child contact and residence issues, and he will probably struggle. If you are going through a divorce, you must know at least the basics and understand where you are at every point within this process.

1. A divorce petition starts the divorce. The person who initiates it is the *petitioner*.
2. The *respondent*, the person being divorced, receives an *'acknowledgment of service'* form to establish whether the respondent agrees to the divorce or will contest it.
3. A legal statement, called an *affidavit*, is prepared by the petitioner to say he or she is going ahead with the divorce.

4. When the court is satisfied that all financial and child care issues affecting the wife, husband and children have been agreed, the court issues a *decree nisi*. However, it is possible that a court will issue a *decree nisi* before these financial and child care matters are agreed.

5. A *decree absolute* can be applied for six weeks and one day after the *decree nisi*. That's when you are divorced, and free(ish), depending on the terms of your financial settlement. Similarly, in some cases *decree absolutes* are issued before financial matters are finalised. A good lawyer would almost always advise against applying for a *decree absolute* until everything is resolved.

A court grants a divorce if satisfied that the marriage has *'broken down irretrievably'* through unreasonable behaviour, adultery, desertion for more than two years, a mutually agreed two-year separation, or a five-year separation.

Most of the 'action' takes place between the third and fourth stages. That means pain, emotional torture, anger and the desire for revenge, leading to sleepless nights and worry as the seriousness of the situation gradually sinks and you start to see mountains of your hard-earned cash evaporating in front of you.

You have to accept that divorce can ruin you financially. Life is unfair, but divorce can be worse! Yet there's a lot you can and should do before you get to even the first item on the list above.

Women are so much better than men at planning their divorce. Most men don't plan, so they lose more. Figure it out for yourself. About 70 per cent of divorces are initiated by the woman, often shocking their husbands, who seemed to have no idea that their wife felt that way. Men are more likely to tolerate an unhappy marriage but women often plan their exit months, sometimes years, in advance. Marriage and the assets within it are seen as a business proposition to this type of woman.

Be proactive, if divorce is inevitable it is essential you file for divorce, rather than leaving it to her.

A single woman had a disagreement with her landlord at the end of her lease. He insisted on keeping the deposit she paid when she started renting for *'general repairs and maintenance'*. She refused to accept these charges but she lost her money. After many months she discovered he was a patient in the hospital where she worked. She deliberately infected his wounds. Her ex-husband commented later: *"I married that woman. At the time I thought that was a dreadful thing for her to do. But I was in love with her. Perhaps I should have taken that as a danger sign. Her behaviour during our divorce was substantially worse than her behaviour towards that landlord. I'd have gladly offered to swap places with him."*

The least you can expect

The less you know about what to expect, the more the family courts are likely to chew you up and spit you out. Imagine being kicked in the testicles repeatedly. Divorce can be worse. Let us put this as delicately as we can; if you're a man, you're going to get screwed, emotionally and financially. Accept this at the outset. Anything less, and you can consider yourself lucky, but best to brace yourself for the worst. When it comes to a vindictive woman's revenge, you will not win. It's as simple as that.

You will feel wronged, abused, taken advantage of, betrayed and deceived. You could be lied to. You could be lied about. She may make frivolous or vexatious claims against you. More seriously, she may make unsubstantiated false allegations of physical or sexual abuse, directed against her or your children.

Get used to the idea that you won't see your children as much as you feel you want to or should. In your role as a father, you will be treated as an irrelevance, except when it comes to providing money. You may decide to fight divorce issues 'on principle'.

Realise now that her lawyers may deliberately make unreasonable demands on you, pushing your buttons so you wear yourself out emotionally. This increases the likelihood that eventually you will agree to just about anything in order to make the pain to go away. They do this because your wife ends up getting a better deal. For many men, principles and ethics are important but in divorce they become irrelevant unless you want to waste a lot of your time and money. So think carefully before you decide to act on principle.

66 *Only the weak are cruel.* Leo Buscaglia **99**

A divorce is not about righting a wrong or proving blame. Indeed, in British divorce there is a principle of 'no blame'. So, no matter how disgracefully your wife may have treated you, as far as divorce is concerned, it is largely irrelevant, unless deemed by the courts to be *'obvious and gross'*.

Divorce for a man is about getting out as quickly, as painlessly and as inexpensively as possible. Your divorce is a business transaction that you will lose, but by listening to a good lawyer, and doing what he or she recommends, you will lose less than you might.

It is in your interests to get this over with quickly but most reasonable men don't conduct a divorce in this way. They sit back and wait to see what happens. They will often make themselves feel even more guilty for wanting a quick exit. They feel they are being disloyal to their wife. Speed, nevertheless, is incredibly important once the decision to divorce has been made. Some women may appear to want a reconciliation. Beware. This may be a smokescreen to delay proceedings.

Read the previous two paragraphs again and again until they are embedded in your brain.

At the beginning of divorce proceedings most men have at least some faith that their wives will behave honestly and fairly. Forget that if she has been abusive to you in the past. It is extremely rare that a vindictive, abusive woman will conduct herself honestly. It is most likely that she will be egged on by friends and advisers to turn up the heat and get her pound of flesh, because 'she's worth it'. When things start moving, especially if she has been abusive to you in the past, she is more than likely to become even nastier towards you. Prepare yourself.

Divorce brings out the worst in everyone. Lawyers represent our 'dark sides'. But remember this too; lawyers don't make the law. Blame your government.

Your wife is entitled to a proportion of your future earnings, and can claim a proportion of your assets. A court is likely to conclude that a 'stay-at-home' wife be credited with a full contribution to the marriage. You may be forced to pay her for many years to come. Don't assume that you own half the house even if it is in joint names.

Whoever takes on responsibility caring for the children usually gets the house. Her divorce lawyer will almost certainly want to negotiate more than 50 per cent of the value of the house if your children are to live there, and in addition you may end up being financially liable for property insurance, repairs, maintenance and property taxes.

Then she may insist on a proportion of the value of your pension. She could even qualify for a proportion or half of any tax-free lump sum you may receive as part of your pension. Her lawyer could also insist that you pay the premiums for an insurance policy protecting her maintenance payments.

Self-employed people report that their income takes a nosedive during a divorce, mainly because they find it so difficult to concentrate on their business, although sometimes this can be beneficial when a financial settlement is calculated. But some businesses go bankrupt, with possible redundancies for any staff which ultimately affects their families. You might as well accept that you won't have any spare money for the foreseeable future and realise you will have to endure a drop in your quality of life while the law protects and maintains the woman's.

Today the cards are stacked against the husband. And the wife knows it.

Why some women divorce

A wife may file for divorce because she is intensely unhappy. She had children to 'fulfil' her. She may see her children as an extension of herself and because they are 'her', she will love them. She may love her children more than she loves her husband. But she is still not happy. She spends money on designer clothes and top-of-the-range cosmetics, she pampers herself by going for health and beauty treatments. She spoils herself with indulgence foods and drink. Yet she's still unhappy. She puts on weight. She's now even unhappier. And older. No matter what she does, the wrinkles still show through, a constant reminder that the days of looking her best are over.

At the same time her husband looks tired. His working hours are too long and he doesn't give her the attention he once did. Therefore, it must be his fault that she feels so bad about herself. Overwhelmed, unhappy, trapped, confused, depressed - it all becomes 'his' fault.

He's that bastard who impregnated her and put her through all that pain of childbirth, even though she was so insistent on starting a family in the first place. He is now a bastard for being so fertile.

She starts to notice all his imperfections. He hasn't fulfilled the potential she saw in him, even though he may have reached the pinnacle of his chosen career, or was happy doing what he did for an employer who appreciated him for the high quality of his work, his reliability and integrity, the fact that he got on with his colleagues, and was well-liked and respected. But to her he was metamorphosing into the bastard she needed him to become in order to justify her extra-marital affair with the plumber. Nothing she ever did was wrong of course. She has convinced herself that her lack of fulfillment is all because of her husband. She argues, if he had been more attentive she wouldn't have been forced into the arms of another man, or men.

By the time she wants a divorce she may be out to get you in every way she can, you bastard. And if you haven't been a bastard, she may have to resort to convincing herself and her friends that you are, by lying about you. You bastard.

> A little girl is overheard telling her friends that her mummy has a personal trainer: *"Every time he comes over, they take a nap."*

The 27-Year Itch, an article in *The Telegraph Magazine* (May 12, 2007), featured the stories of middle-aged couples who divorce after being married for decades. Included was an interview with a woman of 57, married for 28 years to a successful businessman. She had an affair with a man 15 years younger than herself and then sued her husband for divorce. She admitted he was not a horrible man and was a fantastic father to their children. She enjoyed a lifestyle most could only dream of; a big house in the country, a swimming pool, stables, a mink coat, diamonds, regular beauty treatments, exotic holidays and a holiday home in the South of France. Yet she was awarded 65 per cent of everything he had ever worked for.

The divorce lawyer Vanessa Lloyd Platt made a general comment in the article that, for some women, divorce law creates a disincentive to work during a marriage because it could jeopardise a substantial settlement.

She said: *"The wife who gets her nails done, has a nanny and spends her husband's money as fast as he can make it will get a better settlement than the woman who works her guts out."*

The background to a woman's decision to divorce may differ but the process follows a recognisable pattern.

What she may do before she announces divorce action

Below we have created a worst case scenario. Divorces aren't always this bad, but you need to know what an acrimonious divorce could be like. Know what you may be up against in order to develop a plan to protect yourself.

Your wife has legal advantages that you do not have. You have assets that her team will try to take from you. In order to win a larger proportion of those assets she may choose or be advised to do the following before and after she files a divorce petition.

Once her decision to divorce has been made, she will deliberately create emotional distance from her husband. This is designed to 'protect' herself. Some of her behaviours may be dishonourable, dishonest, morally reprehensible or even illegal.

She has to justify leaving you to herself. Therefore she has to hate you first. It's far easier to be angry when you think you can blame somebody else. It doesn't matter that you have done nothing wrong. If she believes you have, it will become real to her. Her desire to seek revenge will be based on what she believes, not the facts. Or your behaviour.

She starts to concentrate on your faults. This may increase the possibility that she will start, or continue to bad-mouth you to your family, friends and perhaps your children. She may blow some of your imperfections out of proportion or make some up.

Before announcing a divorce she may deliberately behave badly and force you to blow your top or provoke you into saying or doing something she can use against you. It's a trap. Don't fall for it. This could be part of her justification for divorcing you. She'll do this even though she has already made up her mind to divorce you.

Her lawyer may seek an occupation order to bar you from your own home. The applicant has to demonstrate that her or her children's health, safety and well-being are compromised. Your wife may make false allegations against you to improve the chances that one will be issued. The police would then have to enforce such an order. Those accusations become a matter of record, but should you ever divorce her, these unsubstantiated 'facts' may be used against you again.

She may report you to the police just for *feeling* threatened by you even when no threats were given or implied. At the very least they combine to create an atmosphere of doubt about you and harm your reputation. They also give her huge legal advantages that can result in larger compensation. Yes, it's legally sanctioned harassment.

She may make other false allegations against you. These are intended to enrage and distract you. Don't let them. Any allegations she makes against you have to be proven. And the more serious her allegations, the more cogent and robust her evidence has to be. Although, without evidence she may simply withdraw the allegations at the last minute, implying she is willing to 'forgive' you. Nothing ever happened but doubts will linger. Job done!

She knows you and will expect you to be reasonable. Indeed, your fairness and sense of decency will almost certainly be used against you. She will expect you to believe whatever she tells you. What she *does* could be entirely different. If she promises something, accept it only when it has been put in writing. If she's not prepared to do this, it doesn't count.

She may start removing joint marital assets from your home. She may hide or sell them and pocket the cash. She may have been advised to spend as much of your money as possible, and to go further into debt than ever before. This strategy may include running up larger than usual balances on all joint credit cards, on items for her personal use such as expensive clothes and furniture. She may insist on a new car, paid for in cash or with a loan in her husband's name.

This is cunning because it could be used to prove to a divorce court that she is used to a lavish lifestyle, which her lawyers will argue should be maintained after the divorce. Maybe she returns some of these expensive items for a cash refund. Multiple wins for a deceitful wife.

Of course, by doing this she could destroy your credit rating at a time when you will be at your most vulnerable financially, making it difficult or impossible to secure a loan to start your life again.

Meanwhile, she resorts to her maiden name after the divorce and is free to apply for credit.

She may give up her job to prove in a divorce court that she has no income. Or she persuades you to pay for her to see a therapist. This is a neat trick because you will be blamed as the reason she felt the need to see a therapist - and you pay for her proof! Some women have been known to lend her husband's money to family members or friends. They get it back after the divorce has been finalised.

For the first time, she may become interested in your financial affairs and could search through your files when you are out of the house. She asks friends and colleagues more questions about your work and promotion prospects and makes a point of talking about you with your financial advisers. She may even clear out your joint bank accounts.

She starts to change her appearance; a crash diet, a new wardrobe of clothes, expensive new hairstyle and a new found obsession with the gym are all signs she's on the lookout for a new lover, or she's already found one. She may try to persuade you to pay or contribute towards cosmetic surgery for herself.

Beware if she appears to be seeing her mother or best friends more than usual. She starts new hobbies to give her an excuse to be out more often. Perhaps she develops a new habit of provoking a row so she can justify storming out of the house. She's going to see her lover! Her cellphone is off at new times of the day, or she answers it, cuts you off instantly and calls you back 30 seconds later, having had time to move out of earshot of her new boyfriend. She may accuse you of having an affair when you are not. But she is!

Mood changes are afoot too. Formerly passive during sex, she may appear to be 'enjoying' being with you far more than normal. If she seems to be having more orgasms than normal - she could be faking it to hide her affair. Or perhaps she starts to come up with all manner of odd excuses not to have sex with you.

She may become less emotionally engaged with you but is 'professionally polite' towards you. Or perhaps her abuse towards you stops miraculously. You may be fooled into believing things are improving between you. The truth is less appealing. A divorce lawyer has advised her to become much friendlier towards you while she prepares her case. It's a ploy to lull you into a false sense of security.

What she may do after she announces your divorce
Many a man has been hit with:

- A court order barring him from living in his own home.
- An injunction forbidding him to come within one mile of his home.
- A ban on all contact with his children because the way he makes his wife feel undermines her ability to look after them.
- A letter from his wife or her solicitor saying that the children no longer wish to see him because he 'frightens' them. Or his wife says they do not love him any more.
- A demand to support her and 'her' children for as many years as her lawyers can negotiate with a judge. This money may be calculated on her lawyer's estimation of what he is capable of earning, not on what he actually earns.
- A claim that she was deceived into signing a pre-nuptial agreement. Lawyers often challenge pre-nups as a matter of course. The husband's lawyer has to defend this and his legal bill goes up.
- A deliberate demand for significantly more in a settlement than she expects to receive, so that he negotiates it down to the figure she wanted all along.

No matter what she says, does or claims, don't say or do anything to retaliate. Calling her names and making threats will probably prolong the divorce proceedings and ramp up your legal bill. Learn to know when to shut up. Don't worry unduly about what she says about you because she's going to bad-mouth you anyway. Make a decision to control how you react, whatever happens.

She is likely to accuse you of all sorts of misdemeanours and more serious shortcomings simply because you were not the knight in shining armour she wanted you to be. Anything she may have done wrong will be seen as her response to your 'unreasonable' behaviour.

False allegations of physical, sexual or emotional cruelty against her or the children have become very common. Their purpose is to help her to gain an unfair advantage early in the proceedings, to throw you off-balance, to make you deeply angry and to frighten you. Expect her to use shock and surprise to destabilise you. You may react with utter disbelief that anyone could lie so brazenly and behave in such a disgusting way. Yet it happens, and it happens often. If she wants to play the victim, she's allowed to. Indeed she will be encouraged to do so.

Women have claimed to have lost a lot of money gambling. The scam is to withdraw the money at a casino, turn it into gambling chips and change it back at a later time.

She may default on loans, claim to be disabled, or file for bankruptcy. Be ready for any personal property you left at your marital home to be destroyed. Some women have been known to give all their husband's designer clothes to a charity shop or say they had put them into plastic bin liners that were mistakenly taken away by the rubbish collectors. Whatever she believes you hold important or valuable in your life are the first things she will dispose of or destroy.

One man told us how he was forced to go to court to face his vindictive ex-wife:

> *"At one point in the proceedings, her lawyer asked for permission to offer me a cheque. It was for £30. I asked what it was for. Her lawyer then explained that they had written to me giving me seven days notice to collect all my remaining belongings from the house. Because I had not complied within the time frame, she sold my entire collection of books. The £30 was what she got for them.*
>
> *I had been away on business for two weeks. She knew all this and timed it to ensure I would be unable to collect them. As an adult, I have only ever cried twice in public. That day in court was one of them. Those books were part of my very soul. She knew that."*

If you have moved away, a nasty woman may insist you attend numerous court hearings. This is intended to make your life as difficult and as expensive as possible. She wants you to waste your money. Ultimately she'll get what she wants anyway, so any wasted money will hurt you at a time when you have the fewest funds.

Should you divorce her?

At least consider the prospect of divorcing her, rather than waiting to see whether she divorces you. The divorcer finds it easier to cope emotionally and doesn't feel additionally burdened with everything rejection entails.

Assuming you have done everything to salvage the marriage, if you no longer want to be married to her and have decided you want a divorce, there are compelling advantages in getting in first. Don't wait to be served a petition by your wife and then be forced into responding and reacting to a stream of ridiculous or unreasonable demands that will almost certainly increase your emotional pain.

Some do's and don'ts before you start proceedings

- Don't ever threaten to divorce your wife.
- If she ever asks you whether you're planning a divorce, don't tell her.
- Don't talk to anyone, other than your divorce lawyer, about your possible divorce. Tell nobody, not even your best friend. Just one casual remark to his wife that got back to your wife is all it could take to cost you dearly.
- Do not leave your marital home unless you or your children are in real physical danger. All divorce lawyers should tell you this. Wait for your lawyer to say when you can leave. If your physical safety or your children's safety is at risk, seek a restraining order or an exclusion order through the courts. Get advice from your lawyer. Inform the police of these court orders. Don't think you can remove your children without evidence. Involving the police helps to create a paper trail.
- Never be seen to leave your children.
- Don't store cash at home. She may find and keep it.
- Set up your own bank account and have your wages or salary paid into that. Ensure there is just enough money in a joint account to cover monthly household expenditure.
- Protect yourself in every way you can. Being too nice about it

could hurt you, though this doesn't mean you should ever be nasty to your wife.

- Whatever you do, stop feeling guilty about preparing to divorce her. Realise that all sorts of emotions will run riot. That's normal.
- Speak about her as Mrs Surname, not by her first name. Alternatively refer to her only as *'the mother of my children'*. This is a practical way to create emotional distance from her to help you deal with the emotional pain you will almost certainly have to suffer.
- Don't blame yourself. Don't blame her.
- Refuse to accept guilt for the breakdown, even though she may want to heap as much blame on you as possible. Don't buy it and don't try to argue with her about it. You will be wasting your breath.

How to prepare and protect

Once you have taken the decision to divorce, get out of the marriage. Speed is important. The longer it takes, the more it will cost you financially as well as emotionally. Yes, it will hurt but you get over it, although you have to decide to get over it. It's a choice.

If she files for divorce first, she is starting from a position of strength and you are in a position of weakness. It's totally unfair but you can't do much about it. So, concentrate on the areas you can influence. Managing your emotions is a critical element of this process. Everything she and her legal team can think of will be done to upset you.

Accept that the mother is always seen to be a better person to look after your children, even if she isn't. She may not even want them, but may insist she does to get at you, especially when she knows what a devoted father you are.

Silence the voice that says: *"Oh, she's not like that."* You tell yourself that she may have been nasty in the past, but not even she would do that. Wake up. She is very likely to behave diabolically.

> During the bitter divorce of actors David Hasselhoff and Pamela Bach, Bach at one point alleged that Hasselhoff had once broken her nose. He flatly denied the allegation. And added that the only man who ever broke her nose was her plastic surgeon!

How to choose a divorce lawyer

Meet with a lawyer, sooner rather than later. Choose one carefully. This can take time. Having to respond to being hit by her divorce petition when you don't have a lawyer is not the best time to choose one.

Instruct only a specialist divorce lawyer who is known and respected in the courts that you may be forced to attend. Someone from out-of-town may not serve your best interests.

If you already have business lawyers, whatever you do, **don't** let them convince you that you should let them do your divorce, perhaps *'as a favour'*. Your lawyer must be a family law specialist. Any lawyer will not do.

Don't worry about their fees at this stage. A good divorce lawyer will save you money. It can be false economy to go for the cheaper option. You do not need to like your lawyer. But you must be able to work with him or her.

Discreetly find out who the best divorce lawyers are in your area. In general conversations with men and women, if the subject of divorce comes up, gently bring the chat around to asking: *"Who divorced who? What happened? How did it all affect the kids? Who was the lawyer?"* After a few of these conversations the same lawyers' names should start cropping up. Make appointments with all of them. And interview them.

Prepare for your preliminary meetings. Think carefully about the outcome you want. Write down what you consider the most salient and relevant points about your marriage history and your proposed divorce. Include the date of your marriage, her name, her address, and the names and ages of your children. The lawyer will be able to read all this faster than you'll be able to relate it.

After you provide the lawyer with the facts about your wife, ask: *"Have you ever met my wife? Have you been instructed to act on her behalf in any way?"*

If so, ask this question *"Is there a conflict of interest here?"* If there is, terminate the meeting. If not, continue with the following questions;

- How long have you worked in your area or city?
- How good would you say you are as a divorce lawyer? What makes you say that?

- How much of your work is devoted to family law and divorce?
- What is your preferred method of defeating your opponent?
- Why?
- What size of divorce settlements do you normally deal with?
- What experience do you have of child residence and contact battles?
- How would you convince me that you are the right lawyer to represent my best interests?
- What detailed information do you need to represent me?
- What is the most valuable lesson you've learnt in representing husbands in a divorce case?
- What aren't you so good at?
- Who do you know in the divorce courts and how might that be of benefit to me?
- What do you feel about mediation?
- What legal traps and pitfalls do most men fall into?
- How do I divorce this woman as quickly as possible and for the lowest cost?
- What do you know about my wife's lawyer?
- How would you describe your relationship with local counsel?
- How happy would you be to approach counsel if there was an issue you were unable to deal with?

Before your meeting, also write a separate list of what is most important to you as an outcome. This is your divorce wish list. Referring to this wish list, ask;

- How achievable are these objectives?
- Why do you say that?"
- What is this likely to cost?
- How do you calculate fees?
- What other charges are there?
- What level of detail is in your fee notes?
- What client testimonials can I see? What former clients can I talk to?

At the end of your meeting and while your impressions are fresh in your mind, jot down answers to these questions overleaf:

- How 'switched-on' does this lawyer seem?
- How candid was he or she?
- How much of a sense did you get that the lawyer understood what you are trying to achieve?
- Did you sense the lawyer was only prepared to provide 'legal counsel', rather than what he or she would advise you to do?
- What indications were there that the lawyer was 'on your side'?
- How aggressive was your lawyer in your initial meeting?
- Is the lawyer simply picking up on your anger and giving you what he or she thought you wanted to hear?

You need your lawyer to help you see sense and maintain your focus, not fuel your emotions. The lawyer must be someone with a workable solution, not someone spoiling for a fight. If the solution requires a fight, that's a different matter altogether.

Your lawyer is your reality check. You need them to be pragmatic, upbeat, in control, realistic and on your side. But also realise that some are slow, lazy and unprofessional and rely on ill-informed clients not challenging their opinions, although that has changed considerably in recent years.

Male or female lawyer? Choose the best lawyer based on the answers you receive to your interview questions. The sex shouldn't make any difference, but it can. Don't assume that a male lawyer will be more man-friendly or that a female lawyer is man-unfriendly. Sometimes, female lawyers are more appropriate if they face your ex-wife in court. If, for example, your wife chooses to tell the judge she can't possibly hold down a job and raise children at the same time, a female lawyer will have a credibility that could help your case immeasurably if she says: *"I do. Why can't you?"*

This is what you do after appointing your lawyer:

- Avoid talking to your lawyer about your emotional state. Instead, hire a therapist. It is not your lawyer's job. In any case, a therapist charges less per hour.
- Get into the habit of asking your lawyer: *"What are my options? What are the risks? In your opinion, based on what you know*

about this case, what would you do in my position? And why would you do that?"

- Lawyers, even good ones, can be terrible at explaining in layman's terms what is happening. They've given the same explanations countless times and seem to assume that their clients understand them. Don't be afraid to ask your lawyer to explain something more clearly if you are uncertain about anything.

- Keep your communication professional and be brief. Wherever possible remove your emotion from conversations and correspondence. If you write an e-mail or letter to your lawyer read it through before you send it and redraft if necessary, to make it more succinct.

- Keep a paper trail with your lawyer. And keep copies of all correspondence and court orders just in case things do not work out with that particular lawyer. Confirm all conversations in writing by summarising your understanding of what was agreed and who was going to do what, by when.

- Don't be afraid to fire your lawyer if he or she does not do what has been agreed and promised.

- A small, but important point - don't annoy your wife's lawyer. Lawyers are just doing their job. They don't usually get emotionally involved. However, if you force them to, because you are rude or threatening, they can hurt you too!

Always remember that your lawyer works for you. It's not the other way round. A well-chosen lawyer has expertise you don't have. So really listen to what you are being told. However, lawyers tend to be ultra-cautious and risk averse. When you have been fully informed of the risks involved, don't be afraid to cross-examine your lawyer to ensure all decisions are reached by evaluating the fuller picture of your situation.

But don't allow your emotions to cloud your judgment and deceive you into believing that you know better. Most of the time you won't.

It's crucially important to develop a strategy clarifying your preferred outcomes. Define what is important to you and what isn't. From your list of outcomes, decide which ones you must have, which would be nice to have, what doesn't matter to you and what you don't want. Study your list and do your best to remove emotion. Set priorities, give the list to your lawyer and work together to achieve those outcomes without allowing yourself to be distracted by any games your wife plays along the way.

What's next?

As a rule of thumb, don't forewarn your wife about your plans. She will almost certainly use whatever information you give her in ways that you would never predict. Nasty women seem capable of twisting things to the point of absurdity. If she has been abusive towards you in the past, the abuse will almost certainly escalate and she will probably attempt to punish you for daring to reject her in this way.

Before you ever let your wife know that you're contemplating divorce, start collecting information and evidence. Find out who is *legally* responsible for your financial liabilities such as the mortgage, car payments and bank loans. Which debts and assets were acquired before your marriage and by whom? Which debts and assets were created during the marriage? How many of your assets are in your wife's name for tax or insurance purposes? With your lawyer's help, you may need to change these arrangements. What debts does your wife have? In whose name are they? What are the limits on your joint credit cards? Consider getting them reduced. Write to your card companies requesting this.

You must not be seen to deprive her of all financial support. This will be regarded as deliberately causing her hardship and judges take a poor view of this. Therefore, only cancel the credit, charge and store cards with the highest credit limits. Do this in writing to be effective on a predetermined date. State that you will not accept liability for any further debt she incurs after that date. Keep copies of all correspondence. Collect, collate and copy all credit card, bank and mortgage statements.

For safekeeping, copy or remove from your home: property deeds, share certificates, loan agreements, passports, including those of your children, and all critical financial paperwork. If you have safe deposit boxes, remove all items for safekeeping.

Change your will if your wife is a beneficiary. Imagine you are involved in an accident and are on a life support machine. Could she 'agree' to pull the plug? Remove her name from any documents listing her as next of kin.

Make copies of all your private electronic data and copy them on to a removable memory stick or burn them to CD. Then delete the files from your home computer. If there is particularly sensitive information on your computer hard drive, consider replacing the hard drive and destroy the old one. She may be able to restore highly important data if it is given to a forensic data recovery company. This data could be used in court against you.

Delay or avoid buying new furniture or carrying out home improvements. She'll probably get the house and all its contents, so it's wasted money.

It might be worth you deliberately declaring bankruptcy. Discuss this with your professional advisers. Certainly find ways to lower your income before you file for divorce. For example, go to college to retrain, paying for the course in full and in advance. You will be able to argue that you will have a much-reduced income while you retrain.

Be seen to earn less, or decide to work fewer days in order to look after your children. Accept a commensurate reduction in your salary to do this. It will show your commitment as a father. When your income is about to drop you might be able to persuade your wife to take a part-time job if she is not already working.

At some point you will need alternative accommodation. What are your options? Create a budget to work out this and the other financial implications of your divorce.

Arrange to make all the necessary changes to take place before you announce your divorce to her. Women do this all the time.

Because possession is 'nine-tenths of the law', slowly remove all your personal documents and items of financial or sentimental value from your home and store them securely. Stop settling your wife's personal debts. Remember, she is equally responsible for joint debt. Pay cash for everything you can from now on as credit card statements may be used to prove you have a lavish lifestyle.

Pay off marital debts that are in your name from your joint accounts. Then take half of everything from joint accounts to ensure that you don't lose what is yours if your wife clears out those

142 · Divorce - The Final Frontier

accounts. Alternatively, remove all sums from joint accounts and deposit everything into new accounts where you are the sole signatory. This is not to steal from her but to protect joint assets. Do this in conjunction with your lawyer because if her lawyer suspects that you have siphoned money away, they may apply for an injunction to freeze assets.

Sell your house before you announce a divorce. Don't buy another so that it's easier to split the liquidated cash. From now on, if you receive any cheques, cash them. Don't deposit the money in your bank account.

Set and activate the time and date function on your camera and photograph all your property. Record the model and serial numbers of everything. If any joint items disappear during the divorce, politely ask your wife where they are. If she claims not to know, immediately report them to the police as stolen. Inform your wife after you have done this, not before.

Buy a pay-as-you-go phone and use it only for your most private confidential conversations such as with your lawyer. Re-route all your mail to a PO Box or your parents' home. Get a new e-mail address from a service such as *Hotmail* or *Yahoo*. Instruct your lawyer to use only this e-mail address in correspondence to you. Never use a computer to access these e-mails if it is also used by your wife.

Keep a log of all your spending, collect receipts for everything and stick them in your journal (see Chapter 8). They will prove that you were in specific places at specific times and may disprove allegations she could make against you. Do not under any circumstances let her know about your journal. Keep a written record of anything and everything your wife does that is unethical or unlawful. Keep a record of what your wife spends her money on. Know what she owns and compile an inventory of assets, including jewellery and investments. What value has she put on her possessions for insurance purposes? Use those values when splitting family assets.

To prove your wife is capable of earning a living for herself and is not entitled to spousal support, make copies of her qualifications, previous payslips and old bank statements showing her salary payments. Find out how much money she has earned in cash. Did she declare it to the tax authorities?

If audio or video evidence is admissible in the courts of your country; secretly record her slapping your children, taking drugs, being drunk, especially in front of your children, using bad language, being physically or emotionally abusive, bullying and threatening, screaming and shouting. In fact, tape anything and everything that shows her behaving badly. Keep the tapes safe, make copies and hide them. Keep an accurate log of the times and dates the recordings were made. But be aware that some judges perceive recordings as too intrusive.

If you can afford one, carry a small digital voice recorder everywhere you go. Use it to record conversations you may be forced to have with her. She will want to appear in court in the best possible light and the recordings could go a long way towards undermining or destroying her credibility and the carefully constructed appearance of being a perfect wife or mother.

If it's true, get your doctor to confirm in writing that you are suffering from stress or depression. Don't be afraid to accuse her of mental or physical cruelty. Did you catch a sexually transmitted disease from her after her extra-marital affair? Get medical proof. You may be able to claim that counselling was needed because you have been so traumatised.

If she threatens you or physically abuses you, report it to the police. Make it a matter of public record and collect as much other proof as possible.

Perhaps you now have a better understanding of why so many women plan their divorces for a long time before they announce it. There's a lot to do.

You may never need to use such evidence, but you never can tell. For certain, if you take all necessary steps to protect yourself, you will be at less of a disadvantage. If your wife is prepared to fight dirty, eventually your lawyer will share some of your evidence with her lawyer. Of course, if she thinks you have more evidence than you have, that too can work in your favour.

Imagine everything you say or do could appear in a newspaper - because it could! So it goes without saying, become a model citizen. If you've got something to hide, tell your lawyer. A lawyer can't help you if surprises keep coming out of the woodwork.

All of the above is about protecting yourself. Don't worry unduly about how 'fair' it is.

What to expect during the divorce proceedings

If you believe your wife will respond violently when you inform her of your divorce, ask the police to attend with you. Explain to them that there is a strong possibility that she will cause a breach of the peace.

If or when you are advised to leave your marital home, take all your personal possessions with you. Don't make the mistake of believing that you will be able to return at a later stage to collect the remaining items. You could be prevented by a court injunction from returning, or she could sell or destroy everything you left behind. If collecting everything is impossible, let her know you have photographed all items. If you weren't able to do that, at least let her think you have.

If she changes the locks or you are locked out of your own home, don't threaten her through the letterbox or scream at her through the window. Remain calm. Leave quietly and go to the police. Inform them that you are being denied access to your own home and request they return with you to enter your home to remove your possessions. You may talk yourself out of contacting the police because you don't want to waste their time or because you are a man and you can sort this out. You probably can't. Anything you do can and will almost certainly be described by her as *'bullying'* on your part. Show the police that you are calm, reasonable and professional. Be sober, courteous and convey a genuine need for help.

Your wife must not know what you're aiming to achieve. You need to be clear about what you want, but your wife must never know. If your priority is to be an active father, don't say so. She may try to stop you. If there is an item of property that you're not too interested in retrieving, insist you have it as part of the settlement. It is something for you to forgo at a later stage. Part of the negotiation process is about bluffing and counter-bluffing. It's what she will do.

Some lawyers have been known to do the decent thing by sharing their client's 'real' objectives with her lawyer's under the mistaken belief that, lawyer-to-lawyer, it will help both parties, and themselves. Make it explicit to your lawyer that they must **never** do this.

Whatever you want has a price tag, but you must decide what

are the most important outcomes to you. If proving a point is one of them, you will have to pay more. If seeking revenge is your objective, you will pay even more.

She will be trying to get information about your activities. Politely instruct your friends, associates and colleagues to share nothing about what is going on in your life. Better still, don't tell them. This will actually help them.

Whatever is important to you, she will try to stop you from getting it. Do not give her any information about how you feel. Don't blurt out anything that gives her information that she can use against you.

She will almost certain want to divorce you on the grounds of your unreasonable behaviour, even though she may have been incredibly unreasonable towards you. Your emotions will tell you not to agree to this. But do agree to it, even though it makes you feel so wronged. It may be unfair, untrue or outrageous, and you might be concerned about what your family and friends would say? But that's irrelevant. Get out of the marriage.

But refuse her request initially. Then get your lawyer to ask her lawyer: *"What is your client prepared to trade for our client accepting 'unreasonable behaviour'?"*

The most fundamental rules of negotiating are:

- Know what you want as your outcome.
- Remember that everything is negotiable. Her lawyers will try hard to get the most they can from you. You and your lawyer need to find out the least she will settle for.
- Never concede a negotiating point without demanding something in return. Give nothing away.
- Refuse to agree any financial deals that are open-ended. Whenever possible, your final deal should include the phrase *'In full and final settlement'*.

If you are forced to go to court

Don't go into court expecting the judge to be interested in you or your well-being. The judge won't care about your case as much as you do. A judge's job is not to do what's 'fair'. It's to make a judgment based on the law and on proof. If your wife has behaved illegally, prove it. If you can't, she will almost certainly get away with it.

Your evidence will be the basis of the judge's decision. The more facts, the more likely you will wind up better off. Keep your emotions under control.

Most lawyers will tell you that, no matter how strong your case may be, a judgment can go either way. Judges are notoriously fickle, unpredictable and even unreliable. A judge will try to reach a fair decision based on their analysis of the evidence, but what they deem fair may differ wildly from what you or a different judge would regard as fair.

As flawed and as vulnerable as any man, judges are not immune to being seduced by an attractive woman in the witness box either. After all, they are only human. Unfortunately for you, judges have huge discretion in these cases.

You will get angry and frustrated. You'll want to seek revenge. You'll want to inflict the worst possible pain. It's natural and it's highly likely that this will be in response to things she says and does.

How to get over it

Before the decree absolute comes through and you are 'free', you may feel that a celebration party would be a great idea. But you may feel anti-climactic and deeply sad as the realisation sinks in that your marriage failed. So many men who did their best to make their marriage work admit they feel so many mixed emotions at that time. Don't be too surprised if you change your mind about having that party.

You will inevitably go over and over things in your mind. It almost certainly won't help you. You may even become obsessed with your thought patterns. This will make you feel even worse and you may well become angry with yourself and with her. Keeping yourself to yourself is not a good strategy.

Excessive eating and drinking more won't help you. This compulsive behaviour will almost certainly lead to self-loathing. Revenge won't work either. The best revenge you can have is a happy life without her. Self-pity and feeling sorry for yourself are inevitable to a certain extent, but don't wallow in your sadness.

If you absolutely have to, write a long letter detailing exactly what you feel, how much you detest or even hate your ex-wife. Check it for factual accuracy. Check the spelling. Check the grammar. Then don't send it!

> *We become what we think about.* Anon

Friends will want to help and now it's time to let them. You would want to help someone you care about, so don't deprive them of the chance to help you. Talk to them about your feelings, but know when to stop. Don't fall into the trap of whinging and repeating yourself. Eventually even best friends will find it tiresome. Know how much you would be prepared to listen to before it becomes a burden. You don't want to be that burden to your friends.

Learn to ask yourself sensible questions, not who was to blame. If you have to, ask what used to be so good about the relationship and what changed? And why you were both unable to work through those differences. If your issues are deep-seated and you are having real difficulty coping on your own, find a good therapist. Don't be macho about working through it on your own. They are paid to listen and to help you to move forward.

Find ways to be happy within yourself from today. Make a plan to be happy. Build into your life things to look forward to, even little things. Think about places you want to visit and research those places. Put all this in your diary. What do you want to do with the rest of your life without any marital obligations? At last, you can do what you want.

Dwelling on the past for too long will destroy your present and your future. Going over and over the same things in your mind will probably not make you feel better about yourself either. So don't do it.

Feelings of inadequacy are common when you're the one being divorced, especially if she repeatedly told you how inadequate she thought you were. It was only her opinion. It's inevitable that if you have a failed marriage you will question your ability to make good decisions in other areas of your life. Accept that there will be times when you are in deep emotional pain. This is a normal part of the bereavement process you are going through. Trying to ignore it could extend the time it takes to get over it. It helps to be aware that your attitude towards your situation will have a huge impact on your ability to cope with it. Make a decision not to feel like a victim.

Ultimately, you may have a greater opportunity to rebuild your finances than your ex-wife. One of the most common feelings experienced by men who endure such emotional trauma is that they are on their own. You are not alone. Millions, and we mean millions, of other men have been compelled to suffer the same hardships. Men's support groups have sprung up in most towns and cities. It might be worth joining one.

The rejection and her deception will hurt. Your self-esteem will have taken quite a knock, but the fear of loneliness could drive you into another relationship before you are emotionally ready. Who ever you meet may appear to be *'the one'*, but you're not in a position to make rational decisions at this stage of your recovery. You will be at your most vulnerable, and trying to get back at your wife by using a string of women is unfair on anyone you 'enlist'.

It's a good idea to find ways not to see your ex-wife. The memories will hurt you and inflame her. Of course, if children are involved that may prove difficult, but not impossible.

The next chapter, *Children as Weapons of Male Destruction*, focuses on what some scorned women will do. They will use residence and contact with children to punish the father.

The trouble is ... it punishes the children too.

Chapter 7

Children as Weapons of Male Destruction

> *Whenever I date a guy I think, 'Is this the man I want my children to spend their weekends with?'*
> Rita Rudner

One million children become the victims of divorce in the United States - *every year*. However, it's not just there that marriage is failing and divorce rates are soaring. There was a time, not too long ago, when it was rare to be a child from a 'broken home' in the average school classroom. In many schools today a significant number of children don't live with both parents. The happy family is becoming a distant memory in our fractured society. Parents are not always staying together *"for the children's sake"*.

> *"Over the past four decades fatherlessness has emerged as one of our greater social problems. We know that children who*

grow up with absent fathers can suffer lasting damage. They are more likely to end up in poverty or drop out of school, become addicted to drugs, have a child out of wedlock or end up in prison. Fatherlessness is not the only cause of these things, but our nation must recognise it as an important factor."
President George W. Bush in June 2001

Some children cope, of course. In one way they have to. It is their life, it's the only thing they know, and they have nothing to compare it with. Seeing *'Daddy'* at the weekend is simply what you do.

This arrangement works surprisingly well in many cases. It is remarkable how many divorced parents learn to bring up their children together while apart - organising school drop-offs and pick-ups, and making sure every child has the correct clothes, favourite cuddly toys or the latest batch of weekend birthday party invitations. Parents say it works because it has to work, despite the constant heartbreak for all concerned. However, it can become really nasty. Some women learn to hate their ex-partners more than they love their children.

Who can forget images of Saddam Hussein, the former Iraqi leader, surrounded by young children and making it clear to the world that if his power plants were bombed these children would be slaughtered? The idea of holding children hostage is abhorrent, yet a UK government survey found that at least 40 per cent of single mothers admitted to using contact with 'her' children as a weapon against their fathers. One wonders what proportion of the rest of the mothers surveyed refused to admit they too behaved in this way.

One can only hope that few of those who abuse their children in these ways are consciously aware of what they are doing to them. Some are too wrapped up in their own emotional pain, while others are obsessed with their campaign of hatred against the men they used to love.

Every day good, loving fathers are denied contact with their children by mothers and the courts. Perversely, this is allowed to happen only in 'civilised' societies. Below is an account of how one man was deprived of his right to be a father to his children;

"I was a victim of domestic abuse for many years. This included physical and emotional abuse. In addition to the 'normal' stress and tension accompanying the break-up of a marriage or an established relationship, to experience in addition the impact and injustice of being served with a Court Order based on unfounded and fictitious evidence, without recourse to the normal checks and balances of the law, (i.e. requirement of evidence, witnesses, and a public hearing) - for me the effects on my health of such manifest injustices were pronounced. I experienced hypertension for seven consecutive months, and could sleep only with the help of sleeping tablets.

My faith in the law and society of my birth were utterly shaken. Five years later I continue to take anti-depressants. My zest and enthusiasm for work and life have never recovered. I discontinued my hobby as an active traditional musician. I was too deflated and depressed to continue. My business, a healthy firm established for 11 years, began to go into decline for want of initiative and energy, and eventually went into voluntary liquidation with the loss of five jobs.

During the darkest moments of hopelessness - deprived of access to my beloved children, ejected like a criminal from my home on malicious, unverified evidence, without recourse to justice or any form of help, I frequently considered taking my life. My age, being then nearly forty, was no doubt a stabilising factor preventing this course of action, but I understood why many a younger man felt there was no other way out. Under the circumstances, depression is inevitable.

Accompanying the depression was a pronounced lack of energy, unaffected by diet change, regular exercise, or heavy doses of vitamins and supplements. The indications were that this was an energy loss with psychological, not physical causes. And these psychological causes were circumstantial, not intrinsic.

On several occasions my GP asked me if I had entertained any thoughts of suicide. I was obliged to answer 'No', as any admission to the contrary might further damage my standing as an effective parent for my children. Many a man has been damaged or defeated first, then presented to the courts as unfit for the role of father.

My sense of futility and helplessness in the face of social workers, solicitors, judges, teachers, police, doctors and other professionals who by their actions (and lack of action) individually and collectively proved themselves so prejudiced against my fatherhood, against equality and fair play, that I felt marginalised, disenfranchised, ostracized, and very angry in a helpless, unfocused way. My mind was frequently distracted and my short-term memory proved unable to function effectively.

My children were deprived of their right to their natural father. Not one single police officer, social worker, doctor or teacher took any single act to prevent this happening. On the contrary, by attitude, by prevarication, by ignorance, by disinterest and by barely-disguised prejudice, the individuals with any say in the matter of my children have effectively removed their father from their lives. Their mother now shares with a man for whom the children are not his principal concern, and who is not in a position of care or authority to direct them or to discipline them when required, since he is principally their mother's new partner, and not their natural father. His affections and presents cannot ever replace their natural father's love. The children are not experiencing balanced parenting. Further, they are progressively being told how bad their father was, their happy past is now being re-interpreted as unhappy, and our family history is being re-written to suit the times."

Below is an e-mail forwarded by a man, from his wife. She had previously made false allegations against him.

"I know you're a good man and have always stood by your family. I needed time out when I got the barring order and that's why I did it, [she continues to have an affair]. I know you don't drink and you would never harm us but I did need time out. I know that the kids adore you.

I told you if we got back together I'd go out whenever I want and see whoever I like. I don't care if you're annoyed that I came in at 4.30 the other night. I will do what I want.

> *You either accept that and move back for good or get on with your life. You might think I can't get you out of the house as easy next time but if I tell the police you forced yourself on me, you'll be gone for good. Even your solicitor told you last time that courts always believe the wife. ... I showed you that I'd get the house and kids. If you go your own way, the kids stay with me, I get the house and most of your money. You can see the kids when I decide. So watch what you say or I'll fucking ruin you.*
> *Happy Xmas*
> *Suzie"*

Much of the statistical data in this chapter draws heavily on the extensive research by Matthew O'Connor, Gary Burch and Michael Cox that formed the basis for the Fathers-4-Justice manifesto, *A Blueprint for Family Law in the 21st Century; and the Case for Urgent Radical Reform*. The 55-page report is available as a download from www.fathers-4-justice.org

Some would say the publicity stunts of Fathers-4-Justice, in which men dressed themselves as cartoon action heroes and scaled the walls of places such as Buckingham Palace, have trivialised the very issues the organisation wanted to bring to the attention of the public and government. Yet, so deep was their frustration at not being allowed to present their case with any effective outcomes that shock tactics were felt to be among the few options left. All 'official' attempts had fallen on deaf ears. They set out do what Mahatma Gandhi described as *"Making the injustice visible"*.

The frightening statistics these fathers have assembled go some way towards highlighting the scale of the problem in British society:

- More than 150,000 children a year are affected by divorce in the UK.
- Two-thirds of these children are aged ten years or under. One in five is under five.
- 257,000 children, were registered to unmarried parents in 2003.

- Only 65 per cent of the 11.7 million children in England and Wales live with both their natural parents.
- 2.67 million children live in lone-parent families, 91.2 per cent of which are headed by the mother.
- 65 per cent of total child abuse; neglect and sexual, emotional and physical ill-treatment is committed by mothers, whereas only 8 per cent of child abuse is by fathers. These figures come from the National Society for the Prevention of Cruelty to Children (NSPCC).
- The legal aid bill for family breakdown matches the NHS drugs bill every year.
- The direct cost of family breakdown to Britain has been calculated at £15 billion annually.
- 70 per cent of the 1.25 million teenagers who break the law every year are fatherless children and young adults under the age of 18.
- 84 per cent of them re-offend within two years.
- It has been calculated that the annual cost to the taxpayer of teenage crime exceeds £10 billion.
- There are more than 500 women's refuges in Britain. Only three exist for men, two of which opened in 2004.

In Britain about 100 children lose contact with their fathers and grandparents every day because of a form of collusion between mothers eager to punish their former partners and the British family courts. In the past ten years about 300,000 children have lost contact with one of their parents. The vast majority of these parents are fathers.

Fathers-4-Justice says there has been a systematic failure by Britain's family courts in their duty of care towards the children involved in separation and divorce. The organisation has described such gender apartheid as *"rupturing the parental bonds of thousands of children"*.

It declares: *"Fatherlessness is the child welfare issue of the 21st century. All decent parents and grandparents have inalienable rights to share in the care and upbringing of their children and grandchildren, and the breaking of the bond between child and parent is a grotesque travesty of natural justice. The systematic exclusion of parents from the lives of their children by the family courts in this country is tantamount to abuse ..."*

A report by Civitas in 2002 blamed fatherless families for increasing crime, drug-taking and educational failure among abandoned offspring. The children from fatherless families were, according to them, more likely to live in poverty and deprivation, more likely to have problems in school, more likely to have socialisation problems, were at a higher risk of health problems, at a greater risk of suffering physical, emotional or sexual abuse, more likely to run away from home, more likely to experience problems with sexual health, more likely to be on income support, more likely to experience homelessness, more likely to offend, more likely to suffer long-term emotional problems and more likely to suffer from psychological problems.

Fathers-4-Justice believes there has been a sustained erosion of the father's right to exercise his responsibilities in raising his own children. It claims a generation of children is growing up without the love, care, influence and guidance of its fathers.

Sir Bob Geldof is quoted in the manifesto as saying: *"Family law as it currently stands does not work. It rarely benefits the child, and promotes injustice, conflict and unhappiness on a massive scale ... It is creating vast wells of misery, massive discontent, and an unstable society of feral children and feckless adolescents."*

The children's best interests are routinely ignored by family courts. Take the example of a Plymouth family in which the father was denied contact with his three daughters for six years because of maternal hostility. The case went on for ten years and involved 133 court appearances in front of 33 judges. The mother's boyfriend allegedly made five threats to kill the father from the witness box. But he was allowed to go home to live with the father's children while the father was imprisoned twice for a total of 129 days for waving to his children. His only crime was trying to maintain a relationship with his daughters against their mother's wishes. The case cost the UK taxpayer nearly £1 million. The result? When the children were old enough to assert their true wishes, two voted with their feet and went to live with their father. That father, Mark Harris wrote a book about his experiences called *Family Law HELL*. As part of his harrowing *'must read'* story he wrote:

> *"No one can do anything to stop a former wife or partner becoming obstructive over access to the children, but likewise, no one expects the legal system to assist her on such a mission. But it does, and with monotonous regularity. If the obstructive parents' support mechanisms were removed, and orders for contact enforced, most cases would resolve quite quickly."*

Fathers have a role as protector too. There are countless stories of fathers who are forced to endure nightmares such as the following, told in the man's own words:

> *"During the marriage, it ended up that both the children and I were suffering abuse from my wife. The first indication of this was when I came home from work. The children would naturally run to say, 'Daddy, Daddy', which is something that all children would do. My wife was very jealous of the relationship that I was developing with my children. We eventually ended up having five. She became extremely jealous and she used to say I loved them more than I loved her!*
>
> *I had to steal time with my children. She would explode and would become verbally abusive. Shortly after this ....she actually did some physical violence by biting into my arm. I have the remnants of that scar today. After she did this, she laughed and laughed for days afterwards. She thought it was very funny. This was also very significant because this was the first time she committed physical violence, and she found that I would not hit her back, and from that point on she knew she could rule by violence. She could dominate the household and she could do whatever the hell she liked and she did.*
>
> *The level of violence actually increased. It was no longer once a month or once a week. It was virtually every single day. It wasn't just me, it was my kids. The sort of things that she would do to me were to beat me with the TV aerial lead and stab me in the hand. She would drug my tea with medication*

and attempt strangulation. She tried to throw a radio cassette player into the bath. Fortunately, the lead was about six or eight inches too short.

About a year before my marriage actually ended, I was diagnosed as mentally and physically exhausted by the doctor. My body weight dropped by two and a half stone. I was having blackouts. It got to the stage where I was actually frightened to say anything in case it invoked her violence and anger and boiled into more physical and more extreme violence.

After the marriage finished, her legal people wanted the children to see a psychologist for assessment before the courts. I had the first interview with the psychologist and I explained my wife's behaviour towards the kids and me. Her first reaction was, 'What did you do to make her do it?' What I did was to stand in front of my children when she came after them. I took the punishment instead of my kids, and I don't apologise for that. I'd do it again. I had the nerve to say 'no', to disagree with what she wanted to do. If she didn't get her way she went on the old reliable tack of taking medication and pseudo-attempted suicides. This time social workers were actually getting involved with the family and they witnessed the assaults on me and the children. However, I never received any support. My wife did, but I didn't, and at one stage she actually moved out of the house and took the kids with her. The health board put her up in a house with the children and that same night she moved a man into the house."

How the odds are weighted against fathers

As so many fathers can attest, fighting to see their own children can be a lesson in futility. If a vindictive ex-wife decides you're not going to see them, she can make it difficult, if not impossible, for you to do so. No matter what she does to you, in her mind you will not have been punished enough even though you may be innocent of any wrongdoing. Her actions are often supported by the family courts.

Despite conclusive research that the biological father is the least likely person to abuse children, and all types of abuse increase significantly when biological fathers are absent from the family, the opinions and the role of fathers are not considered. Women often tell the courts that the children don't want see their father. Even though the children are not old enough to know what is in their best long-term interests, these claims invariably delay the court process as welfare officers then have to become involved to ascertain the true needs and wishes of the children. In the meantime, the mother may shape or tailor the child's views. Family courts often take the word of the mother, and reduce a father's contact.

Ex-wives tell outright lies, make false allegations and as a matter of course exaggerate what fathers may or may not have said or done to convince a judge that the father was constantly unreliable or unreasonable. It is made so easy for a woman to accuse a father of being a threat to her children, or imply it, even when she knows this is a deception and a lie. Yet the judicial system doesn't actively punish those who choose to lie and deceive. In any other circumstances perjury is regarded as a serious crime, punishable with a jail sentence.

Mothers have a de-facto veto, also known as the *gatekeeper* role, over the father-child relationship. Any parental conflict is usually 'solved' by the courts by removing one of the parents from the relationship with the child. In almost all cases this is the father because the mother has already been awarded residence with the children and the father has been deemed to have a subordinate role. The courts constantly aim to maintain the status quo, meaning that whatever is happening already will almost certainly be made to continue. A woman can relatively easily use a range of well-known tactics that slowly erode and chip away the father's involvement with his children. This process gains momentum and becomes easier over time, thus excluding him even more.

A mother may claim that her emotional instability, because of the way she feels about her ex-partner, makes her incapable of looking after her children. The courts routinely accept this argument and deny the father contact with the children. The mother's best interests are put before the children's need to have a father to love and care for them. Her role is deemed to be undermined by father involvement.

A Law Commission working paper stated: *"There is a tendency to assume that if access is not working, it should be reduced, whereas some of the factors mentioned would point in the opposite direction."*

The courts actually further inflame conflict. Intense frustration and anger are regularly experienced by loving fathers, deprived of their moral rights to protect and raise their own children. So if you have children with a woman who decides to punish you because you love your children, brace yourself for extreme emotional as well as financial abuse.

A high proportion of fathers are then caught in a parental poverty trap. After a financially damaging divorce settlement and with no legal aid for fathers earning more than £12,000 a year, the legal costs associated with attempts to have contact with his children can be prohibitive - a minimum of £2,000-£5,000 for just six months. We know of one man, a doctor who had to pay £80,000 for his own legal fees, plus his former wife's costs of £120,000. Protracted litigation can cripple a responsible, loving father who wants only to be allowed to look after his own children. That money would obviously be better spent on his children. A father can spend a fortune on legal fees but cannot be assured of success because maverick judges are given a wide band of discretion in making their pronouncements.

Yes, it is possible to save vast sums of money by not using a lawyer and presenting your own case in court by becoming a *'litigant in person'*, but judges usually hate this. They find it irritating to have to explain court processes and the law to men who may be doing the best they can in an alien environment.

Regardless of how cases are conducted, miscarriages of justice are a regular occurrence. You simply cannot rely on the system to make the best decisions for the children or the parents, and the father in particular. Here are some examples and others collected by Fathers-4-Justice to show how some decisions defy belief:

A judge said of a man who sought more than two hours' contact per fortnight that *"It may well be that the father is being too possessive"*.

How about another judge who sentenced a father to four months' jail for giving his children Christmas presents during a scheduled contact meeting, in breach of a court order?

Yet another judge found that a father had been falsely accused by his ex-wife of sexually abusing his daughter. These allegations had also been made to close friends and to a vicar. The judge then criticised the father for not putting it behind him! He said: *"It would be hoped that father might have been able now to put this matter on one side. It seems that he is not yet able to do so ... the father would inevitably feel intensely bruised and battered by the allegations of sexual impropriety ... despite his understandable sense of outrage at the allegations he had really learnt nothing from the whole process."*

In order to pay his ex-wife the onerous maintenance she was claiming, another judge is reported to have said *"You will have to work longer hours and see less of your children."*

On a report, *Managers as Fathers: Hopes on the Home Front*, by Delaney and Delaney, Fathers-4-Justice wrote: *"The dominance of women in family services, and the corresponding scarcity of men, is among the most powerful of all the forces which exclude fathers from the lives of their children today, for in this we see the outward and visible sign of what begins to be perceived as an essential truth: that in family life, men are an irrelevance at best, and at worst a danger."* It is the view of many that the situation for men has worsened since that report was written in 1990.

The situation is now said to be so bad for some fathers that when contact has been denied, often for no specific reasons, the mother will get legal aid to defend her actions, but the Legal Services Commission will frequently decree that the non-resident parent has an *"unwinnable case"* and will then refuse legal aid to him.

Her vendetta - how she may use your children against you

The vindictive mother's personal vendetta becomes more important than her children's welfare. She will rationalise it in any way she can. But this is still child abuse.

Part of the denial process is blaming others, and if she can recruit supporters, including her children, she may mistakenly believe having allies will lessen her guilt. Her denial regime also includes believing that what she wants is exactly the same as what her children want. She needs to think this to justify her abusive behaviour.

To start with, she wants her children to know how much she hates their father. In many cases, she will assume that if she feels this way, so will her children. But, of course, children love their fathers unconditionally. So many malicious mothers have been known to brainwash the children to hate the father and this sometimes takes place over prolonged periods. It is difficult to spot and even more difficult to prove.

Some women tell the children their father is a loser because he lives in a tiny dilapidated apartment while they live in a nice big house. Conveniently, she fails to tell the children that their father pays for their nice house and that after a punitive financial settlement he cannot afford anything better than his shabby hovel.

She tells them their father doesn't love them as much as 'Mummy' does because he doesn't take them on the expensive holidays she does. Again, she doesn't tell them that their father pays for those holidays. And sometimes paying for her boyfriend to go along too. And other women deliberately relocate just to create more hardship for the remaining parent.

Behind his back children are told that their father is stupid and that he abandoned the family, even though the mother was having an affair, which led ultimately to the divorce.

Some mothers have even told their children to call 999 in the UK, or 911 in the US, to say they are scared of their father. They may not be, but they *are* scared of their mother! Clearly, children are very easily manipulated by a deceitful parent.

Expect a vindictive ex-wife to tell your children repeatedly about what is wrong with you. She mistakenly believes that the more bad things they hear about you, the more they will love her. If she has shown vindictiveness towards you in the past, be aware that she may attempt to brainwash your children into hating you by making false allegations of physical and even sexual abuse. Bad-mouthing is commonplace.

If your children are young, they are more inclined to believe what they are told to think. As children grow older, the woman may manipulate or trick them into believing the father is uninterested in them, is unreliable and doesn't love them. Sustained and deliberate alienation by one parent against another has been defined as parental alienation syndrome, or PAS. It can take many forms, it is controversial and it divides the professionals. However, it is essential to learn to recognise any of the following signs that may indicate that your children are being brainwashed or manipulated to turn against you:

- Notice if your children become less affectionate towards you and are afraid to say what they think.
- Do they quickly look towards their mother for approval before they say anything to you?
- If you have been denied contact with your children and they are becoming more hostile towards you, it is highly possible that she is using brainwashing techniques.
- Do they seem to hate anything to do with you?
- Do they seem frightened of you for no apparent reason? She may be telling the children you are violent when you are not and never have been. Those lies understandably make them feel frightened of you. The father has no idea what she has been saying. Perhaps she hopes that when he finds out it will trigger violence for the first time, so that she can say: *"There, I told you he was violent."*
- The child's regular refusal to see you may be caused by undue influence from the mother.
- Do the children automatically and always take her side, even when you know for sure that she is wrong about something?
- Do they scream abuse at you for no reason that you can think of, call you unwarranted names or withdraw and appear uninterested?
- When they are with you, do they lose their sense of fun?
- Do they expect presents but are unwilling to give you even a little respect?
- Their mother may try constantly to reduce contact, making it increasingly easier for her to create emotional distance between you and your children. Less physical contact leads to a lower psychological connection and reinforces the mother's belief that *"Nobody can love you like your mother does."*
- Another commonly used and highly subversive tactic from the mother is to encourage the children to call you by your first name. On the surface it sounds informal and friendly. In reality, it's often a deliberate ploy to wean the child away

from thinking of you as their father and create even more emotional distance. If this happens to you, ask them what their friends call their fathers. Of course, it will be *'Dad'*, not the first name. Then you can gently explain that it's normal to call you *'Dad'*.

• She may promise to renew contact when it's a *'better time'*. That's almost certainly a dishonest ploy to weaken even further the relationship you have with your children.

Some women 'remind' their children of that time when their father abused them. Even though he did not. This 'reminder' is repeated so often that eventually the children believe it must have happened, even though they have absolutely no recollection of it. This is pure brainwashing.

By the time they go to court, the children remember very clearly the abuse that never took place. It is well known that vindictive mothers coach their children to say certain things against their father during child residence battles.

Divorce Poison, by Dr Richard A. Warshak, is a ground breaking book that catalogues the extreme measures some parents - men and women - are prepared to take to get back at ex-partners, for actual or perceived transgressions. The author details systematic campaigns of hatred and revenge intended to inflict maximum harm with little or no regard for the well-being of the children. The book offers a great deal of practical help for both partners to counter the effects of this divorce poison. A must-read for any parent caught up in child residence battles.

In his book, Warshak recounts an experiment with a group of pre-school children who were asked to recall a time when someone called Sam Stone visited the classroom. His visit was part of the experiment. The next day the children were shown a dirty teddy bear that was not in the room when he visited. The children were asked: *"Remember that time Sam Stone visited your classroom and spilled chocolate on that white teddy bear? Did he do it on purpose or was it an accident?"* By the end of the experiment 72 per cent of the youngest children falsely accused Sam Stone of wrongdoing!

When the vindictive mother of your children knows you love

them, these types of actions sometimes become her most effective weapons against you.

However, you have a weapon too. To help your children to question any negative things their mother tells them about you, make sure they meet and spend time with people who think well of you. These can be colleagues, family members, friends and all their children. Let them see you being liked and appreciated by others.

If you can prove she is deliberately alienating your children from you, she runs the serious risk of being denied the right to care for those children. So discuss possible solutions with your lawyer. However, you would need to prove your case, and that means gathering evidence.

The evidence

Don't waste your energy feeling down about how someone you used to love could lie in such a way. To defend yourself effectively you need to be able to prove her manipulation and abuse. As previously stated, amassing evidence should be a top priority before you commence divorce proceedings. Here are some additional tips:

- Do as much as you can to prove she is a habitual liar. This could undermine her credibility and help you in court.
- What proof can you produce to suggest she is unfit to be a mother?
- Recordings of verbal abuse may not be admissible in court, but accurate transcripts often are.
- Store all her abusive or threatening text messages. Do not send messages yourself that could be used against you in a similar way.
- If she ever tries to turn your children against you, write down in your journal the evidence of anything she says, dating it and accurately capturing the essence of what she said. Over time this could provide invaluable evidence to be used to protect your children from being deliberately alienated from their father.
- How often do your children have cuts and bruises and are

subject to accidents when you're not around? Photograph their injuries.

- Women are often advised by their lawyers not to be seen to have a relationship or cohabit during divorce proceedings because her new partner's earnings can be taken into account when a financial settlement is calculated. Therefore, it is potentially in your interests to gather such evidence if she is in a relationship with someone else.

> " *Strategy without tactics is the slowest route to victory. Tactics without strategy is the noise before defeat.* "
> Sun Tzu

The value of proof cannot be over-emphasised, even though you may never need to use it. Gather evidence of her abuse and bad behaviour for as long as you can. Record her sustained nasty conduct in every way you can.

When you know you have a chunk of evidence that will show her in a bad light, it can also have quite a calming effect on you, because you know you have something up your sleeve. Keep it all to yourself and your lawyer, however. Hold off from telling your wife's lawyer of its existence. Let your wife and her lawyer continue to make their unreasonable demands.

Then, when you are approaching the final negotiations and her threats to go to court intensify, this is the point when your evidence is sent to her lawyer. Your lawyer will tell her lawyer that you are happy to proceed, and that, with her sustained threats and unreasonable demands recorded, you are prepared to allow a judge to decide. Your lawyer will explain that you have done everything you can to bring the matter to a conclusion but have now been forced to use this evidence, as every other course of action has failed.

Depending on the evidence you have collected, she will almost certainly have second thoughts about going to court. She will want to save face, and her own skin. The prospect of washing all her dirty linen in public may be very unappealing. This is the point at which you are most likely to gain leverage in your negotiations. Very subtly let her believe you have more evidence than she thinks. Her fear of even more truth coming out will temper her demands. After all, she may publicly deny any wrong-doing herself, but she still knows what she has done to you.

66 *Don't compromise yourself. It's all you've got.*
Janis Joplin 99

Don't ...

Some fathers, despite their best efforts, lose all contact with their children. As we said, the judicial system is prejudiced against the father's moral right to raise his own children.

However, many fathers often make fundamental mistakes that can harm their chances of contact. A lack of knowledge of the judicial system and a misguided sense that fairness will prevail can cause untold frustration and anger. The system is not fair to fathers. Accept this and learn to navigate your way around it.

To help you improve your chances of increased contact, listed below is a collection of 'don'ts'.

Before your separation or divorce, don't leave the marital home. Never be seen to leave the children. In child residence disputes the status quo issue is an important one. Judges usually prefer to change arrangements as little as possible to ensure that the children's lives are not disrupted unduly. You must maintain contact so that your status quo is assured.

Don't be separated from your children during the divorce. Don't allow your wife to convince you that they need to be with her during your divorce. Show that they are used to sharing time between her and you. Similarly, unless your children are in grave danger from her, don't ever stop them from seeing their mother. Being passive is not the answer, but trying to be nastier than she is will not help you either.

Don't ever use your children as a weapon against your wife. Don't bad-mouth her, even though it is highly likely she would be prepared to do that to you. Let such behaviour be a reflection on her. Don't stoop to her level. Therefore, never let your children hear anything bad said about her. Some fathers talk disparagingly about their ex-partners to other adults in front of their children, subconsciously wanting them to hear how horrible she is. They fool themselves into believing it's acceptable because they aren't actually saying these things directly to their children. No, that's still child abuse.

Don't lose your temper, because at all times she is trying to wind you up. If you fall for it, your outburst will be used against you. She wants you to argue. She wants you to feel pain. She wants to punish you. Don't allow yourself to get sucked into all that. Learn to step back and see everything for what it is. Learn to shrug your shoulders at her latest antics and focus on your children's well-being.

Your anger may be inflamed, but don't ever take it out on your children. Don't let them become hostages to your hostility. Nor should you shout or swear at your ex-partner in front of the children, no matter how severely you are provoked.

Don't let your children feel you are interrogating them or using them as informers. Don't turn your children into go-betweens either. If things need to be said, say them face-to-face to your ex-partner, or send messages by text, e-mail or via a trusted friend, or, if absolutely necessary, through a lawyer. Whenever possible, organise pick-ups and drop-offs so you will not have to meet each other.

Don't assume your children have been brainwashed to hate you just because they are not behaving the way you want them to. They may be having a bad day. Incorrectly blaming or criticising your ex-wife could come back to haunt you.

Don't try to change your children's minds. They have to do that themselves, though it may take time.

Don't allow your children to be taken out of the country if there is a serious risk they will not return. However, use only the legal process to do so, and don't make the mistake of taking the law into your own hands by snatching them in an effort to protect them. You then become the abductor, regardless of your motives.

Ex-wives have been known to exclude the entire family of the children's father from their lives, claiming this is in the children's best interests. It's important not to let grandparents be denied contact with their grandchildren. They too can apply to the courts for contact orders.

Whatever you do, don't punish your children for your deep feelings of hurt. They hurt too, remember.

Contact with your children

Depriving fathers of contact with their children is commonplace. Assuming you are looking for increased contact, and she is blocking your attempts, you will find ideas in this section to help you.

Try planting the seeds in her mind that if you don't see the children she will suffer, because she will never have any time off for a life of her own. If you are on speaking terms, gently sell her the idea that it is in her interests that you have equal responsibility for looking after the children.

Through a lawyer, your written approach could be: *"I want to be an active father, to share our parenting, to be a meaningful part of their lives. If you refuse to allow me to do that, I'm not going to fight you any more. Wasting more money on legal fees will ultimately punish the children. My love for the children won't ever change."*

Parents who have managed to divorce sensibly often say how shared child care works better for both parents and for the children simply because it gives the ex-wife and ex-husband time to themselves when they are not having to look after the children. It's possible she will realise that her life will be more difficult if she is a full-time carer. If she suspects you are forcing it on her, she will fight you in any way she can. Sadly, there are no guarantees that this will achieve your objective. But it might work for you.

Things to do:
- Be reliable for your children.
- Make sure you're involved at their school.
- Keep a detailed log of your attendance at the school parents' evenings and school concerts that you attend. Record how often you put them to bed, ferry them to and from school, take them to doctor's appointments, and anything else that shows your active and sustained involvement in their upbringing.
- Continue communicating with your children through recorded delivery letters or via your lawyer, if necessary, to provide proof that you have maintained contact.

- E-mail their mother volunteering to babysit. Keep her written refusals.
- Keep a written record of when you do see your children and for how long.
- Play with your kids. Lose yourselves together in play.
- Encourage your children to invite their friends over too. It's their time, not just yours. Time with your children is not meant to satisfy your need for their company. Seeing you is part of their life - they are not pets.
- Send birthday and Christmas cards and gifts via your lawyer. Alternatively, send everything via recorded delivery so that she can't ever claim things did not arrive. Of course, this does not guarantee they are ever passed on to your children.
- Write them a letter every day, or make an entry in a specially created scrapbook, which you may be able to show or give to them one day. Include all sorts of photos, cartoons, postcards and pictures of them.
- Create a website for your children to access. Or, upload regular video diaries to video based websites. But make sure the site you choose does not include unsuitable video material for children.
- Carry copies of legal documents with you when your children are in your care in case the authorities are called by your ex-partner for spurious reasons.
- Tell family and friends: *"I want to be a good father to my children. But I'm not being allowed to."* Don't add any comments about what a horrible woman she is.
- If you can still afford it, seek professional financial advice about creating a trust fund that matures when the children become adults. By the time they grow up and you present them with a significant cash sum, perhaps to fund their first property, you will be able to show that you have looked after them in your own way during all those years when you were forbidden contact with them.

" *When a brave man takes a stand, the spines of others are stiffened.* Billy Graham "

If you are unable to resolve child care arrangements between you, attending a court hearing may become inevitable. These cases are held in a civil court, not a criminal one. You may have to attend a *'finding of facts hearing'* to ascertain *'the balance of probabilities'*. If she has made false allegations against you, part of doing so is to incense and frighten you. She will, however, be required to prove her claims. The more serious the allegations, the more substantiated the evidence has to be.

On the brighter side, one day your children may learn the truth about their mother's refusal to allow them to see you.

Communication with your children

Children don't always understand what is going on. They won't experience the same emotions as you or your estranged or divorced wife. They can't understand irrational behaviour. They are often confused, scared and emotionally disturbed by the mother's behaviour. They can't appreciate why they feel so bad, especially when their mother makes such a big issue of how much she loves them. Many will conclude that they themselves must have done something wrong. They could fear that you will abandon them too.

Tell them: *"Even though mummy and I no longer live together, we both still love you very much."*

Assess the risks of telling your children too much too soon. If they are old enough, explain to your children what is happening without bad-mouthing your wife. Don't tell them more than they can handle emotionally. It's too easy to tell them everything and justify it by saying: *"I just told them the truth."* That is often dishonest honesty. If it hurts the child's feelings, it is not appropriate. Always reassure your children about the love you have for them and how that will never change. Don't just think it and assume they realise it already. However, don't tell them over and over again either, as it may soon come across as desperation. Avoid making too big a deal of things with your children.

Without putting them under any pressure, create an environment in which they can talk about what they feel. Find out how your children feel about themselves. Give them space to talk to you and be seen to listen without judging or telling them they are wrong. Ask them: *"What else do you want to talk about?"* Gently encourage them to talk to someone they like and know well about anything that may be troubling them, if they don't feel they can have that conversation with you.

If your children tell you that their mother has been saying nasty things about you, simply say in a low-key way: *"I think she's mistaken."* Tell them what you think is the truth without making any negative comments about their mother, and leave it at that.

If you are rejected, the rejection may not be about you. It's perhaps the best way your children have of coping with intensely painful circumstances that are not of their choosing. Regardless of any horrible things your children say to you or about you, never tell them you don't want to see them. At their most obnoxious, be kind. If they won't resist, hug them, but never force affection on them.

Children will often play one parent off against the other. They're learning the divide-and-conquer manipulation techniques used by their parents! Children can be extremely opportunistic. If children ask you for something, and you sense they are chancing their luck, ask them back: *"What did your mother say about this?"* It at least gives the appearance that you are working together. Swallow your pride sometimes and tell your children that if their mother said something you aren't going to countermand her.

> *"What hurts children the most is when parents place children in the middle of their battles. In some cases children witness their parents' violent disputes. Or their parents encourage and take sides, to deliver angry messages, or spy on the other parent. Taken to extremes, such practices may be part of the systematic effort to turn children against the other parent. Even in less extreme cases, this type of behaviour will harm children."* Dr Richard A. Warshak in *Divorce Poison*

As much as you feel you may be falling apart, the children need you to be strong for them. It is not a child's responsibility to look after your emotional wellbeing. It's your role to look after theirs, no matter how bad you feel.

Yet some women are so wrapped up in themselves that depriving the children of their father is seen by some as an acceptable punishment against the father. Some might be horrified if they were made to realise that this punishment hurts the children more. A woman of this type just forgets the needs of her own children. Her feelings become more important than their needs. But, of course, she will say and do whatever it takes to convince a court that satisfying her neediness is in the children's best interests.

Your children are entitled to the unconditional love, kindness and support of both parents, whatever she may ever think or say to the contrary. So, no matter what is happening, reassure your children that you love them and say that will never change and you will always be there for them.

Fathers-4-Justice says: *"It is vitally important for a child to retain a meaningful, loving relationship with both parents, and it is a failure of the legislature not to provide, in the 21st century, the legal right for parents to contribute to the day-to-day care of their children."*

It's simple. Children do better when their father is actively involved in their lives. And loving grandparents are never bad for a child. Yet when a vindictive woman decides against all this for her own selfish reasons, she invariably still gets what she wants, supported by the courts.

Chapter 8

Protection Strategies Against Malicious and Vindictive Women

Let us now explore strategies and techniques for handling physical, verbal, emotional, psychological, sexual and financial abuse from a nasty woman. The woman in question may be a colleague, your boss, your girlfriend, partner or wife. You may be male or female. Some malicious and vindictive women are violent and dangerous, and, in extreme cases, your life may be in danger.

From the beginning, the premise for this book has been that there are genuinely innocent men and women who are targeted by a small but dangerous category of malicious women. These women are the primary aggressors. In many cases their behaviour can be ruthless, cruel, deceitful and manipulative. Their targeted victims may or may not be aware of what is being done to them. Many are routinely bullied, threatened and physically or emotionally abused, but they simply don't know how to deal with it. Her victims often suffer in silence because they may believe they are the only people in the world being treated in this way. They feel impotent or paralysed into doing nothing about stopping the abuse.

The abusive woman may have perfected her illusion of loveliness so that her victim is unlikely to be believed by friends, family or the authorities. *"You must be making it up,"* they may think, or they will believe you must have done something to provoke her.

Emotional pain, rather than physical hurt, is often her weapon of choice. It's far easier for her to smile demurely, deny all accusations and feign surprise that anyone could possibly think she is sadistic or has deliberately tried to hurt someone, than to indulge in stabbing, shooting, poisoning or bruising. Emotional pain lasts longer and often hurts more intensely, and because it is invisible, the victim is less likely to receive comfort or sympathy. And destroying a man's life by abusing him emotionally isn't yet against the law in some countries!

In the past you may have ignored your instinct. Nevertheless, even if you are wrong some of the time, it will be worth trusting your instinct more. You could save yourself from being manipulated. Whatever you can do that makes it less likely that she will pick on you, and every time you recognise her tactics, and every time you deflect her attempts to hurt you, you become a little stronger and a little more confident. This, in turn, makes it more likely that you will listen to what your gut instinct tells you.

Physical abuse nearly always escalates. A slap will get harder. A punch will hurt more. When that fails to deliver the desired result, she will probably start using small implements, then larger and sharper ones. See where this can go, before it does.

This and the next chapter have been written to lead you to a better understanding of your present position and to assist you in disentangling your frazzled emotions from the facts. This achieved, you should be better placed to assess your options, define your desired outcomes and create and implement a plan.

And then pray it all works! Because the sheer creativity of truly malicious women makes it impossible to predict what she may do next, no book can possibly account for all scenarios or present comprehensive and infallible tactics for coping with every eventuality. If she's out to get you, she will make sure she wins - by whatever means necessary.

In this chapter we tackle the following:

- How to be better at recognising her covert aggressive behaviour. By doing so, you will be far better placed to develop a strategy to reduce or stop her behaviour.
- Are you being abused, or is it your imagination?
- Realise the part you play in her abuse. What it is about your own personality and behaviour that may be encouraging her to abuse you? Does she see you as weak?
- And are you abusing her - perhaps without even realising it?
- What are your options? How can you protect yourself against someone who seems hell-bent on making your life a misery? Where do you start? What can you do? What can't you do?

Being a male victim

Male victims of female abuse come from all walks of life, social backgrounds and cultures. They are however, often sensitive, caring men who are victimised because they fail to conform to macho male stereotypes. They are sometimes wrongly dismissed as wimps for being caring, sensitive, good fathers and providers.

They often want help for the abuser, even though she rarely accepts she needs any help, yet these men suffer society's stigma for not protecting themselves. All too often they are the ones removed from, or asked to leave, their homes. Because they are men, the abuse they suffer is not believed. They have few or no support systems and no 'listening ear'. These men are often the victims of callous gender prejudice by society in general and the 'caring' agencies in particular.

Many of these men become depressed in their isolation, feel suicidal and sometimes take their own lives.

Every time you recognise abuse as it occurs and learn to challenge the behaviour in ways that don't fuel further abuse, you can slowly decrease the likelihood that she will keep doing it. Please note, there are never any guarantees of this.

Are you being abused?

She claims to love you, so why do you feel so bad about the relationship? It could be that you have been shown disrespect or abused for so long that feeling bad now feels normal. However, if you are constantly put down, threatened or physically assaulted, it is not normal.

If you rationalise her behaviour as *'the way she is'*, that's not normal either. Perhaps you have learnt to cope by becoming anaesthetised against the pain, but that's yet another coping strategy, it's not normal behavior. These coping strategies have an unfortunate side effect - the abuse continues, and in a high proportion of cases, it worsens. Ultimately, taking the cruelty without doing anything about it will not help you in any long-lasting or meaningful way. For a reality check, how much of the following do you identify with?

- Do you live in fear of what she may say or do next, and do you find yourself agreeing to things because it will make life easier?
- Does she explode into uncontrollable rages for no apparent reason?
- Perhaps she is all over you one moment but claims to hate you the next.
- How often do you feel confused about your relationship or sense that something is wrong, but you can't quite articulate it?
- Do you try to please her, yet find nothing is ever good enough for her?
- How often does this lead to general feelings of emotional exhaustion?
- Do you find yourself feeling unappreciated, depressed or anxious but can't figure out why?
- Do you feel trapped in your marriage?
- Have you found yourself seriously contemplating suicide as a way of escaping from the relationship?
- Have you suspected, but been unable to prove, that she has stolen money or property from you?

- Has she deliberately damaged your property?
- Does she spend your money irresponsibly, running up debts that you have to pay?
- Has she threatened to harm you, your children or any family pets if she doesn't get her own way?
- Does she criticise you and put you down in front of family or friends?
- How often is she sarcastic to you and if challenged claims she was 'only joking'?
- Do you feel that she insists on controlling your life, what you do, who you see or what you spend money on?
- Are you afraid of making even small decisions in case she disapproves - as she invariably does?
- Does she become jealous when there are no grounds?
- How often has she accused you of infidelity although you have always been faithful?
- Has she falsely accused you of anything or reported you to the police when you have done nothing wrong?
- Does she blame you for practically everything and refuse to accept any responsibility for her own actions?
- Has she threatened to harm herself in some way or to commit suicide if you don't do what she demands?
- Does she claim that you are lucky she's prepared to have you as a partner, because nobody else would be interested?
- Does she call you horrible names, possibly in front of your children?
- Do you find yourself making excuses for her behaviour to family, friends, colleagues and strangers?
- Do you have difficulty sleeping?
- Have your eating, drinking and sleeping patterns changed while being with her?
- Do you suffer from stress, excessive tiredness, depression, or pains in your chest, arms, lower back or stomach?

If you find that you do indeed experience a significant proportion of the above, you are being abused. Being made to feel that you are the one being unreasonable for feeling this way is another sign that you are being abused. Her behaviour is not normal. She may need help, but so do you.

Men in abusive relationships try various methods to diffuse potentially violent situations. They may:

- Go into another room or lock themselves away in a safe place.
- Leave the dwelling and go to family or friends.
- Sleep in their car, shed, garage or wherever they can find shelter.
- Promise to do whatever she asks or demands.
- Accept responsibility for all sorts of untrue accusations.
- Cover up for their violent partner.

These are all survival tactics, but they will not stop the attacks. What most of these men fail to do is *record* the incidents, injuries or pattern of events. They fail to tell any family members and they make excuses for their injuries even when they attend a hospital or see a doctor. They fear the humiliation and stigma of disclosure even when the abuse is life-threatening.

Don't fall into the denial trap, the mistaken belief that the abuse will go away if you do nothing to stop her. She may just try harder to hurt you. You will create 'pressure cooker syndrome', and when you blow, she'll win, possibly using the law against you.

When you have been assaulted by a woman, especially one to whom you have an emotional attachment, it is easy to rationalise why you would choose to do nothing, but that is almost certainly a mistake.

There is never an excuse for physical violence against anyone.

Unfortunately, some extreme women often decide or imagine someone is a threat to them and will then enlist or demand help from the police to destroy their 'enemy'. The police may suspect they are being used inappropriately but they cannot be seen to ignore the heartfelt pleas of a woman who claims to be the victim, although she is in fact the aggressor.

You have some options. You can allow the violence to continue hoping it will somehow wane without any action from you. You can pray she leaves you to pick on someone else. Or you can take responsibility for your own future happiness. Remind yourself that it is not your job to suffer for her benefit.

When you finally realise what she has been doing, she may decide to become destructive and angry before leaving to find her next target, if she hasn't already lined him up. Unfortunately for you, she will probably use and abuse you shamelessly first, and she will do it for as long as she can get away with it. If a female bully picks on somebody and the deed goes unchallenged, she is more likely to do it again. She induces apprehension, fear of rejection, loss and humiliation. She wants you to feel on edge.

She will never volunteer to relinquish power over her victims.

The misery she inflicts on you during the time you are together is not her problem. By not standing up to her, you deserve, in her mind at least, whatever she decides to dish out. However, if you do confront or challenge her, your ultimate punishment could be even more extreme. She may try one day to get you back, somehow. These are the sociopathic women with personality disorders that we described in Chapter 4. We will explore practical ways to manage a variety of abusive situations in the next chapter.

For the purposes of this discussion, another type of woman exists. She is the sort who may be deeply disillusioned and unhappy, and may feel unappreciated, rejected and invalidated by her partner. As her partner, you may or may not be aware of what you have done to trigger her abusive behaviour. You may or may not be guilty of any wrongdoing, but she feels the need to take it out on you anyway.

As we said in earlier chapters, generalisations are always dangerous, but many of these women can be emotionally very needy, lack confidence and possess low self-esteem. They may have a history of attracting men into their lives who put them down and took advantage of them, emotionally or physically. She may have suffered abuse as a child, therefore, she may have carried her unhappiness and suppressed a raging anger for decades. She wants to be strong for herself one day, but until she is, she may choose or settle for a man on whom she can rely to be strong but gentle, accommodating and generous, and who will look after her.

It has been said that all intimate relationships are based on an initial 'trading of needs'. If those fundamental needs ever change, the relationship can suffer or even collapse. Perhaps at the beginning of your relationship she had a higher opinion of you than you had of yourself, and you held her in higher regard than she held herself. As all that changed, the relationship changed.

Over time she realised you were not the perfect man she thought you were, meaning she was proved wrong. She became convinced that you had failed to make her happy, although this is never a partner's responsibility in a genuinely loving relationship. So finally she erupted in the relatively safe environment of her own home with the suppressed anger and rage she had kept in check for years. Your sincere attempts at kindness, generosity and going out of your way to please her have became proof that you were weak. You therefore deserved to be trampled on.

Realise this - if it hurts, it isn't love! Constantly putting her needs ahead of your own is not love. She is hurting you.

However, when you decide to challenge such a woman, you must fully evaluate the possible consequences. You must find ways to stop the abuse without provoking her rage and possibly putting yourself at risk of serious physical assault.

Before we explore the possible strategies and tactics you may be able to use in order to protect yourself against such women, it's worth taking a closer look at you.

Why did she pick on me?

One of the most common questions male and female victims of malicious and vindictive women ask is: *"Why did she pick on me?"* Many go on to say: *"I have never done anything to deserve this. I don't understand. I have racked my brain for years trying to figure her out."*

The good news is that nasty or sociopathic women almost always target 'nice' people. This is at least one thing you can feel good about! Conscientious people are the least likely to challenge or confront her. The woman relies on you giving her the benefit of any doubts you may have about her or her motives. She sees your reasonableness as your biggest weakness. As we said on the first page of this book, these women with little or no conscience target men and women with too much conscience. They are very likely to play on someone's desire to please and will often tie up their victims in emotional knots to wield power over them, using clearly identifiable tactics to abuse them.

You may have been picked out because you tend to put women on a pedestal. You are a carer, a nurturer, a rescuer, or a good Samaritan. You may be chosen because you are generous with your time and money. You may be someone who always sees the good in people. You don't like confrontation. *Anything for an easy life* could be your mantra. You're not one to complain. If there's poor service at a restaurant, you tend to let it go. You go out of your way to avoid conflict. Life's too short to get upset.

You probably don't like to confront her, especially when you are not absolutely sure you are right about her, but, of course, creating self-doubt is part of her toolkit.

It is quite possible, too, that you have a history of attracting difficult women into your life. Consider these questions:

- Are you attracted to women who claim to want your help? Or want something 'fixed'? But when you give help, do they resent what you have done for them because you proved they were incapable of sorting out their problems for themselves?
- How confident are you that you always know when you are being manipulated, perhaps because you are too trusting?
- Are you the sensitive type? Do you take things too personally?
- Do you regard yourself as a kind, generous, nice person?
- Do you expect everyone to behave fairly because you do?
- Are you a GAG, (a Go Along Guy or Girl)? If you go along with too much, don't be surprised to find it leads to more trouble.
- How quickly do you cave in when there's conflict?
- If a woman (or anyone, for that matter) puts you down, do you tend to let it go by not saying how hurt you are?
- Are you afraid she might think less of you for reprimanding her about something, even though this is basic assertive behaviour?

- Similarly, do you find yourself agreeing to requests when you would prefer to say no?
- When you are being abused, do you find yourself looking down or looking away in an effort to disengage or cope with the pain of the moment? You could be sending a different message. She could interpret this behaviour as submissiveness - confirmation that she is winning.

Precisely why is being a *'people-pleaser'* important to you? Take some time to reflect on this. Your upbringing may have a lot to do with it. Did you learn this lesson too well? Putting the needs of others ahead of your own for too much of the time makes you a target for unscrupulous women.

Some women appreciate a sensitive man. Others will see your sensitivity as weakness. You are the perfect partner for the first type, but unfortunately you are also the perfect victim for the second; for the time being at least, until she moves on to her *next* victim.

If you are easy-going, preferring to be non-confrontational, and she is motivated to fight you either overtly or covertly, you are telling her ahead of time what the outcome is likely to be. She knows she's going to win. The reasons why she so desperately feels the need to win are complex, but let's stick with what you need.

Know that the more accommodating or submissive you are to her demands, the more she wins. In most cases she knows she's being difficult or utterly unreasonable. Perversely, the more she gets away with, the less she respects you for allowing her to treat you so badly. If you consistently fail to stand up to her - and this is not to be confused with being aggressive towards her - you are convincing her that you are weak, and therefore you deserve her present and future contempt. This is why abuse invariably escalates if it is not combated.

> *"My ex-wife came from a well-off family. My background was far more humble. She kept telling me she married a 'fucking council boy'. I was therefore 'beneath her'. It took me years to realise that I was actually more intelligent than her, which was possibly why I earned far more than she did, or ever would. She had a massive chip on her shoulder, and for a long time she successfully transferred it to mine."* A divorced man

If your partner or colleague has been abusive for a long time, she is used to getting her own way and has convinced herself that you are *'pathetic'*. What is more, her choice of someone *'so useless'* also reflects badly on her. As far as she is concerned, she deserved someone so much better. Yet, from your perspective, you have done everything to love, care for, support and give her everything she wanted. For many of these women, nothing will ever be enough.

Are you the abuser?

Making you think you are the abuser when you are not is one of the tactics of a woman who uses covert aggression, but it could be that you *are* the one being abusive without even realising it. Before concluding that she is malicious and at fault, you need to examine your behaviour closely to see if she has genuine grounds for complaint.

Making improvements in your own behaviour may be necessary and may solve or reduce your problems with her. So, in what ways could *you* be contributing to the abuse you receive from her?

Nothing ever happens in a vacuum. She may have convinced herself that you are abusive because she accidentally or deliberately chooses to misinterpret some of your behaviour.

For the sake of fairness, why might she feel angry enough towards you to justify her abusive behaviour, at least in her own mind? Here's a little food for thought:

- How aware are you of the effect your existing behaviour may be having on her?
- Do you constantly put her down?
- Do you neglect her?
- Do you treat her with disrespect?
- How confident are you that you are not dragging her down with what you consider to be well-meaning advice or *'constructive criticism'*.
- Do you bombard her with solutions to her problems when she has not asked you for your help?
- How often do you stop her doing things for herself because of your over-eagerness to *'help'*?

- How often are you trying to prove she is wrong? Or do you think you are just explaining why you are right?

Imagine you were in court accused of abusing her, what evidence could there be to secure a conviction? It's worth thinking about because one day that could just happen!

Even if you have not been actively engaged in abusive activities, you may still do something that feels abusive to her. Women who have been abused have a vast databank of painful memories, which they learn to suppress or delete from their minds. Sometimes, though, you might say or do something totally innocuously that triggers one of these painful memories. The incident from her past will rush back and flood her with all manner of emotional pain. You could not have known you would have such an effect, but re-activating that memory, in her mind you become her abuser.

Generally speaking, some good men can be incredibly insensitive about a woman's feelings. Many a man, of course, would be genuinely mortified if or when his thoughtlessness was pointed out to him. Indeed, a man may behave with the best of intentions towards a woman he loves dearly, yet she may feel deeply unloved, unappreciated and angry at the ways she is convinced he shows disrespect towards her. Many women feel this lack of respect for reasons that men find difficult or impossible to understand.

A male friend had a relationship with a woman in which they used to call each other names. They were very unpleasant names. He thought it was fun and believed she thought it was too. It became a competitive sport. Then just when he was winning, she would burst into tears. He couldn't understand. He said: *"I think she does the crying thing to win."* So he had to be put straight. He was told that men and women are socialised differently. Boys are called all sorts of horrible names in the schoolyard, and most males learn to engage in this playful, put-down banter without taking it too seriously. There are obviously exceptions, but in many cases being called the most appalling names is a sign that you are liked more, not less.

That does not tend to happen among girls, for whom being called names is purely aggressive with none of the being *'accepted as part of the group'* aspect that it acquires amongst boys. Many women don't 'get' this type of banter, it just hurts.

He said *"But she encourages me and she gives as good as she gets."*

Perhaps, but the deeper meaning of the activity was different for her. For some women, agreeing to engage in such banter is sometimes an effort on her part to be liked more. She wants to be accepted and may do what she thinks will bring her closer to her man. This man didn't realise the damage he was doing to her and to their relationship. He was deeply upset; he later apologised to her and stopped the behaviour immediately.

She may need to see that you're capable of standing up to her. She wants you to be strong but she doesn't want to feel threatened by you. If she feels threatened by anything you say or do, the threat, whether intended or not, would be vividly real to her. Her fear could be extreme. In your mind it may be totally unwarranted and wholly irrational, but look at it this way; if you tell an arachnophobe that their fear of harmless spiders is silly, the best you might get is: *"I know that already, but it doesn't make any difference."* You just make them feel more stupid and your statement could easily be perceived as an 'attack', even if you felt you were just making a statement.

We are assuming you are not a nasty man, but you may be abusing her in other ways. So; when you point the finger of blame at someone, take a look at how your other fingers are pointing back at yourself. Ask yourself how you could be contributing to the abuse you receive from her.

What she knows can hurt you

She knows you extremely well, perhaps better than you know yourself. You have been studied by her and your sensitivities have been noted for future exploitation. She knows how to make you feel small. Knowing your vulnerabilities and fragility becomes her strongest weapon. She will focus on your weaknesses, your anxieties and your 'hot buttons' in order to hurt you. Any snippet of information she picks up from you can, and almost certainly will, be used in evidence against you. Be aware of this at all times, realise what she is doing, and why.

However, before you can develop an effective coping strategy, you need to ask a few more searching questions:

- What have you already told her that gives her a better understanding of your anxieties and insecurities?
- How might she use that information against you?
- What does she know about you that you would much prefer others didn't know?

So what are your options?

An abusive relationship is a little like being at sea in a storm, out of sight of land, in a speedboat loaded with your family, hurtling along at breakneck speed, the throttle jammed open. You're taking on water. You all cling on for dear life. The children are petrified, you are trying to comfort them while you battle with the steering, knowing that one false move will make the boat capsize. There is no let-up in the weather. You think you're heading in the right direction but you worry about how much fuel you have left.

You have no choice but to weather this storm. When you thought things couldn't get any worse, an enormous wave suddenly crashes down on the boat. This is the moment you are all going to die. But, no, you survive.

Unfortunately, your bad day just got worse. That wave dropped a man-eating shark into the boat. Or did the wave transform your wife into that shark? She's thrashing about and screaming abuse at you because it's your fault the sea is so rough and the wind is so strong - but wasn't it partly her idea to take the boat trip in the first place?

Taking sharp turns at high speed in such a sea is highly dangerous because it increases the likelihood of capsizing. It's the same with an abusive relationship. If you or your abusive partner are forced to change too much too soon, it may create more problems than it solves. Confronting her and issuing threats or ultimatums are the equivalent of taking a sharp turn in choppy seas.

But what can you do? An ocean-going oil tanker, despite its size and its potential for causing catastrophic environmental damage if it smashes into rocks, takes a long time to change its course. The captain knows that a safe manoeuvre can be achieved only at a slow pace.

If you want to change or improve your relationship with the lowest risks to you and your family, you have to do it slowly. Hence the comparison. This way your abusive partner may even be unaware of what is happening. Again, there are no guarantees you will be successful.

Create a protection journal

Creating a paper trail is essential if you ever have to defend yourself against false allegations that she may make against you during a court battle or in a report to the police. The police have to take all allegations seriously and nasty women know this. Many women have no qualms about telling outrageous lies to punish the men they hate. Regardless of how preposterous her lies may be, people will assume you are guilty of everything the woman says. In these circumstances you would need to prove your innocence. Most men find this incredibly difficult, because they make a string of fundamental mistakes. They don't tell anyone what is happening within the relationship, they don't complain to anyone, they let the abuse continue, and, crucially, they have no evidence or proof of her abuse.

Therefore, if you are in a relationship with an abusive woman you must keep an accurate protection journal, capturing everything she says and does against you and/or your children. If she ever threatens to report you to the police, take that as the best cue you will ever get to start a journal. This is one of the most important and effective recommendations in this book. Create a journal that accurately captures her abuse. Without one....

> *"The facts have become irrelevant. Everyone knows that restraining orders ... are granted to virtually all who apply ... In many [divorce] cases, allegations of abuse are now used for tactical advantage... It has become essentially impossible to represent effectively a man against whom any allegation of domestic violence has been made."* Elaine Epstein, former Massachusetts Bar Association President

A well-documented record of all her abusive actions and threats against you or your children is the best insurance you can have if she ever falsely accuses you of physical or sexual abuse. If you are ever forced to defend yourself in a court of law, your journal will be a very powerful defence document.

Do not write your journal on a computer. It is difficult to prove time and place with electronic documents. Use a book or a medium-sized diary. Write your entries on the corresponding pages of the diary. Whatever book you decide on, it is important that the pages are bound into the book (not a spiral ring binder). You must be able to show a court that no pages have been added or removed at a later date. They must show a 'timeline'.

Keep a written record of every incident, however small or insignificant you may think it is at the time. Include when she physically assaults you, calls you names, makes threats or behaves in any way that would undermine her credibility in a court of law. It is best not to include what you said to her as this may be used against you in some way. This is a document to protect you. Don't incriminate yourself.

Add how she made you feel about her threats. If you feel traumatised, at risk, afraid, nervous or sick, briefly write down those feelings. Were any children present? What effect did the abuse have on them? Did they cry? Did they hide or run away?

Record the names of any witnesses. Add their contact details, names, phone numbers and e-mail addresses if you have them. It may sound melodramatic but it is nevertheless true that these details would be invaluable to the police if something serious should happen to you.

For every entry in your journal, write down the time, date and details of these witnesses. Make your written entries in pen, not pencil. Explain exactly what she threatened or actually did to you. If you have been injured, however minor those injuries may be, write down exactly what she did. Take photographs of your injuries if you can. Use a mirror if necessary to take the photographs of yourself. Digital cameras are perfect for this. Stick these photos inside your journal, together with an explanation of what she did to cause the injuries.

Was she drunk or on drugs? Was it in front of your children? Family members? Colleagues? The people you have mentioned in your journal may be prepared to confirm in court that you had such conversations. This will corroborate your side of the story.

For example, write the date and then: *"Jenny screamed at me yet again, and punched me hard on the arm because I wasn't prepared to go shopping."* Or perhaps: *"Debbie worked herself up into a frenzy and threatened to commit suicide."* Or: *"Today Jean and I had another row. It came out of nowhere. I managed to remain calm. But I got so sick and tired of her behaviour that I left to avoid any further confrontation. Within the next half an hour she must have called me more than 20 times. I didn't pick up the phone. I just couldn't take it. One of her 17 text messages threatened to destroy me."* Another entry might say: *"Spoke with Ian about it. He, yet again, asked me, 'Do you really need this much grief in your life?'"*

Do not make excuses for her, stick to the facts, be accurate, don't lie. Because your journal is so important, make sure your partner never knows about the journal and cannot find it. If she does, she may be tempted to hide or destroy it. For added security, scan or use a digital camera to photograph every page, then copy and paste all these photos into a password-protected computer document. Burn it on to a CD and keep it in a safe place. Burn additional copies every time you update the journal. Send copies to your lawyer for safekeeping. The small charge solicitors may make for such a service is a tiny price to pay for this level of personal security.

Don't worry if you don't do much writing. Just do your best. Your financial future or even your freedom could be at stake, so don't talk yourself out of protecting yourself in this way. It's important. If you never need to use it, no harm has been done, but if you ever do need it, you will *really* need it.

If you decide to share your experiences with a trusted friend. Be very careful what you write. Including 'Private and Confidential' at the top of your letters or e-mails may help protect yourself against any accusations of slander or libel she may make against you. Writing disparaging, unproven accusations can be fraught with legal difficulties, so be careful what you write. Private e-mails could possibly be used against you in court.

Most male victims of domestic violence tend not to do any of this. They suffer unnecessarily as a consequence. In the next chapter we explore why this happens and why a failure to report violence to the police may not be a wise decision, for you or other innocent men. In addition, you will learn specific strategies and tactics that may help you to manage her physical, verbal and emotional abuse.

For now, accept the following when facing up to the realisation that you are being forced to deal with an abusive woman:

- You are not you alone. Many other men suffer abuse by women.
- The abuse will continue or even intensify for as long as she gets away with it.
- Male ego deceives you into believing that you can handle whatever she does. Your ego is well-meaning, but wrong.
- You cannot control someone else's behaviour. However, you can influence that behaviour, by controlling your own and controlling the ways you react to her.
- You can choose to walk away mentally or to disengage by learning not to take everything personally.
- Create more options in your life so that you aren't so reliant on her.

Accept that in many cases, good men are often punished more severely than those who care less.

Chapter 9

Getting Out of Her Clutches

There were two zookeepers. One was old, wise and experienced. The other young, inexperienced but enthusiastic. One day, they are outside the bear enclosure. The bear was in an extremely bad mood and was roaring and making quite a commotion. The young zookeeper asks the old, wise zookeeper *"What's the matter with him today?"* The wise man responds by saying *"Oh, he's broken his climbing frame again and he's sitting on a rusty nail."* The young zookeeper says *"So why doesn't he just get up?"* to which the wise old zookeeper said *"Ah, that's easy. It doesn't hurt him enough yet."*

How much worse does the abuse and misery have to get before you get up from your own rusty nail? For the bear, the solution was simple – all he had to do was stand up. Standing up for yourself in an abusive relationship is more complex. Yet nothing will improve until you make the decision to do something about it. Then you need to figure out the best way to achieve your desired result without putting yourself at risk of further abuse or retaliation.

Being in an abusive situation goes far beyond just your relationship with an intimate partner. It also includes dealing with abuse in the workplace, from a *'bitch boss'* or *'bitch employee'*, and dealing with any other difficult women you may meet.

Towards "Goodbye"

Disentangling yourself from the clutches of a controlling woman is rarely straightforward. So many abusive women are adept at finding a multitude of ways to cling on to a relationship even when it's obvious that it is not working and is not a mutually happy one, but feeling she has power over her victim often makes it worthwhile to her. She is highly unlikely to relinquish her control voluntarily so you have to take it back without her 'permission' or negotiating terms with her. There is no one-size-fits-all solution. Every case is unique, but *yours* is probably different!

The most effective way to protect yourself against an abusive or controlling woman is to end the relationship. Then refuse any and all further contact with her. It's an extreme solution but, in many cases, it is ultimately the best solution.

You need to consider whether her sustained abuse is her way of forcing you to dump her. She may want you to end the relationship. When you don't, she then escalates the abuse. If this is the case, her lack of moral courage to end the relationship herself is perhaps her way of maintaining her victim status. If she is making your life a misery and you do not feel able to end it, we suggest you look very carefully at why you allow yourself to suffer in this way. All too often men tolerate outrageous behaviour because they believe they have some sort of obligation to be nice to everyone. Low self-esteem, fear of reprisals and fear of being alone in the future are common reasons why men stay in bad relationships. If family members and friends have tried to tell you that she is bad for you, listen to them. They care about you and are trying to help you.

If you are married to this woman and have children with her, revisit your options in chapters 7 and 8. Many of the strategies in those chapters are applicable whether or not you are married to a trouble-some woman. If you have a history of non-confrontation, taking the initiative to end a relationship with a long-term abusive girlfriend can be difficult too, especially if she has played on your sympathy and pity, or has threatened you over a prolonged period. She may take it very badly and cause havoc. But keeping her in your life could become much worse - a horror story waiting to unfold.

If you have tried to make her happy but keep falling short of her unreasonable demands and expectations – face up to it, you will probably never be 'good enough' for her. Nobody will ever live up to her expectations. Being her doormat is guaranteed to cause you future pain.

Some men and women are known as 'monkeys' – they won't let go of a branch until they have grabbed another first. They need a new partner before they can let go of the previous one. If you are one of these, be careful: leaving her for someone else is not always the best solution. Your 'ex' will almost certainly accuse you of being deceitful, thus reinforcing her role as a victim. Furthermore, you might find that your new girlfriend will be made to suffer as a consequence of her involvement with you. Not a good start for a promising new relationship and your 'ex' will know this, as this example illustrates;

> The 'ex' bombarded her former boyfriend with countless texts, one of which claimed she had recently had an AIDS test – and they needed to meet urgently! It was an untrue, but desperate attempt to frighten him into engaging in dialogue. When that didn't work, she started showing up in the same bars and restaurants when he was on dates with his new girlfriend. That relationship progressed and many months later, imagine their surprise when they went to a luxury spa resort in Asia only to find that the 'ex' had also booked herself into the same hotel at the same time! This was too much for the 'new' girlfriend. She ended the relationship because he was not prepared to stand up for himself.

As much as she sometimes claims to hate you, being dumped could fuel her wrath. You will almost certainly have to endure bad-mouthing, false accusations and additional threats or actual violence. She may involve the police if she feels particularly aggrieved or feels she has no control over your actions. Expect this and take counter-measures, such as those described in Chapter 8.

No matter what you do, how you do it, how kind you try to be, or how blunt you are – she will choose to describe your behaviour as cruel or unkind. Expect a savage response because you have 'rejected' her. Although do not inform her that the relationship is over by text message; that's universally accepted as a cowardly way out!

If you live together seek legal advice about what you can and cannot do in order to separate. You may have to give her written notice to leave. Only a lawyer can tell you your legal status. Do not act without specialist legal advice.

If you do not live together and she has a set of keys to your home, change the locks immediately before you break up. Do not rely on her returning them. Many a man has regretted behaving fairly only to discover that she entered his home without permission and damaged or destroyed property. Numerous news stories have told of women who have shredded every item of a man's clothing, or called a premium rate phone number and left the phone off the hook for days when she knew he was away. He then discovers a phone bill for thousands and 'proof' that he is 'addicted to porn lines' when he was not. Invariably such media stories are written as though they are 'amusing'. You won't find them amusing if they happen to you.

If you still live with your parents, explain to your family members that things are not going well between you and her, and politely instruct them not to allow her into the house under any circumstances. Explain that she can be highly persuasive, so no matter what she says, she must not gain entry.

How you break the news to her can have a profound effect on her reaction. Accusing her of wrong-doing is probably the best way to evoke fury. So don't! You need to handle the situation with sensitivity. Give your partner a way to *'save face'*. Men, as well as women have used the *"It's not you, it's me."* formula because it works. An alternative approach could involve saying something along the following lines: *"This isn't working for me any more. I have tried as hard as I can to be a good partner, but I now realise that I can never be good enough. I don't see us having a future. Our relationship is over."*

This approach does not accuse her of anything and the word *'you'* has not been used. This is important. Make it ALL about how you feel.

Show regret and don't talk too much. Don't allow yourself to get drawn into a discussion about it. She may try to create an argument to prove you wrong about her, or try to convince you to change your mind. When you get involved in such a discussion she may try to make you feel guilty or create an environment to justify getting angry with you. If you do this, you are giving her an opportunity to behave destructively towards you in the future.

If she has a history of abusive behaviour and she agrees to go quietly and easily, beware! She may have revenge and retribution on her mind.

Soon after you have ended the relationship, request in writing the return of all your property. Create a list of the items she needs to return to avoid all ambiguity. Expect her to try to instigate an argument about it. At the same time, tell her she can have all her property back at a mutually agreed time. Do *not* state that she can have her stuff back on condition you get yours back. You may need a copy of your document to prove that you are not denying her rights.

Preferably, collect all her property together yourself and pack it up carefully. Then arrange to have it delivered to an agreed address at a specific time by someone on your behalf. Try not to do it yourself. She may claim that you deliberately damaged items. Therefore get an independent witness to verify that everything left you in perfect condition.

Once you decide to break up from a vindictive woman it is important you avoid ALL contact with her. Refuse to meet a violent or abusive woman, especially on your own. She may have an ulterior motive that could harm you in some unforeseeable way. Women have been known to arrange to meet their ex-partner in a public place and start screaming and shouting at him, making wild and false accusations at the top of her voice. In extreme cases she will insist that someone call the police on her behalf because she is being attacked or abused by him. The man has no idea that he is being set up in this way.

If she stalks you, she is trying to destabilise you, to create fear, anxiety or stress. If the situation becomes intolerable, do not speak with her. If communication is necessary, ask a companion to speak to her instead, and ask her to stop her behaviour. Sometimes, stalkers are not actually breaking any laws, although in some jurisdictions this has changed. If you live in a country or state where anti-stalking laws exist, report her to the police. In your statement explain how she is making you feel stressed or threatened by her stalking.

Expect constant text messages, voicemails and e-mails. Do not respond to them. If she sends you abusive messages, keep copies. Many women want to find ways to engage you in a dialogue, either to persuade you to change your mind because she 'promises' never to treat you badly again (when you know that all previous promises have been broken) or as a way of trying to get you to say or do something she can use against you. Forcing you to talk to her not only furthers her control over you, it also means she will be able to draw you into an argument. She wants, in fact she *needs*, to win against you. Don't allow yourself to get sucked into her game. If she involves the police you will need paperwork to prove that you are the victim, not her, as she will claim. Again, your journal will be invaluable here.

If she makes false allegations against you to the police, write a brief letter addressed to the chief constable or the most senior police officer in your region. Go straight to the top. Explain in one or two sentences that the police were called by [her name] on [date]. Ask for the names of the officers who attended. Then say that you are concerned she may have made false allegations against you. Ask to be informed of exactly what she told the police. Remove all emotion from your letter. Don't make any comments or accusations against her. Your letter will be passed through the police hierarchy, ensuring that a response will be sent to you from your local police station.

When you receive the written response, consult your lawyer to discuss your options. Again, creating a paper trail is very important if you are to defend yourself adequately against a woman who is 'out to get you' in this way.

As stressful and draining as all this can be, console yourself with the realisation that whatever you are forced to endure in the short term would be insignificant compared with the problems you would face if you were married to her!

Assessing your risks

Whether your relationship is over or you are trapped within an abusive one, knowing where to focus your depleted energy can be difficult and it obviously depends a great deal on the scale, nature and history of the abuse you have suffered. Many of the issues are the same as for a married man contemplating divorce.

A good start is to assess ALL the risks you face, preferably before you end the relationship. Develop a plan to minimise each and every one of the risks you identify. You may be tempted to dismiss some of the risks we highlight by telling yourself *"Not even she would ever do that."* Don't count on it. An act of wanton destruction of your personal property may happen without warning and at any time. The element of surprise is a common behaviour trait amongst malicious women. The risks you face include:

- Your physical safety
- Items of financial or sentimental value may be damaged, destroyed or stolen.
- Your personal and professional reputation could be questioned or damaged.

Expect her to bad-mouth you and make false allegations even when you are innocent. With this in mind, inform friends and colleagues after you have ended your relationship. Tell them it went badly wrong and that she may behave erratically. Ask to be informed of anything she may say about you. Don't bad-mouth her. If such comments ever got back to her, she could use them to justify what ever she decides to do to you. Think carefully and list every potential risk you face; physical, financial and emotional. Then prioritise them.

Your physical safety

By the very nature of this topic, we need to consider extreme abusive behaviour. Your personal safety must remain at the top of your priorities. If you have children, their personal safety becomes a secondary consideration. This is pragmatic, not selfish. It's the same as airline safety instructions that tell you to put on your own oxygen mask before helping others.

In a worst case scenario, if you confront a woman with psychiatric problems and get it wrong – you could be killed.

> A young man felt the need to leave the UK in an effort to avoid an ex-girlfriend after she threatened to murder him with a knife. He described her as a '*very scary woman*', yet she claimed to love him. Years later, he is still convinced that she would have carried out her threat. To this day she is known as "*Psycho Sarah*" within his family.

If she has ever threatened physical violence, she may only be one step away from actually hurting you. You *must* take it seriously. Consider yourself lucky to have been given advance warning. You ignore such a warning at your peril. Anyone who threatens to hurt you is a threat to your safety. Do not let your emotions or misplaced loyalty cloud your judgement. Do not delude yourself that she will not act on such a threat. Realise that men have been killed either deliberately or accidentally by women they loved. Your first priority must always be your personal safety.

Fear that you will evoke further rage and violence is a common reason why male victims of domestic violence do nothing. In many cases, they simply don't know what to do anyway.

Removing yourself from harm's way is an essential part of preserving your physical safety. Recognise the times when she is more likely to lash out at you. Stay out of striking distance. If you are threatened with physical violence or are experiencing on-going physical abuse, sleep in a spare bedroom. Fit a bolt to the inside door (although expect her to remove it), another alternative is to block the door with a heavy item of furniture – such as the bed. Prepare yourself for her demands to enter the room, probably on the most preposterous of pretexts. Not getting her own way will almost certainly lead to her making more and more threats as she becoming increasingly desperate to 'win'. This is potentially a good time to record her antics on video or audio to demonstrate how you are forced to live with this '*domestic terrorist*'.

If she assaults you, do not strike back – even in self-defence (unless you are in mortal danger). Violent women routinely scratch, bite, pinch, slap, kick and knee men in the groin. Much of the time it is designed specifically to provoke a physical response from the man. No matter what she does to you, if you lay a finger on her, you can be sure she will report you to the police for being physically violent to *her*! Prepare yourself to be accused of being violent towards her anyway, even if you have never touched her. She may also claim to the police that she felt 'emotionally threatened' by you. Even if you have done nothing to warrant any of her claims the police may feel obliged to arrest you. This is yet another reason you need a keep a journal.

After she threatens you, do not tell her what you are going to do about it, and do not threaten her in any way. Giving her advance notice of your actions may provide her with the opportunity to accuse you falsely of a crime in order to undermine or damage your credibility. Therefore;

Step 1. Record in your journal exactly what she said or did, where and when it took place.

Step 2. Collect as much evidence as you can such as photos, correspondence, audio and video recordings.

Step 3. Embark on a strategy of advice seeking.

Step 4. Report her to the police.

Keep your journal up-to-date and in a safe place; preferably not in your own home.

Creating a paper trail cannot be emphasised enough. Keep copies of all letters, e-mails and text messages from her, as well as everything you receive from advisers.

Make a point of asking advice of your trusted friends, family members, your doctor, social workers, priests, your employer and the police. Ask them *"Based on what I have told you confidentially, what would you do in my situation? And why? Who else do you think I should be talking to about this?"* Write down in your journal who you have spoken to about the abuse you suffer, and what they said about it.

Consult your lawyer for advice on whether you should go to the police. Explore your options. Ensure your lawyer takes this seriously. Confirm what you are advised in a letter or an e-mail back to your lawyer. If you do not have a lawyer, make an appointment to see one at your local citizen's advice bureau.

Ask these people what they would do in your situation to bring this behaviour to an end. By asking for advice, you are simply seeking a workable solution to a potentially serious problem.

Your personal safety is a basic human right. Asking advice is non-confrontational. And it opens up options you may not have considered. By seeking advice in this way you are also ensuring that others get to know what is happening. In the event that you are seriously injured, she will be accountable. By speaking to a range of different people you will start to amass different insights. Decide for yourself which pieces of advice are most relevant to you and then take action. Not making a decision is rarely, if ever, your best option.

If she is already abusing you physically, report her to the police. Do NOT try to deal with this situation yourself. She is breaking the law. It's a job for the police or the courts.

Each time a man is assaulted by a woman and does not report it, he makes it more difficult for all male victims to defend themselves effectively. It also helps to perpetuate the myth through skewed statistics, that some women are not as violent as they are.

And do not talk yourself out of going to the police. Fear, embarrassment, misplaced loyalty, under playing the seriousness of the situation, believing because you love her, you *can't* take action, thinking you can *sort it out* yourself without actually doing anything about it, the possibility of losing contact with your children and not wanting to bother the police, are all common excuses and reasons we have heard from so many men who visit *Amen* for help when their circumstances have spun out of control.

Some men have ended up being stabbed in their sleep because they did not take effective action soon enough. Other men report being *accidentally* elbowed in the face while asleep, others have been hit repeatedly in the face with high-heel shoes, also while asleep. One man took three days off work after such an assault, rather than admit to his colleagues what she had done. His silence inadvertently ensured the abuse continued. Other men have been kicked in the testicles, had boiling water thrown over them, been struck by blunt implements and had kitchen knives thrown at them. Many other assaults were described in earlier chapters.

It is essential that you nip this type of behaviour in the bud. If you do not take appropriate action, you run an increased risk of being physically assaulted by her. And possibly receiving serious injuries.

It is particularly important to see the police. If you have been assaulted, you **must** report it. How you conduct yourself when you meet police officers is critical. Your primary objective is to be taken seriously. Accept that some men who have reported even serious abuse have been disbelieved. Present yourself professionally. Be polite. Stay calm. Be seen to be reasonable, sober and respectful. Your secondary objective is to get practical advice to protect yourself and your children. Your third objective is for the police to begin a paper trail of her abuse.

Calmly explain that you have been threatened, and wish to protect yourself against a probable attack. Wait to be asked who has threatened you before you tell the officer. *"What can I do to protect myself and my children against [whatever she threatened to do to you]?"*

Take your up-to-date journal with you to the police. This will go a long way towards demonstrating that you are the victim. And increases the likelihood that you will be taken seriously. Make copies of the relevant pages in your journal and take them with you. Politely decline any requests to leave the journal with the police. Offer to leave the copies instead.

Make yourself known to any officers responsible for domestic violence. Write down their names and ensure you have a number you can call in an emergency.

Expect a backlash when she finds out that you have been asking for advice or gone to the police. She may become savage. She will be furious that other people now know what she has been doing. Calmly explain that you have tried repeatedly to get her to stop the abuse. Tell her that you want her to be happy, but you have run out of ideas. You've tried everything. Therefore you decided to get advice from others including the police. Tell her all you want is for her to stop her abusive and violent behaviour.

Then you can add, if she doesn't do this, you probably don't have a long-term future together.

If you ever require medical treatment, do not cover it up because you love her (or think you do), or because you fear you will be punished. Tell the nurse or doctor exactly what happened to you. And who inflicted the injuries. They will be required to make a record of what you say. Stick to the facts. Do not make excuses for her. Simply tell them exactly what, where and when it happened.

If she physically abuses you, say *"This isn't working for me any more. I want this to stop. I have asked for this to stop. It has not stopped. Whatever happens between us in the future is because you won't stop behaving in this way. I have tried so hard to support you and be a good partner. Apparently I have failed you."*

She may demand you tell her who you have been talking to. Refuse. She thrives on information. Deprive her of it. Tell her nothing. This is a case when 'less is more'. Let her imagination fill in the gaps in her knowledge. It is highly likely she will start spreading lies about you to protect her own reputation. If indeed she hasn't been doing so already.

If the 'caring' agencies fail you, write to your member of parliament, senator or congressman to explain how you have been mistreated by an organisation that has made wrong assumptions about you. Insist on an investigation into why your needs were not taken seriously.

Other threats to your physical safety

You also need to consider who else is a threat to you. Some women of the type we are discussing are very likely to persuade others to do some or all of their dirty work. These women can be very persuasive.

> In March 2007, millionairess businesswoman Ann Hunter, aged 50, of West London was sentenced to 8 years in prison for persuading her boyfriend Anton Lee to hire a hitman to murder her ex-partner Colin Love aged 54 and maim his new wife. Thankfully the hitman he found was an undercover police officer. Judge Brian Barker described her as a *"Callous and manipulative"* woman.

Ms Hunter had developed what was described in court as *"an uncontrollable hatred"* for his new wife. She allegedly told the 'hitman' she only needed the woman to be maimed – blinded or put into a wheelchair - not murdered.

There may not be many of these women around, but they do exist. You *could* be dealing with one. If she is serious about *'getting back at you'* (for real or imagined transgressions) she may enlist help. New, besotted boyfriends, lawyers, the police, girlfriends, private investigators, the media, thugs and/or hit men are all possible accomplices.

Your personal property

In extreme cases, she will do anything she can think of without conscience or remorse in order to harm you. And she will do it in ways that are the most hurtful to you. If she knows your car is your pride and joy, expect it to get scratched by a key along its entire length. If your reputation is important to you, expect her to lie about you to mutual friends, colleagues or your clients. She will focus her venom on what she knows to be your weak spots.

As discussed in an earlier chapter, do an inventory of all your most valuable possessions. Record the serial and model numbers of these items. Photograph them to capture their condition. Remove everything that is particularly valuable and store in a safe place where she will not be able to find them. Similarly, remove all of your essential documentation such as property deeds, birth and share certificates and your passport.

Bully girl

When a woman uses bullying tactics she is trying to exert power and control, or regain it. When she starts to lose control she will almost certainly *'up the ante'* and behave more and more desperately, but now that she cannot operate in secrecy as she is accustomed to, she may be less certain of her options. Her best form of defence therefore invariably becomes *'attack'*. Whatever she does or threatens to do is her attempt to re-assert her power and control. Recognise this behaviour if it happens. It's a sign that she is afraid of *'losing'*. Keep your observations to yourself (and to your journal) and prepare yourself for more trouble.

One man described what he did when his girlfriend threatened to commit suicide if he didn't do what she demanded of him. *"Without telling her, I called her father. The first she knew about it was when he showed up on her doorstep a few hours later having travelled 100 miles to see her. She went absolutely ballistic with me. She never tried that with me again. But a few months later I had to finish the relationship."*

Working for a bitch boss

Meryl Streep epitomised the bitch-boss from hell in her role as Miranda Priestly, editor of *Runway* magazine in the movie *The Devil Wears Prada*. The character was allegedly based on Anna Wintour, the formidable editor of *Vogue*. At least you know where you stand when the boss has a reputation for being ruthless.

On the plus side, bitch bosses are unlikely to inflict physical abuse, but the worst types wield and abuse their positions of power and authority in covert, underhand ways. Learning to recognise when you are being abused and manipulated is therefore essential if you are to protect yourself (and your career) against such a woman.

Bitch bosses love to confuse, infuriate, intimidate, belittle, bully, coerce, and harass. They set people against each other, and routinely move the goal posts to set people up to fail. They deliberately create friction and frustration and have no problem making false accusations, lying, cheating, deceiving, using humour at her victim's expense, innuendo, put-downs, sarcasm as well as veiled or explicit threats.

Changing jobs is the ultimate solution of course. If you are being forced to endure any of the above, get out. Find a better job. Over time, you could end up paying a very high price for staying. In many cases, a significant proportion of a bitch bosses' team suffer from depression, anxiety and stress-related illnesses. Some even experience nervous breakdowns as a result of her behaviour.

She prefers to recruit and surround herself with people who will not pose a threat to her position. She wants *'yes'* men and women. Needless to say, her behaviour is bad for a business, and productivity invariably suffers as a result of her antics. The incompetent get promoted to their levels of ineptitude, whilst the best people are sidelined, ignored or passed over for promotion.

Assuming she is behaving unprofessionally, abusing her position for her own selfish purposes or acting against the best interests of the organisation, you have a duty to yourself to develop a survival strategy.

A large part of that strategy is collecting the written evidence that you may need in order to prove that you are not guilty of any false allegations she may make against you or your vulnerable colleagues.

Don't assume your colleagues feel the same way as you. Don't say or write anything that could get back to her.

Use your journal to record her attacks, put-downs, threats or unprofessional conduct. Include witnesses to this behaviour.

If she has a habit of saying one thing and then criticising you for not doing something else, it might be worth starting to send her brief, written summaries of what she has told you to do, and confirm agreed deadlines. Give her the opportunity to 'correct' you by saying *"If I have misunderstood you, please let me know what I have missed."* But expect to be accused of not taking enough initiative!

Assuming she isn't someone you can talk to about stopping her abuse, you need to build up written evidence of sustained abuse over a long period. If you ever have to share this evidence with your superiors or in an employment tribunal, you will be more likely to be taken seriously and win your case. However you can never be sure so consider carefully, the possible consequences of challenging her through official channels before you do so.

You need to assess carefully what she could do to harm you and your reputation before you do anything. Expect her to accuse you of being a disruptive influence. She may want to turn you into a scapegoat. Questions will be asked about your competence and you may face any number of other false allegations. The more she feels threatened by you, the more serious her allegations against you could be. She will need to prove them of course. Could she?

For example, some of these women routinely use innuendo and remarks of a sexual nature, expecting their colleagues to 'join the game'. It's too easy to fall into such a trap. If you are a man with an untrustworthy female boss, never say anything that can be construed as a sexual remark – ever. Even as a response to anything she says. It is easy for her to twist what you say into a possible sexual harassment case – where *you* are the guilty party. This just one example of what she could do to protect her own position.

Once you make your decision to go ahead with a complaint against her, rather than submit a formal one, write to your human resources or personnel department, asking for their advice about the difficulties you are experiencing. Write 'Private and Confidential' at the top of your e-mail, memo or letter. Do not make any accusations at this stage because you could find that your note is forwarded to your boss, even though you wrote a private note. The less inflammatory you are at this stage, the safer it will be for you. Make no reference to your journal or your evidence.

If they fail to respond in a timely way or go to your boss, with the inevitable threats you may receive from her, you will have a much better idea of the potential struggle you face.

On the other hand if you are taken seriously and sense that you will be given a fair hearing, it might be appropriate to take things further, knowing that you have detailed evidence up your sleeve should you ever need to use it.

Bitch employees

Unfortunately, she doesn't have to be a boss to cause mayhem in the workplace. There are countless examples of malicious women behaving in the exactly the same ways against their bosses. When they don't get what they want, they claim victimhood, unfair dismissal and prejudice. Reasonable employers are routinely targeted by unscrupulous female employees. Protect yourself and the reputation of your organisation by keeping accurate written records of every disciplinary action against all employees. Follow procedures meticulously. Smaller, more casually run businesses must be particularly careful not to breach employment law. A malicious former employee can cause irreparable financial damage to a small enterprise by taking advantage of an employer's informality.

It is essential to create and follow your company's internal procedures and all legal requirements scrupulously if you are looking to get rid of a difficult employee. Work closely with your Human Resources department or specialist advisers to ensure you cover yourself and the company. Employment law is highly complex and has a habit of changing regularly.

Lying by omission

A dishonest woman will try to cover her tracks. One of the most widespread ways of doing this is being economical with the truth. She may lie by omission. Without ever accusing her of anything, if you sense she's not telling you the full truth, show a higher level of interest and ask her questions that require her to give more detailed information. Do it in a polite, matter-of-fact, non-confrontational way. Become aware of when she's being vague or evasive. If she doesn't give you a straight answer to a straight question, ask her the same question again. Silence is an incredibly powerful technique. Just wait. See what she says or does next. Does she change the subject, deflect what you said, accuse you of something unrelated or throw a tantrum? These are common techniques designed to distract you away from her failure to respond to your question.

Bring the conversation back to where you want it to be to ensure it doesn't go where she wants to take it.

Dishonest women also believe that if they sound incredibly enthusiastic or forthright, she will sound more honest. That is also a technique to hide something from you.

If you are simply trying to defend yourself, a sign that your new, more assertive behaviour is having an impact is when she starts accusing you of being 'controlling'. What she has probably started to realise is that her own control freak behaviour is no longer working as it once did.

Conflict conversations

It's been said that women always have the last word. Any subsequent remark by a man officially becomes the beginning of the next argument!

Realise that a difficult woman wants to win. And winning can mean so many different things to her. Part of winning could mean wanting you to feel threatened, frightened, stressed, confused, frustrated, neglected, anxious or overwhelmed. Part of her plan may involve forcing you to question yourself while you desperately try to find a logical solution to the relationship problem. Much of her behaviour is deliberately engineered to ensure there is no solution! This illogical behaviour ensures that the victim is distracted from noticing what else she is up to.

Of course if you complain or challenge she can then accuse you of being 'too sensitive' or you're someone who 'can't take a joke'. She wins again.

George Simon, author of *Wolf In Sheep's Clothing* compares dealing with this type of covert aggression to coping with a whiplash injury. *"Often, you really don't know what's hit you until long after the damage is done."*

Coping with her verbal outbursts

She is fighting you. You are in the middle of a battle, even though you may not realise it. She's an expert at verbal judo; she has to be. Especially when her victims start to recognise her attempts at covert manipulation. She is capable of twisting almost anything anyone ever says to suit her purposes.

Often when she is *'spoiling for a fight'* she wants to goad you into reacting. If you do, she wins. By escalating conflict she will try to justify her anger, frustration or resentment against you, when it may be nothing to do with you. If she shouts, swears at you, threatens you or calls you names, doing the same back to her won't improve your situation. In fact, she wins.

If it makes you feel bad about yourself, she wins again. Refuse to allow yourself to fall for her ploys.

She will wear you out. And you won't win. Winning is unlikely anyway, because the moment you gain any advantage, she will almost certainly escalate the conflict to a new level. So don't waste your breath or energy trying to fight her in these ways.

If she says something derogatory about someone else, don't assume its true. Calibrate it. Check it out. Take on the role of an investigative journalist.

Confronting her is unlikely to resolve your situation either. This will provide her with the opportunity to lash out at you verbally to *'prove'* you wrong, or she will accuse you of being aggressive, even when you are not. As far as she is concerned, she must demonstrate how right she is about how wrong you are! She is likely to say what ever she can think of in the moment to get what she wants.

In her brilliantly titled book *Tongue Fu!*, Sam Horn offers many ways to deflect, disarm and defuse all kinds of verbal conflict. As a general rule, this approach is far more effective than direct confrontation. Some of her suggestions have been included below.

To start with, become aware of what she is trying to do. When you learn to develop a better insight into her motivations, you will feel more in control. Ask yourself *'What is she trying to achieve right now?'*

When you are forced into a confrontational situation, which she knows you hate, she is trying to push you into a defensive position (which, of course, adds to her sense of control). You may try to use logic to show that she is wrong about her latest accusations, but she's playing by different rules, where logic is irrelevant. She just wants you to wear yourself out. And then cave in.

She will ask you questions you cannot answer *'correctly'*.

Assume at the outset that everything she says is designed to prove you wrong and make you feel bad. In the previous chapter we talked about how changing the course of an oil tanker can only be done slowly. You need to be clear about what you want to achieve and how to manage her outbursts. This is part of a longer term, slower strategy. In order to achieve this, you may need to develop a different mindset or approach.

So what do you do? How do you respond to her verbal attacks? In John Gray's book *Men are from Mars, Women are from Venus,* he writes that women just want to talk about their worries and what upsets them. But men as *'fix-its'* instinctively assume that by doing so they are being asked to provide a solution. This is not the case. She just wants to talk. So the first thing to remember is don't bother telling her what she needs to do So, even if the solution is obvious to you. Keep it to yourself.

The next thing to keep in mind is very simple, but may be very hard: talk less. Don't interrupt her. Bite your tongue if necessary. Her attacks are not logical and therefore require no response on your part. Do not feel obliged to provide one.

Not responding verbally is not the same as ignoring her. Don't look away when she is ranting and raving against you. Even though this can be very difficult, be seen to listen attentively. This will decrease the likelihood that the argument will escalate. In many cases (but not all) the act of trying to calm down an angry woman is perceived by her as an attempt to patronise her. So don't try to calm her

210 · Getting Out of Her Clutches

down. Let her vent. Be quiet, even though you might think she is totally wrong about what she is saying. In any case, she is unlikely to be open to anything you say, so don't tell her she is wrong. When you don't challenge her, she will assume you think she is right. Let her – for the time being at least.

When you feel she is running out of steam, ask her *"What else do you want to get off your chest?"* Again, let her talk for as long as she wants to. Don't interrupt her. Just listen. Take it all. When you think she has finished say *"Have you said everything you want to say?"* If she hasn't, say *"What else do you want to say?"* Let her. By being given the opportunity to speak uninterrupted she may calm herself down.

There are also ways you can try to defuse the situation. For example, you can say *"It's a shame we don't get on any more. Do you remember the time when... ?"* And then remind her of a time when you had a great time together. Remind her of times when she felt really good about herself. Try saying something nice about her. Or ask her something about herself. These are known as 'positive anchors'.

She may try to give you ultimatums, forcing you to make a choice. Don't play her game. Respond by saying *"I'm not prepared to make that choice. You can choose."*

Expert manipulators use these tactics for one very simple reason: they work. But they don't have to! They won't work if you don't let them.

When tempers flare, many men make the mistake of walking away. This is almost guaranteed to inflame her rage even more. A woman who feels that she is not being listened to will choose to interpret a man who walks away as employing a 'power play' that is designed to deprive her of her right to be heard. Some men certainly do that (as do some women) but in many cases men do it simply to avoid the conflict and the resultant stress it induces.

If you have great difficulty in coping with her when she is being particularly abusive, take a 10 minute break. Tell her before you walk out that you need to think about what she just said and that you need to go for a walk or sit in another room in order to give it the attention it deserves.

What to say – and how to say it

When she let's you speak, don't behave predictably by telling her why she is wrong about whatever she said. It won't help you achieve your ultimate objective.

Ask her more questions. Do so quietly, a little more slowly, at a lower pitch and without nervous hesitation. You will come across as stronger, without being seen as aggressive. You can start by saying *"I have no control over anything you say or do. What you decide to do is entirely up to you. You are responsible for your own actions."*

Here are a few questions you might like to add;

- *"What do you think the solution is?"*
- *"What needs to happen for you to feel happier?"*
- *"How sure are you that if those changes took place, you would be happier?"*
- *"What are you prepared to do as your contribution to finding a solution?"*

When she is in a quieter mood ask

- *"What did you used to like about me?"*
- *"What has changed?"*

Don't assume all the responsibility for the solution. Include her. Say *"What can we do about this together?"* If she demands a response from you at any time say *"I'm listening to what you are saying. I want to think about it. I'll get back to you."* Don't be drawn by her demands. If necessary, repeat *"I'll get back to you."*

What not to say

When she attacks you verbally, there may be many responses that spring instantly to you mind. DO NOT REACT. Pause, take a deep breath, and keep in mind the following don'ts:

- Don't be sarcastic.
- Don't use loaded words and phrases.

- Don't challenge her or inflame the situation by shrugging or smirking at her.
- Don't allow yourself to get drawn into an argument.
- Don't fight her because it will wear you out.
- Don't say so much. Less is more. You give her fewer 'footholds' to argue, threaten, or disagree with you.

Saying "No"

One of the most valuable lessons in dealing effectively with any difficult person is learning when and how to say *"no"*.

Do you tend to be a bit too polite for your own good? And say *"yes"* too often, when you really want to say *"no"*? But nice people don't say *"no"*, do they? That's what so many people learn from an early age. A history of saying *"yes"* when you would have preferred to say *"no"* is probably a major contributing factor to the problems you are currently facing with this woman.

When you aren't used to saying *"no"*, it can feel really awkward. It's as if you are rejecting the person. You're not. You are just being assertive. You have a right not to do what you don't want to do.

After she has made yet another unreasonable request or demand, pause before you respond to her. This will make you appear to have thought about the answer. If you don't know whether to say *"yes"* or *"no"*, say you want time to think about it. One of the most powerful phrases you can use is *"I'll get back to you on that."* You don't have to make a decision immediately. Even when she insists.

Say *"no"* calmly and politely. The secret is not getting drawn into explaining why you are saying *"no"*. You don't ever have to explain yourself. Simply stick with *"no"*. If she's not used to you standing up for yourself in this way, expect her to demand an explanation. Don't give it to her. If you do, you simply turn your decision into a discussion. She may then try to persuade you to do what she 'asks'. Then when that doesn't work, she will use your 'excuse' to threaten you into doing what she expects from you. Hold your ground.

If she continues to make demands simply adopt the 'broken record' technique. After each demand simply repeat the same word *"no"*. Do it politely and calmly.

Learning to say *"no"* more often is one of the simplest yet most effective ways to regain control in any relationship (and not just those with an intimate partner). Each time you experience even a minor success by refusing to allow yourself to be taken advantage of, you strengthen your self-esteem and self-confidence. Perversely, others will start to think more of you, not less as you might have feared.

Another part of *"no"* is never agreeing to collude with her deceptions. If she has done something wrong and wants you to help her conceal it, refuse to do so. If she insists you do something you aren't happy about simply say *"I am not prepared to do that."* Don't give her your reasons.

Change your language

Stop asking for things by saying *"Can you...?"* or *"Can I..?"* Instead develop a new habit of saying *"I want..."* Say what you want, then add *"How prepared are you to do that?"*

If she calls you a name, pause. Look at her and calmly say *"Repeat exactly what you just said."* See how she responds. It's unlikely she will repeat exactly what she said. If she does, politely say *"I'm curious, when you say derogatory things like that, what are you actually trying to achieve?"*

If you are ever interrupted, out of frustration you may be tempted to say *"Shut up. You never let me finish."* That's aggressive. A more assertive alternative would be *"I am going to finish what I have to say....."*

When she is being unreasonable, consider saying *"This isn't working for me. This behaviour must stop. If your abuse doesn't stop, we don't have a future together."*

When you explain what the consequences will be if her behaviour continues, follow up with this question *"How much does this help you understand what is likely to happen as a result of your behaviour?"*

By gently forcing her to take responsibility for her actions she will normally back down. By slowly and quietly changing the dynamic of your arguments she may become less likely to pick a fight with you and move on to someone who she can manipulate more easily.

Put-downs

If she puts you down in front of others, it's worth considering the following approach: *"We need to talk about how you put me down in company. Would you like to do it now or would you like us to talk about this privately?"* This communicates to those present that you're not prepared to accept what just happened. You will be seen to be reasonable. And it will tell the abuser that she hasn't got away with it. If she says with bravado that it's OK to have a conversation in front of everyone, say the following *"Are you absolutely sure about that?"* Then pause. Don't be the next person to speak. It will unsettle her. And it will tell the group that you are trying to be reasonable.

"When you put me down, what do you think you are achieving? How sure are you that trying to put me down is going to help you feel better about yourself?" It doesn't matter what she says in answer to such questions.

Look her straight in the eye, hold the look for a moment and say nothing. If you threaten her in any way, she will almost certainly taunt you more to test you. And if you don't carry out your threat, she knows that she can walk all over you even more. She wins yet again.

If you make a threat and don't follow it through, you will be seen to be weak. She may then try to push you into an argument. Consider turning to the people present and say something like *"I have asked [her name] to stop abusing me by saying cruel and untrue things about me, but she still insists on doing it. This is not acceptable behaviour to me. How do you suggest I get her to stop? Please let me know what you think later."* At that point, you might want to excuse yourself and walk away.

One man told us that his wife constantly put him down in company. For years he took it without ever saying anything until one day he responded by saying *"Please tell everybody more about how I am so inadequate. I really don't mind. Who knows, it might tell everyone more about you than it does about me. So, go ahead."* She stopped the behaviour, in public at least.

Managing emotional and psychological abuse

She will probably know you better than you know yourself. This means she will know your psychological weak spots, your anxieties and insecurities and is likely to store all this knowledge in preparation for the time when she can use it against.

When you're being bombarded with venom, hatred and anger it can be incredibly difficult to see what is really going on. Sometimes we are psychologically in an *'associated state'*. This means we are so immersed in the pain we can't see the situation clearly. Putting yourself into what therapists call a *'dissociated state'* can help you deal with the situation more effectively.

Imagine you are in the throes of a ferocious argument. Feel the pain, frustration, anger, hopelessness and the sheer hopelessness of the situation. Can you *'see'* the argument in your mind's eye? If so, can you see yourself in the scene as though you are a spectator, or are you viewing the scene through your own eyes?

If it hurts to think about something like that, especially if you have found yourself in those environments on a regular basis, it's highly probable that you were watching the scene through your own eyes. Now do the following if you can. Not everybody finds this easy, so if you struggle, don't worry, it may take a little practice. Imagine the same scene again where you are facing her and can see her through your own eyes. Try to mentally transport yourself to the far side of the room so you become a spectator of the argument in your mind's eye. Try to see yourself as well as her in the mental scene having the ferocious row.

When people learn to do this, many experience a massive shift in the way they feel about it. In this dissociated state, it is far more likely you will experience a lower emotional attachment to the situation. Therefore, in an effort to cope more effectively during these extremely stressful situations, try to remove yourself mentally to the far side of the room to assess what is really going on. This can be a very effective technique to cope with difficult situations.

Are malicious and vindictive women *'mad, bad or sad?'* It's usually a combination of all three. But each time you stand up to her, without being confrontational, and help her to realise that her behaviour has a consequence, you begin the process of re-building your self-esteem and re-establishing yourself as someone who refuses to be treated disrespectfully.

Those with whom we assemble, we will soon resemble.
Anonymous

Chapter 10

Happy Talk

> *I believe that the very purpose of our life is to seek happiness. That is clear. Whether one believes in religion or not, whether one believes in this religion or that religion, we all are seeking something better in life. So, I think, the very motion of our life is towards happiness.*
> His Holiness the Dalai Lama, from *The Art of Happiness*

Anthony Robbins, the bestselling author and personal development coach tells a story about when he was learning to drive a racing car. During a practice session he took a corner very badly. No matter how hard he tried to turn the wheel, he saw a wall of tyres approaching at 150 miles per hour. Then BAM. He hit that wall. The car spun out of control, with tyres flying everywhere.

He was a bit shaken but unhurt, although he admitted his ego got a bit of a bash. When he'd calmed himself, the instructor sat him down in front of a screen to replay video footage of the crash. The instructor asked him lots of questions about what had happened. Then he said, *"Do you know why you crashed?"* Robbins felt it was a bit of a dumb question and said, *"Of course I know - I could see the wall coming at me at 150 miles an hour and I hit it!"*

"Ah," the instructor said, *"That's your problem."* He then added, *"The best racing drivers focus all of their attention on where they want the car to go – not where they **don't** want it to go. If you had made a conscious effort to look down the track and not at the wall, you would have dramatically improved the chances of making that corner."*

This story is a powerful reminder to us in our lives. How much do you focus on the wall when you really should be focussing further along the track? Where is *your* current focus? How much of your thoughts and energy are devoted to reacting and dealing with your problems, dwelling on the life-sapping emotions generated by a difficult woman in your life? Is she succeeding in robbing you of your life energy?

> *People spend a lifetime searching for happiness; looking for peace. They chase idle dreams, addictions, religions, even other people, hoping to fill the emptiness that plagues them. The irony is the only place they ever needed to search was within.* Ramona Anderson

Everyone wants to be happy. And that includes the nastiest of people. Whatever they are prepared to do to others in order to achieve happiness for themselves, is the best they've managed to come up. This is a key point: they really are doing the best they know how.

In earlier chapters we discussed how sociopathic and vindictive women use strategies to induce sympathy from those they target. Having people feel sorry for them goes at least some way towards helping them feel at least a bit better about themselves. But they can never receive enough sympathy to overcome their innate feelings of deep unhappiness. For many, this unhappiness was handed down through the generations by their abusive, unhappy parents. The cycle continues like a contagious disease that gets passed on to the men and women least resistant to their vicious virus.

On the face of it at least, we have *'never had it so good'*. The *'good life'* is enjoyed by millions all over the world. Good jobs, good money, good grown up toys, good homes, good holidays, good health care. But *'good'* stuff doesn't necessarily lead to happiness. If it did, there wouldn't be so many deeply unhappy people. Unhappiness afflicts the rich, poor, educated, uneducated, intelligent, dumb, young, old, male and female alike.

> *Happiness? A good wine, a good meal and a good woman. Or a bad woman. It depends on how much happiness you can handle.* George Burns

Look closely at the people in your life. Look at yourself. And ask *"How truly happy are they with their life?"* And *"How happy am I?"* Behind the façade of a nasty man or woman, you will almost always find someone who is deeply unhappy. Some may have justifiable reasons to be unhappy – yet for every unhappy person you meet, you can also find genuinely happy individuals who have suffered far more.

Unhappy people seem to possess an inner darkness and have convinced themselves that happiness exists *'out there'*. This 'black hole' deep inside their soul constantly sucks in all the energy and happiness from everyone around them. But no amount of that energy will ever be enough to satisfy them or to make them happy.

If only they could have 'more' now. Surely **that** would make them happy? More of the latest designer clothes, a better job, more money, a more loving partner, more children, more expensive holidays, a newer car, then they would be happy. They have to believe other people can and will make them happy and when those people fail to deliver what they demand or expect of them, the unhappy person then has someone to blame.

And that blame is often sufficient justification to make their target's life a misery. They effectively say to themselves, *"I am not happy, YOU haven't made me happy. Therefore it is YOUR fault I am not happy. And you are going to pay. I will then be happy."* It is flawed logic, but it's the best they've been able to come up with. After all, nothing else has worked.

Of course, when her abuse doesn't make her happy, the abuse then intensifies as she consciously or sub-consciously forces herself to 'try harder' – may be THEN she will be happier!

'More' is rarely, if ever, the answer. In fact, truly happy people realise that happiness comes from within. And external material possessions often play a minor role in their happiness.

They know that *"The best things in life, aren't things."*

It's only the unhappy people in the world who are nasty. Happy men and women are not malicious or vindictive because they really don't need to be.

Nasty men and women often become increasingly desperate to achieve happiness and to rid themselves of the intense pain they continue to carry. They will often try anything to do so. Look at any addict, of any type, and you will usually find a deeply unhappy individual. Consumed by their unhappiness they may drink themselves into a stupor, inject themselves with heroin or shove even more cocaine up their nose. So many of them want the world to believe they are having such a great time. If they need to fake happiness for themselves to appear more appealing to their targets, they will do so.

They may indeed feel happy for a short while, but it is only a temporary 'fix'. Another 'fix' should do the trick. But it never does. The underlying unhappiness never leaves. Whatever they do, it is never quite enough. They fail to recognize that the short-term high, delivers a longer-term low.

We are often far too busy pursuing happiness to have time to experience it 'now'. Unhappy people focus most of their energy on what they *don't* have, and take for granted anything they do already have.

> *Happiness is like a cat, If you try to coax it or call it, it will avoid you; it will never come. But if you pay no attention to it and go about your business, you'll find it rubbing against your legs and jumping into your lap.*
> William John Bennett

Happiness lessons from the so-called 'Third World'

A UK poll conducted for the BBC found that the proportion of people who described themselves as 'very happy' has fallen from 52% in 1957 to 36% today. This is despite massive increases in personal wealth. In the BBC poll respondents were asked whether the government's primary objective should be 'greatest wealth' or 'greatest happiness'. 81% wanted 'greatest happiness' as the goal, only 13% wanted greatest wealth.

Here's a challenge for any government; what would you do to create a society where your population didn't take mood-altering drugs, or go binge drinking every weekend because people didn't want, or need to? What impact would that have on crime figures where it has been estimated that in Britain alone up to 70% of all burglaries are committed in order to pay for a drug habit (which is, ultimately, the result of unhappiness).

Bhutan in the Himalayas is the only country on this planet that takes the happiness of its people seriously enough to build it into its government policy. While more developed countries measure GDP (Gross Domestic Product) as a means of benchmarking its wealth compared to other countries, Bhutan introduced its GNH (Gross National Happiness) in 1972. Public places are devoid of advertising messages, (what some call 'colour pollution'). Its government decided that *MTV* should be banned from its TV screens (television itself was only introduced in 1999) because it was felt that it did not contribute to overall happiness. Unsurprisingly, for a Buddhist country, inner spiritual development is seen as just as important as the accumulation of material wealth.

Most of the Bhutan population do not earn much. But they are happy. Cynics (from the West) say it will not last. That may be the case if unfettered commerce is allowed to attack their culture, but the Bhutan government knows that a happier population means nicer people and fewer nasty ones.

Is it a coincidence that in recent years spirituality in its many forms has seen a resurgence in the West? More and more people have a nagging sense that something is not right about their life. Consumerism makes huge promises that it doesn't deliver. People are looking for inner meaning, inner calm and inner peace.

But as ever, the 'West knows best'. Even when it might not.

It's so easy to dismiss or even scoff at the approach of a tiny country such as Bhutan. Bhutanese women are generally happy. Could there be a link between that happiness and the fact that they have not been brought up to believe that all it takes to be happy is to buy the latest miracle cream, a new wardrobe of clothes, etc. etc. etc? Nor do they latch on to the latest diets in a vain attempt to look the way they have been told to look. They are happy with who they are on the inside.

Western society in particular sells a monumental lie: you can buy happiness. Each time we hand over our cash (all major credit cards also accepted!) we are sold a hollow promise. We are told that more (or newer) material possessions will make us happy.

And it doesn't work. We all pay in so many other ways.

Happy people don't feel the need to spend money on products that promise to make them feel better about themselves. They already feel OK with who they are. They don't feel the compulsive need to 'buy' their happiness.

Happy people are therefore bad for profits. In that case, it makes a lot of commercial sense to ensure that potential customers don't feel happy about who they are. This was realised early in the 20th century when the ability to mass-produce products exceeded the natural market for those products. Since then, advertisers and marketers have studied to a shocking degree, what drives our decisions to buy every conceivable product and service.

Today guilt, shame, lust, envy, desire, hope, even hatred are used to entice us to buy into the marketers' promises of happiness and fulfilment. We all like to think that we are immune to their techniques. Advertisers are happy for us to think this, because they also know from their extensive data that their glossy, expensive ads have the desired effects; higher sales and increased profits.

Anyone who hasn't worked in advertising, cannot begin to imagine the effort and money that is spent (and often squandered) on convincing us that we 'need' what they are selling. The most beautiful models are photographed by the best photographers and cinematographers, using the most experienced hair and clothing stylists and the most skilful make-up artists. Everyone uses the best equipment to create images of sheer perfection. And that's before the digital artists get to work on enhancing what you would have thought could not be improved.

Advertisers and marketers continue to invest millions into finding more ways to persuade us to part with our hard-earned cash. Vast sums are spent on research to unlock our purses and wallets. And if that involves making us feel less than perfect – then that's what will happen.

Let's take 'aging' as an example. In just about every 'non-civilised' society on the planet, older people are honoured and respected for their experience and wisdom. They are looked after with pride by younger members of their families. But in the West, young is 'good', old is 'bad'. Think about it. If growing old gracefully (or even disgracefully) was accepted as normal, who would need to spend all that money on creams and potions to fool ourselves and others that we are younger than we are?

66 *There is no path to happiness, but happiness can be a path.* Thich Nhat Hanh, Buddhist scholar. 99

Suffering – and going beyond it

Your happiness depends on how you deal with the suffering you have been experiencing. This is so fundamental that one of the world's most widespread religions, Buddhism, is actually based on dealing with suffering: its 'four noble truths' are:

1. There is suffering.
2. There is an origin of suffering.
3. The end of suffering is possible.
4. There is a path to the end of suffering.

Everyone suffers. Some suffer more than others. Some suffer less. Some think they suffer more than others. Others carry, or have carried, horrendous suffering over prolonged periods. In *Man's Search for Meaning*, the psychiatrist Viktor E. Frankl tells his account of life at Auschwitz, the concentration camp in which millions of Jews were slaughtered by the Nazis during the Second World War. He recalls an incident where a fellow prisoner sleeping next to him appeared to be experiencing an horrific nightmare. Frankl reached forward to wake him, but then realised that even the worst nightmares experienced during sleep couldn't even begin to compare with the horrors of the living nightmare they endured every day. He withdrew his hand, and let him sleep.

Life doesn't make sense sometimes. Good things happen to bad people and bad things happen to good people. As M. Scott Peck states as the first sentence of his classic *The Road Less Travelled*, *"Life is difficult."*

And not everyone deals with their suffering as well as they might. Particularly malicious and vindictive people deal with it the worst.

Unsurprisingly, Viktor Frankl writes a great deal about suffering. This short passage seems to capture an essence of its nature:

> *"..a man's suffering is similar to the behaviour of gas. If a certain quantity of gas is pumped into an empty chamber, it will fill the chamber completely and evenly, no matter how big the chamber. Thus suffering completely fills the human soul and conscious mind, no matter whether the suffering is great or little. Therefore the 'size' of human suffering is absolutely relative."*

    Happiness is not having what you want, but wanting what you have. Rabbi H. Schachtel

This is being written outside a coffee shop in the warm sunshine of Cape Town in South Africa, surrounded by black, Asian and white people, which only a few short years ago would have been impossible within the apartheid system. Only a few miles offshore is Robben Island where Nelson Mandela and fellow prisoners served decades in prison for being black and for daring to stand up to the injustices they saw around them. How is it possible for people like Mandela, who suffered so much and for so many years, to have such compassion for their oppressors? How did they adopt a happy outlook on life when everything about their lives was designed for suffering?

> " *For to be free is not merely to cast off one's chains, but to live in a way that respects and enhances the freedom of others.* Nelson Mandela "

We have been conditioned to seek complexity and dismiss simple truths. As complex as we are, human beings are simple creatures; all human behaviour has a positive intention. And ultimately, everything anyone ever does is in the pursuit of pleasure and happiness, or is an attempt to avoid pain and suffering.

Unfortunately, in our obsessive determination to pursue pleasure and happiness, we so often create negative consequences that are far more harmful than the unhappiness we started with. By alleviating the *symptoms* of our unhappiness temporarily, we often intensify or prolong the actual unhappiness. A vicious cycle.

Many have learned to cope with their pain by taking it out on others. In the context of this book – that means on *you.*

Before we look in more detail at some of the simple differences between happy and unhappy people, ask yourself the following questions:

1. As specifically as possible, why do you think you are as happy or unhappy as you are?
2. On a scale of 0-10, how happy would you say you are, most of the time?
3. On a scale of 0-10, how unhappy would you say you are, most of the time?

Dr Robert Holden, the founder of The Happiness Project and author of *Happiness Now!* has the following thoughts;

"Unless you are happy with yourself you will not be happy with who you are with. Your relationship with your Self sets the tone for every other relationship you have.… Eventually everyone must pay for your own self-hatred; either that or you change your mind about yourself."

"As we become even more strongly addicted to the pursuit of happiness, we are in no way prepared for happiness when it happens… We've been conditioned into believing that happiness has a price tag

- you must suffer in some way before you can be happy. Who you are isn't about how much you've suffered. We all 'suffer' from a highly critical condition of CSJ – constant self-judgement....Nothing is ever enough, if you judge you are not enough."

The following pages highlight the differences between happy and unhappy people. They apply equally to men and women. As you read, reflect on which qualities more accurately describe yourself and your mindset, and which ones accurately represent the mindset of your girlfriend, wife, friends and colleagues? Learn to recognise those around you who are generally happy people and those whose default setting is 'unhappy.'

Whatever a nasty person says or does, so long as you aren't being nasty yourself, it is invariably nothing to do with you. She may go to great lengths to try to convince you otherwise - to lay guilt and blame on you. It's about *her* and her attempts to become happy. It's not about you.

Understand that she is in pain and is doing the best she can. It's her problem that *she* has to deal with. Don't mis-interpret what we're saying here: we are NOT saying - don't care. Just stop caring TOO much.

Inside the mind of an unhappy woman

Unhappy women see life as a struggle. Her focus is on all the elements that make it a struggle, whilst idealising the way she thinks her life 'should' be. When reality doesn't conform to this 'dream', she tends to blame others for her situation and circumstances and will whinge and complain about it to whoever will listen. She sets herself up to fail.

She tends to be so immersed in her unhappiness she can't see the bigger picture of her life. This leads to a loss of perspective. Or she may be guilty of thinking far too much and doing far too little. With a lack of focus about moving forward she is often obsessed with over-analysing the past. And will often paralyse herself into doing nothing to improve her situation to make sure she doesn't make a mistake.

By doing so she establishes in her own mind her status as a victim. Wallowing in self-pity, she ensures the world knows she is a victim, even if she is not. Seeking and demanding perfection in herself and in others, this is probably the easiest way to ensure that she can never be happy. It is impossible to be a happy victim. Seeking outside professional help is seen as a sign of weakness – or not worth the money which may be better spent on new clothes.

As far as she is concerned, she has a monopoly on feeling bad and feels she has the most to lose. Oblivious to the feelings of others, she is only interested in herself, her thoughts and feelings. Favours they 'give' are rarely given without 'strings attached'. She constantly keeps 'score' and knows exactly who owes her for what. Yet she possesses convenient memory loss when it comes to what she owes others.

> *There is a wonderful mythical law of nature that the three things we crave most in life - happiness, freedom, and peace of mind - are always attained by giving them to someone else.* Peyton Conway March

By insisting that others conform to her expectations and wishes at all times, she attempts to control the uncontrollable and demands certainty for everything. She has more rules than she knows what to do with. There are rules for herself, but mainly rules imposed on others. She constantly finds fault with everyone – except with herself.

She refuses to acknowledge that her current situation is the result of all of the decisions she has or has not made up to that point in her life. She always wants everything 'now', and is unable or unwilling to delay gratification. This means she consistently misses out on the 'looking forward' stage. Even though she wants it 'now', she rarely ever enjoys the 'now'. She is unaware or refuses to accept that 'the journey' in life takes far longer than 'the destination'. She is only interested in 'destinations', and therefore misses out on all of the potential of joy getting there.

Loathe to share information because knowledge is power, she makes everything a contest, and seems to thrive on turning even the mundane into a crisis, focusing attention on her and giving herself a superficial sense of having 'power'. She insists on knowing everything that is happening around her and hates being left out of 'secrets'.

She is more interested in taking life's short cuts. Invariably she hates what she does for a job. She probably feels she is not paid enough, and expects or even demands to get back more than she is prepared to give. She says she would work harder if she was given more money first. Money is her prime focus. It doesn't really matter to her who has earned it.

She squanders her time and money, whilst complaining that she doesn't have enough of either. Yet she is always 'so busy', either to impress others with her own sense of importance or as a strategy to stop her thinking about what isn't working in her life. She will use as many devices as she can think of to attract attention to her plight. Although she may want happiness, invariably she is far too busy to actually do anything about being happy. So wrapped up in thinking about her unquenchable thirst for happiness she is metaphorically sitting motionless in a boat floating on a huge lake of the cleanest crystal-clear water imaginable, but is slowly dying of thirst.

She claims to be chronically fatigued on a regular basis, or wants people to think she is, thus reinforcing her status as a martyr. She refuses to link her fatigue with the fact that she routinely has too little sleep. This contributes to her lack of energy which encourages her to pump herself full of caffeine and sugary foods (which also makes her fatter than she would prefer) to give instant energy bursts. A few hours later she experiences a sudden drop in energy as the sugar wears off. More sugar and coffee is then added! Increased irritability follows. She also fails to see the link between her personal stress levels, her irritability, the way she relates to others and how they treat her. Afraid of being hurt she sees others as a threat, even when no threat exists.

She craves true intimacy and affection, yet devotes herself to pushing it away to protect herself in case she gets hurt. She may capture a man by appearing affectionate, but inside she knows that loving anyone else unconditionally is far too risky. She therefore creates impregnable fortresses to protect herself. Her defences are so tight that nothing good can get in either. She wants everything, yet tends to end up feeling she has nothing. This is partly because she isn't interested in the well-being of her partner, she doesn't care about his happiness, success, aspirations or comfort. It's *"Me, me, me"* all the time. She will routinely take *love* from those around her. She may offer less than 25%, yet demand at least 75% of this *love* within a relationship.

One of her closest friends is a green-eyed monster. Her jealousy is the result of major insecurities, and she will accuse her partner of infidelity even though he is being faithful. Her intense jealousy invariably drives him away, sometimes into the arms of another woman, thus 'proving' that her suspicions and jealousy were entirely justified.

She is prepared to hold on to what she doesn't like, afraid that what ever replaces it will be worse. Above all, she is afraid of being alone, in case she meets herself.

Personal development is a waste of time, treated dismissively as *'that psycho-babble rubbish'*. She simply doesn't want to gain a better insight into her plight. Her mind is closed to possibilities that involve her assuming responsibility for her results.

Generally pessimistic, assuming the worst in situations, she is unenthusiastic, easily bored, possesses low self-esteem and lacks self-confidence. She expects others to 'give' her happiness. *"I'm bored. Entertain me."* is how she thinks. When feeling particularly down, she will do nothing, and inevitably ends up feeling worse.

She would far rather be right than happy and actively seeks out conflict to justify releasing her suppressed anger or rage. She generally contributes more to the 'problem' than to the 'solution.'

Being a slave to her emotions, it never occurs to her that she could change those emotions. She is certainly not prepared to accept that she could find something to feel good about right now, in this moment, if only she decided to do so. Instead, she has convinced herself that happiness starts on the *outside* and is supposed to seep inwards.

> " *Happiness is having a large, loving, caring, close-knit family in another city.* George Burns "

Happy men and women

In contrast, happy women (and men) know that happiness starts on the inside and radiates outwards. They choose to be happy, yet are realistic enough not to expect a high degree of happiness all of the time. Their happiness is within them, regardless of their situation. They know that it isn't what happens to them that matters, it's how they respond that counts.

If their circumstances are not of their choosing, they are proactive and take action to improve the situation. They have the confidence in their own ability to turn things around and make things better. Happy people are open to the idea of seeing how something works out without requiring a guaranteed outcome from the very beginning.

They blame no one and know they can achieve almost anything if they apply themselves to it. Even if they fail, they will have gained something in the attempt.

With a youthful outlook on life, despite their true age, happy people manage to preserve their playfulness, joy and enthusiasm. They don't care if they're not 'good' or accomplished at what they enjoy. They like themselves and feel comfortable with the person they have become over the years. This is not the same as being narcissistic.

They know how to have real fun and are able to lose themselves in 'play'. It's part of looking after themselves by ensuring they maintain a healthy work/life balance and manage their energy and stress levels so they don't burn themselves out. They know when to stop. They also know instinctively that being active makes them feel good, whether or not they are aware of the physiology of physical exercise, which releases endorphins into their bloodstream, making them feel better naturally. Happy people are action-orientated. They know that even the most outstanding athletes don't win all of the time. By doing more, they inevitably end up getting more and better results. Not all of these results will be outstanding, but they increase the likelihood that some will be.

When they are feeling a bit 'down', they know that the best way of getting themselves out of it, is to do something – anything! They don't just sit around the house, moping. They act.

Genuinely happy people don't overeat and don't indulge excessively in illegal mood-altering drugs or alcohol. They don't need to.

Looking after themselves is a priority. They know that food, exercise and getting enough sleep are critical to their sense of well-being. They make a personal commitment to do what it takes to be physically, mentally and emotionally fit. They schedule quality time to do this each and every week. They always have enough time to do what is important to them.

Because they understand what 'enough' means to them, they don't feel the need to consume or buy the latest fashions or unnecessary faddish toys. Able to delay gratification, they also benefit from the added advantage of enjoying everything twice: once whilst looking forward to it (which costs nothing), and once again with the actual experience.

Generally, they feel good about themselves and who they are, regardless of what shape or size they may be. If that shape or size starts to bother them enough, they accept the responsibility to do something about it, and then do it.

They refuse to beat themselves up emotionally and just concentrate on being and doing the best they can. At the same time, they won't allow people into their lives who consistently 'drain' them. They have learned to protect themselves against toxic people and poisonous influences.

These are the people who love their jobs and would probably do it for free because they aren't driven by money. Money just seems to come to them. Prepared to give more than they gain, they invariably find they receive more than they expect. Even when they don't love their jobs, they accept them and do their best without complaint.

Happy people are generally relatively uncomplicated. What you see is what you get. They have no hidden agenda and don't feel the need to impose rules on anyone else. If they have to reprimand someone, they do it respectfully, kindly and in private.

They don't always need to be right, and willingly accept that they don't have the monopoly on all good ideas. Not afraid of failure, they realise it's just a part of life. They listen to the opinions and views of others without feeling threatened. They are also open to feedback, which they take without resorting to defensiveness.

They become what they do and what they think about. They have 'good intentions' in everything they do and wish harm on no one.

They always look for, and see, the good in others. Without needing to keep score, favours are given freely with little or no expectation of 'repayment'. Happy people are always happy for other people's success, and are proactive about helping others to feel happy. That in itself, makes them happier, too. They always seem to have time for others and actively collect friends and happy memories.

When it comes to love, even though they may have been hurt in the past, they aren't afraid to love unconditionally.

Happiness is made up of lots of little moments. Happy people know that everyone can make a decision to be happy right now – in this moment. They have learned to enjoy the 'now'. Unhappiness is no one's destiny. It is up to each of us to choose happiness and focus on that, rather than what we don't have. Choosing to be a happy person means accepting full responsibility for who we are and what we achieve in life. It means accepting that we are supposed to feel good about ourselves and not feel guilty when we experience happiness.

In short, happy people just are.

> *If you were happy every day of your life you wouldn't be a human being, you'd be a game show host.*
> Gabriel Heatter

How many of the unhappy and happy traits did you personally identify with?

Remember - unhappy men and women are simply doing the best they can to cope with their life. Become more aware of what good things happen to you every day. Be kinder to yourself and those around you.

Happiness is a choice, and is free to anyone who embraces it, so long as you don't try too hard to be happy.

Chapter 11

Full Esteem Ahead

> *Sticks and stones may break my bones, but names will never hurt me.*

This couldn't be further from the truth. Names hurt.

The human body has a remarkable ability to heal itself quickly from even serious physical wounds. New tissue starts to regenerate immediately. Broken bones, once 're-set' will naturally fuse together within a few weeks. Even the humble scab protects a cut to the skin to help speed recovery.

But being called names is a different matter. We like to think we can deflect them. We delude ourselves into believing that horrible criticism is like *'water off a duck's back'*. In reality, each time we are called a hurtful name, especially by someone who claims to love us, or knows our weak spots, it flows into our *Reservoir of Suffering*. At the bottom of this reservoir is our self-esteem. It just sits there minding its own business. But as each new 'hurt', gets poured on top, that self-esteem is crushed by the sheer weight and pressure bearing down on it.

Our self-esteem is drowned by the combined effect of these slurs and put-downs. Because many come from those closest to us, we tend to accept them as being true. Much like a ship-wreck at the bottom of the ocean, our self-esteem is confined to the depths of our despair.

Commercial divers lift precious artifacts from the depths of the sea to the surface by attaching buoyancy aids to help with the lifting. So it is with salvaging your own self-esteem – one of the most precious cargos you possess.

Your self-esteem can float (even fly) again. Salvaging a self-esteem that has been damaged can take a long time, and requires a concerted effort on your part. Especially when you consider how many forces are at work to push it down again.

Propaganda experts know that the lies and distortions they spread become *facts* if they get repeated often enough, but the same process can work for the good too. Repetition is the key to improving your self-esteem. You must create an environment for yourself that nurtures you, and provides constant reinforcement by the constant repetition of more empowering thoughts and beliefs. This can take time. If you were abused for many years in say a long, miserable marriage, expecting to regain a healthy self-esteem within a matter of only a few weeks, is unrealistic.

How's your self-esteem right now?

Low self-esteem affects your relationship with others, your physical and mental health and your attitudes towards sex. It can also lead to eating disorders, drug or alcohol abuse. And stress. With stress come headaches and stomach aches, accompanied by a recurring sense of feeling overwhelmed. Constant tiredness and wanting to sleep or just to lie down during the day are all symptoms of stress. Sleep is thought of as an escape.

If you have been subjected to physical or psychological abuse and your self-esteem has been eroded over a long period, it is almost certainly worth seeking professional help. Sadly, those who are in most need of expert help, are the least motivated to do anything about it. They feel so bad about themselves, so depressed, so lacking in energy or so overwhelmed by a pervading feeling of hopelessness, that they cannot take the steps necessary to get help. They may even convince themselves that they don't deserve such help anyway.

They have learned to believe they are as bad as they have been told. In some cases, especially among men, they will sometimes perceive getting help as a sign of weakness; proof that they are indeed as pathetic as they have been told.

Some convince themselves that they have too many problems, not enough time, or not enough money to do this 'right now'. These are excuses of course, not reasons. Such feelings and patterns of thought are a recognised sign of someone who needs to find professional help. See your doctor first. Ask to be referred to a specialist. It could be the best decision you make about re-starting your life. Find some books on self-esteem and self-confidence. Adopt the quick-fix ideas and strategies later in this chapter. These will become the oxygen that will fuel your recovery and inflate those buoyancy bags to lift your self-esteem. So, make a decision to adopt small improvements every day from now on. Invest in yourself.

Your inner critic

Sadly, after years of being put-down, or being made to feel bad about themselves, many people develop a most unfortunate coping strategy. They learn to put themselves down before anyone else can 'get in first'. By doing this, they fool themselves into believing that they have insulated themselves from the hurt of others, but it's the equivalent of punching themselves in the face. So many men and women with low self-esteem beat themselves up constantly, creating invisible deep-rooted bruises and emotional scarring.

Unfortunately, they've heard insults and put-downs so often from someone who professes to love and care about them, that they MUST be true, right? Wrong! But even though they are not true, we start to believe them. What is worse, your inner critic may even start to agree with these put-downs!

We all have an 'inner voice'. This voice can be supportive or destructive. The inner voice of those with low self-esteem tends to become their most savage and vicious critic, even worse than the nasty woman in their life.

If you're thinking right now, *"I don't have an inner voice."* That was it!

Ideally, our inner voice should be encouraging, helpful and supportive. Think of this voice as a potential coach. If you were an international athlete how well do you think you would perform if you were constantly told how incapable you were of winning any races, or improving on your previous *'personal best'*? Who would want a coach like that? But it's surprising how many of us allow our inner voice to drag us down. Its motives are sometimes honourable. This voice exists to help and protect you. Unfortunately, it doesn't always do a great job. Well-meaning it may be, but it can get a lot of things wrong about you.

For example, if your inner voice thinks you won't be able to achieve something, it may be negative to the idea of helping you in order to protect you from feeling so bad when (not if) you fail. But that's no help at all, in fact it's a hindrance, because the voice knows that if you don't try something, you cannot possibly succeed. Therefore, the voice proves that it is right, and you are kept in your place.

Whatever you do to re-build your self-esteem, much of that effort will be wasted if you don't redefine the relationship you have with your inner voice. No matter what progress you make in other areas of your life, if your inner voice is highly critical, it will scupper most of your efforts, dragging your self-esteem back down to the bottom of your *Reservoir of Suffering* where it may believe your self-esteem belongs.

You are the result of all your thoughts, all your reactions and responses to whatever has happened in your life. You are the sum of all the decisions you have made and all of those decisions you may have been too afraid to make.

That voice has been with you for so long, you have probably never questioned the accuracy of anything it has said to you, or its motives. Your inner voice can be your own personal ambassador, but often it's an assassin.

What scripts has your inner critic used against you, perhaps for decades? Does it tell you what you aren't capable of? Why you don't deserve to be happy? How and why you are unworthy of anything better? Why you deserve the abuse you receive?

This voice will often repeat all of the negatives you've heard from others in the past. Sometimes that voice will make it impossible for you to succeed in order to ensure that it is right and you are wrong. That critic can become a toxic dump. The words it continues to use could have been poisoning your psyche for decades.

How often does it express itself so forcibly that it sounds like it is stating facts about you when they are only opinions? How often have you challenged what is said to you? And how often has it told you not to confront anyone else because you *'will'* end up feeling bad or worse than you do already? There is no actual certainty that anything *'will'* happen, but we blindly accept whatever this critic tells us as fact. If it is never challenged, your inner critic will govern the decisions you think you are making and ultimately create a life for you that inevitably proves your inner critic is correct!

This inner voice routinely interprets a situation, or something someone says and persuades you to respond in a particular way. That voice has perfected the art of making everything sound so true and reasonable.

Your reactions may not be based on the reality of the situation. Your inner critic merely assigns a meaning to the situation that may or may not be correct. It could be based on wildly inaccurate assumptions. Sometimes your inner voice will even tell you what other people are thinking about you, but this voice does not have telepathic powers. It is probably wrong, but again, we never seem to question or challenge the accuracy of anything it says to us.

How much does that voice run your life? Does it keep reminding you of everything you got wrong in the past? How often does that voice stop you from enjoying your moments? What you think, and what you do, based on your thinking, has a massive effect on whether you undermine or enhance your self-esteem. It's really worth knowing what effect your thinking is having on yourself. It's not what others tell you, it's how you decide to interpret what they say that matters more.

We all like to imagine we think logically. However our thinking often gets distorted to reinforce what we already believe, and those beliefs are not always correct. They are not always healthy. In fact, some of them at downright harmful to us. Learning to recognise and decide what you allow your inner critic to tell you can help move you forward and improve your self-esteem.

How to take control back from your inner critic

When you improve your self-esteem, you increase your options. You will feel better about doing so, which in turn helps you improve it even more. You must realise that your inner voice is yours. It is not the full you, it is just a small part of you - you own it. This means you can control it. It is almost like having a pet; you can own a puppy but you have to take responsibility to train it not to pee on the floor or to bite visitors. Use obedience training on your inner voice too. It takes time, effort and energy, but it pays off in the longer term.

How might you behave differently if your critic was not trying so hard to control you? Remember that this voice is not you. It's someone who wants to control you. Give your inner critic a name. It doesn't have to be a flattering one. You can disagree with this voice. You can argue with it. Although, it's probably not a good idea to do this out loud unless you know you are alone! Confront your critic. Prove your critic wrong. Tell your critic to shut up. When you hear negative comments from your critic. Yell at it *"Delete, delete, delete."* or *"Shut up and get lost"*, *"You're poison. Go away."* Come up with your own comments if these aren't strong enough for you. When your critic starts to have a go at you, tell it to stop. If it carries on anyway, internally yell at it *"Stop. Stop."* What if you could turn down the volume of your inner critic, or even switch it off entirely? Actually, you can. Give it a try. You own it, and you can do with it whatever you want. Do what *you* want, not what *it* wants.

"You're always so stupid." And variations of such personal attacks are routinely used by an inner critic as universal put-downs. How often has it called you *ignorant, insensitive, lazy* or *selfish*? Many of these critical statements are simply wrong and often very harmful. They become so common that most go unnoticed, but not unfelt.

Become far more aware of what you tell yourself. Let's suppose, for example, you have learnt to believe that you are stupid. How might you prove such a comment is totally incorrect? Do it now. For the purposes of this exercise, write down a list of situations or incidents where you have behaved in a way that demonstrates conclusively that you are not stupid. What good decisions have you made in the past? What good results have you created? What are your best achievements? You may find it difficult at first to come up with answers to these questions, but you have definitely achieved a great deal in your life. Surrounded by negative comments from others and hearing your inner critic repeat such attacks the truth about your achievements can be obscured. Universal put-downs that go unchallenged, contribute to at least a dampening of an otherwise healthy self-esteem. When you hear your inner critic using words such as *"always"*, *"never"*, *"you should"*, *"you must"* – challenge it and demand proof that what it says is true. When you become more self-aware, you may discover that these words are used far too much.

Remove the words *"should"* or *"must"* from your own vocabulary. Become extremely aware of those who try to use those words on you. Increased awareness will help you question the motives of those around you. These are 'loaded' words and easily lead to feelings of shame, guilt and disapproval. So become more aware of others who accuse you of *"You always....."*, *"You never ...."* They are trying to exert power over you. Don't let them.

In the same way that your critic has constantly and repeatedly put you down over the years, it's essential that you learn a new habit of repeating healthy thoughts. You might think this is silly, but it really works. Notice more of your successes. Every time you do something right, quietly congratulate yourself. You're slowly starting the process of proving your inner critic wrong, and clearing space in your mind for a constructive coach to contribute.

Practical ways to boost your self-esteem

Stop putting yourself down. From now on, make a decision not to allow your inner critic to say anything that undermines you. Ever. And stop letting your inner critic blame you for everything. It's wrong about you – yet again! It may take some time to re-train yourself and silence your inner critic but you *can* do it.

Decide to become more assertive. Being assertive is about respecting yourself as much as respecting others. Aggressive behaviour is not to be confused with assertiveness; aggressiveness is the equivalent of marching into somebody else's country. Assertiveness is standing your ground to ensure nobody marches into yours.

It was mentioned in an earlier chapter but is worth repeating; learn to say *"no"* more often. Wean yourself off the notion that you have to say *"yes"*, when you would prefer to say *"no"*. The fear of disapproval often stops us. In reality, we tend to think more of people with clear boundaries and who will not allow themselves to be taken advantage of. Someone who expects you always to say *"yes"*, may be 'put out' or unhappy with your decision, but over the longer term you may earn more respect from that person.

If someone puts you down, or makes jokes at your expense, politely say *"Please stop doing that. I don't like it."* If they dismiss your request, repeat what you said calmly and politely. If they insist on making fun of you for being *'so sensitive'* simply get up and leave the room if you can. Just because you let people do it in the past, it doesn't mean they should be allowed to continue. It's better that they choose to think you have no sense of humour than to allow them to make you feel bad (or worse) about yourself. Just stop everybody from getting away with it. Do it calmly. There is no need to get irate or emotional about it.

Stop making assumptions about what people think of you. You cannot read their minds, so don't be so sure they think poorly of you.

Stop letting others have what they want at your expense. Each time you allow this to happen, it chips away a little more of your self-esteem and reinforces any feelings of inferiority you might have.

Identify the toxic people in your life and make a decision to minimise the time you spend with them. If you can't avoid at least some contact, make a concerted effort not to tell them about your plans and aspirations so they won't try to talk you out of pursuing what you want. Who are the people that make you feel good about yourself? Invest more time with those and not individuals who make you feel bad about yourself.

Who do you perceive as the authority figures in your life? Parents are inevitably on the list. Gaining approval from these authority figures is usually important for most people, but when those authority figures have practically made a career out of putting you down, perhaps it's time to delete them from your list of people that you want approval from. After all, they've never done it before, so it's unlikely they will ever do it in the future.

Make a list of everything you like about yourself. Find out what your friends like about you. Ask your friends what they think you're particularly good at. Write down everything. Ask only those you trust. Don't ask the individuals who have been responsible for putting you down in the past.

Some other things to think about; what is working in your life? What isn't working as well as you might like it to? And what actions can you take to improve the areas that aren't working and how those things make you feel? Make a point of congratulating yourself each time you do something well. This helps you become more attuned to what actually works in your life. Reward yourself more often. List your achievements; everything from swimming a width of the swimming pool to running a marathon. Everything. You might find it difficult, so try carrying a note pad around with you for a while so you can write down your past achievements as you think of them.

Do more of what *actually* makes you happy, as opposed to what you *hope* will make you happy. Decide to do something new every day. Add together a lot of little things. This can lead to big improvements. Create a list of all the places you want to go to and all the things you've always wanted to do. From this constantly evolving list, find something each day to look forward to. Use your list to set yourself a new, personal 'enjoyment' goal every month; that's 12 new goals in a year. To make this happen, plan ahead more. Make appointments with yourself. And don't cancel on yourself. Your needs are at least as important as anyone else you would make promises to. By actively finding ways to reward yourself AFTER you've enjoyed yourself, you reinforce the healing effect that these happy moments have on your life.

Ask yourself questions like these:

- If I could do anything I wanted, and were guaranteed of success, what would I do?
- What new skills could I acquire?
- What new hobby could I immerse myself in?

New activities can help you break out of the self-destructive thinking that often leads to harmful introspection. Worry and guilt have been described as the 'pointless emotions'.

Another way to feel better about yourself is to volunteer some of your time to a worthy cause.

There are some extremely high-performing individuals in the world. Invariably they are incredibly busy, yet they look after their physical wellbeing by investing time in themselves for exercise and relaxation. You can do the same, but only after you decide to make 'you' a priority.

Invest time in making friends with yourself. Even though you may not feel like it, find ways to interact with other people. Make a decision to get out more. If you want help about meeting people, you might want to get a copy of Roy's little handbook *Meet Greet and Prosper*. When you know the techniques for *'working a room'* you might learn that it's easier than you thought.

If and when someone gives you a compliment, have the grace to accept it. From now on, **never** invalidate it by dismissing what they have said, even though you may intend it as being humble. It disrespects the giver of the compliment. Simply say, *"Thank you. That was a nice thing to say. I appreciate it."* Never say, *"Oh, it was nothing."*

Become more aware of what you allow into your head. Avoid harrowing movies and books or humiliating television programmes. Seek out uplifting entertainment.

66 *I will not let anyone walk through my mind with their dirty feet.* Mahatma Gandhi 99

Accept that you *can* change if you want to do so enough. All change can be a bit uncomfortable or even frightening at first. Acting *'as if'* you have confidence in what ever you do can be a major contributor towards actually being more confident. By making small changes and improvements, as your confidence grows you become more inclined to make even more changes and improvements. Slowly you will start to notice a change for the better in the way you feel about yourself.

Sometimes we can't seem to help what we think about. Especially if or when we are in emotional pain. If, for many decades, you have been put down, used, abused, taken for granted, made to feel guilty, frustrated, bad, wrong, fat, stupid, lazy or selfish, it can be extremely difficult to feel happy about yourself. Perhaps you have been told such things for so long and so many times it seems the only sensible thing to accept is that they must be true. It is possible that everyone who said those things is wrong. You may not realise this, but you *can* change your emotions. All it requires is making a choice. You can *decide* to feel something more empowering and more useful to you.

Try this brief exercise. Sit or stand; look down at the floor; make your shoulders rounded and take on the appearance of a depressed person. Now, without changing your physical posture try to feel happy. You will probably find this difficult to achieve. Next, stand up straight; look up; breath deeply. Then, again without changing your posture, try to feel depressed. It's difficult to do so. One of the simplest and most powerful ways to improve the way we feel is to simply stand up straight.

May be it's time to forget what has happened to you in the past. The entire world is open to you. You can do anything you want – if you want to do it enough.

Learn to accept that it is OK just to be you.

We become what we think about. So, practice visualisation. See yourself being more confident and handling situations better. See those around you with happy smiling faces. Expect to be successful. This will improve the likelihood that you will follow through on your new behaviours. Experience feelings of quiet confidence and happiness. Practise your new behaviour with people who don't know you.

Finally, become the person you are meant to be.

Last thoughts

Compiling this book has involved a great deal of research and extensive interviews with victims and abusers. What alarmed us the most were the huge number of examples we were given that demonstrated beyond any doubt that *'women with malicious intent'* operate everywhere. So many kind and gentle men and women we spoke to had personal experiences or knew at least one person who had horrific experiences of trying to deal with such women (and so often unsuccessfully).

One woman we talked to, so accurately defined these malicious women as *tapeworms* because they eat their victims from the inside. So, make a decision to stop allowing yourself to be manipulated and abused by being eaten away in this manner.

The most disturbing part is how in so many instances, malicious women simply get away with it, free to find their next targets.

Become more aware of your own weak spots to minimise the likelihood that you will be targeted by a malicious bully. Stop being an emotional punch bag.

Learn to recognise when someone is attempting to *'hack'* into you, in the same way that a computer hacker may try to gain access to your computer and use or abuse the data stored on it, or how a computer virus will try to worm its way into your hard drive and cause as much damage as possible. You need to develop your own *anti-virus* protection to recognise possible attacks and refuse access to these harmful and malicious viruses. Don't allow yourself to be infected by them any more.

Remember, we are not responsible for what others say or do. However, we *are* responsible for how we choose to respond to what happens to us.

We sincerely hope that this book brings these issues to a wider audience, generates constructive debate and that in some small way (or even in a big way) stops or at least minimises the destructive effects of these *'women with malicious intent'*.

Finally, regardless of whether you're a man or woman, or whether you have been attacked or abused, perhaps in a truly horrific way over a prolonged and sustained period, regardless of what he or she says, does, or threatens, no matter how hateful, malicious, vindictive, deceitful, violent, angry, unreasonable or how unjustified and unfair it has been, learn a new way of responding to those memories and their behaviour.

Remember, some of these women are not deliberately vicious, it could be that they are simply doing the best they can under their own painful circumstances. You don't have to go as far as liking them – just try to understand them. From understanding can come empathy and compassion.

You too may feel deep pain – real pain. You may feel threatened, frustrated, angry, outraged even, but regardless of how 'right' you believe you are, we all need to learn one very simple mantra, and decide to live by it. As impossible as this may seem - and this applies equally to yourself,

"Do no harm."

> *To laugh often and much; to win the respect of intelligent people and the affection of children. To earn the appreciation of honest critics and to endure the betrayal of false friends, to appreciate beauty, to find the best in others, to leave the world a better place, whether by a healthy child, a garden patch or a redeemed social condition. To know even one life has breathed easier because you have lived. This is to have succeeded.*
> Ralph Waldo Emerson

Appendix - Due diligence checklist

This checklist is comprehensive - deliberately so. Don't feel compelled to attempt all of it. Just select what is appropriate to you, and don't even consider doing all of it in one session. The following is not infallible and should not be used in isolation, but if you discover that your girlfriend is not ticking a significant proportion of the important boxes for you, it could be time to consider seriously that your relationship should end. Remember, too, that if you feel the need to ask her these questions, she must have the opportunity to ask you the same ones. The same rules of full disclosure and honesty must must apply.

Personal information

Full name. Date of birth. Place of birth.

Family

- How would you describe your relationship with your mother? Your father? Your brothers or sisters?
- How would you describe your parents' relationship?
- How happily married are they?
- How has that affected your own views about marriage?

Medical

- Are you on any mood-altering medication? If so, what?
- In particular, do you use or have you ever used tranquillisers or antidepressants? If so, what were the circumstances?
- Do you have or have you ever had compulsive or obsessive tendencies?
- Were you ever abused as a child? Mildly, moderately or severely?
- Have you at any time received professional counselling or therapy for that abuse?
- How successful was this for you?
- What history of mental illness is there in your family?
- In particular, have you suffered or do you suffer from clinical depression, schizophrenia or bipolar disorder?
- Have you ever been diagnosed with any other personality

disorders? If so, which ones? What treatment have you received?
- Have you ever threatened or attempted suicide? If so, what were the circumstances?
- Have you ever had an eating disorder such as anorexia or bulimia?
- What treatment did you receive?
- What other therapy have you ever received? How did it help you?

Drugs and alcohol
- What are your views on the use of recreational drugs?
- What personal experience do you have of recreational drugs?
- Have friends, family or work colleagues ever tried to tell you that you may have a drink or substance abuse problem?
- If so, how did you react?

Sexual health
- Have you ever contracted an STD (sexually transmitted disease)?
- If so, what and when?
- Have you ever had an Aids/HIV test? Why?

Legal
- Have you ever used an alias or a false name? If so, why?
- Have you ever been cautioned by the police? If so, what for?
- Have you ever been arrested? For what?
- Do you have a criminal record?
- Has a family member, partner or friend ever threatened or actually taken legal action against you for any reason?
- Have you ever been sued by anyone? What were the circumstances and the outcomes?
- Have you ever threatened to call the police to 'get back' at someone?
- Have you ever threatened to harm someone in any other way?
- Have you ever made allegations of sexual or physical violence against a previous boyfriend or husband?
- If so, what were the circumstances?

- In particular, have you ever been reported or arrested for violence against men?
- If so, what were the circumstances?
- Have you ever deliberately harmed yourself in any way?

Financial

- How financially responsible would you say you are?
- How financially irresponsible are you?
- How many credit, debit or charge cards do you have?
- How many store cards do you have?
- How much credit card debt do you have?
- What other debts do you have?
- How long have you had this debt?
- What are you doing to pay off whatever debts you have?
- Have you ever borrowed money from friends, partners or family members?
- Did you repay them all and in full?
- How important is it to you to repay all your debts quickly?
- Have you ever been taken to court for the non-payment of debts?
- Have bailiffs ever attempted to recover money from you? What were the circumstances?
- Have any courts ever made financial judgments against you?
- Have you ever been declared bankrupt or gone through an individual voluntary arrangement (IVA)?

Emotions, attitudes and values

These questions give an insight into *how* your partner thinks.

- What have you ever done that you wish you hadn't?
- What and who do you hate? And why?
- When was the last time you felt really happy?
- What would make you happier? Why?
- What do you most like about your friends?
- What is it that you most want to improve about yourself?
- How often are you "short" or "prickly" with strangers?
- In what circumstances do you believe that treating strangers badly is appropriate?

- Who has hurt you? What did you do about it?
- If you had your time over again what would you do differently in your life and why?
- What are your biggest regrets?
- How do you cope with not getting what you want?
- When do you believe it is acceptable to criticise others?
- How important is honesty and trust to you? Why?
- How do you consistently prove your own honesty and trustworthiness?
- How often do you change your mind when you make promises?
- How much do you care about what other people think of you?
- How responsible are you for your own actions and behaviour?
- Have you ever stalked anyone?
- If so, what were the circumstances?

Past relationships

- What type of people have you tended to attract in the past?
- How and why have most of your past relationships ended?
- When you think of failed relationships you've had, what part did you play in their break-up?
- With how many former lovers are you still friends?
- In what ways have you taken revenge against a former lover?
- In what ways have you used your sexuality to get what you want from past relationships?
- What does 'commitment' mean to you in a relationship?
- How do you usually sort out relationship problems?
- In what circumstances is it acceptable to put someone down or criticise them in private or in public?
- How do you feel about your partner having just a friendship with a former lover?
- When things are not working in a relationship, do you try to stay together? If so, why?
- In what circumstances do you walk away from a relationship?
- On average, how much are you the problem and how much are you the solution when you have had disagreements with any of your ex-partners?

- How many times have you been engaged to be married, but did not marry? What went wrong?
- How many engagement rings have you kept for 'sentimental reasons'?
- Have any former partners suffered from depression and attempted or committed suicide?
- Who are the people who have caused you the most pain?
- How often have you been jealous?
- How often has your jealousy been totally unfounded?
- How many times have you cheated on previous partners?
- Have you ever secretly accessed a partner's e-mails or cell phone to read private messages?
- Have you ever rifled through a partner's private documents?
- When would you find it acceptable to lie to a partner?
- Have you ever read someone's private diary or journal?
- Why do you believe it was justified?
- How often have you felt neglected in a relationship?
- How 'needy' would you say you are?
- If you have ever lived with someone before, has your partner ever thrown you out? What were the reasons?
- If I asked that person, would they say the same? If not, why not?

Marriage and family
- What does the institution of marriage mean to you?
- How much do you want to be married? Why?
- What do you believe marriage would contribute to your life?
- What are you prepared to give up in order to be married? And how do you feel about that?
- How important is monogamy to you? Why?

Future life together
- How important is having children to you?
- As specifically as possible, why do you want children?
- What would children add to *our* lives together?
- How would you define the role of a father?

- If I went out to work and you chose to stay at home, perhaps to look after our children, how would you expect me to contribute to the marriage?
- How demeaning is the idea of looking after a marital home if I was the person who went out to work?
- How would you want us to divide our labour?
- What needs to happen to ensure that you don't ever *feel* as though you're being taken advantage of?
- How much might you resent putting your career on hold in order to have children?
- If you had children, how much would you want to continue working? Why?
- If you had a choice of career or children, what would it be and why?
- What would you do if you discovered you were pregnant today?
- How would you expect me to respond?

You and me

- Why do you want to be with me?
- What do you want more of from me?
- What do you want less of from me?
- What do you believe I get from our relationship?
- What do you contribute to our relationship?

Carefully listen to what is said to the last two questions in particular. How much of what you hear is actually about what your partner wants from the relationship and not what they actually contribute?

About the authors

Roy Sheppard

For many years Roy was a BBC TV and radio presenter and reporter. And a visiting lecturer at Cranfield School of Management's full time MBA course.

As a journalist, he has written for national newspapers and magazines and interviewed countless global business leaders, politicians and celebrities. He is author of the following books; *Press Pause on Your Life, Your Personal Survival Guide to the 21st Century, Meet Greet and Prosper, Rapid Result Referrals* and the audio programmes *The Secrets of Successful Freelancing* and *Network to Win.*

Today he works as a conference moderator, often chairing complex, unscripted discussions for many of the world's largest and most successful organisations.

Mary T Cleary

Mary founded Amen in December 1997 to help male victims of domestic violence. Over the years, as a nurse, she treated a succession of men who suffered injuries that could not have been caused 'by accident' as most men claimed. They were too embarrassed and ashamed to admit that they had been wounded, sometimes quite horrifically by their wives or girlfriends. By travelling with ambulance crews to the scenes of domestic violence, she discovered that on occasion, injuries were sustained by men. Since 1997 Mary has devoted herself to helping these men in practical ways, and raising awareness in the media and with governments about how men continue to suffer from on-going and widespread gender discrimination.

About Amen

Amen is a global authority on the issues affecting the men and their children who are victims of domestic abuse. Amen's male and female volunteers provide;

- A helpline
- Advice, support and legal information
- Support group meetings
- Networking men with others in similar circumstances
- Counselling/therapy services/bereavement counselling
- Court accompaniment
- One-day training courses for health professionals
- Lobbying national and international bodies

In Ireland alone, women's organisations receive over 25 million Euros a year in public funding. Men's organisations receive next to nothing. It's the same story around the world.

Through its website (www.Amen.ie), Amen reaches out to male victims globally with its help and support.

Appeal
If you have been a male victim of domestic violence, or can identify with the plight of men who have, please make a donation to Amen. You can be assured that the money will be well-spent on helping improve its services.

To make a donation please visit www.Amen.ie/goodguys.htm

Newsletter
To receive an occasional e-mail newsletter dealing with the issues raised in this book, please subscribe by sending an e-mail to: Newsletter@ThatBitchBook.com

Recommended reading
Visit www.ThatBitchBook.com/books.htm for a recommended reading list on the topics raised within this book.

For men who adore women; WowCardz

When you see someone who evokes a 'Wow!!', just pass them one of these fun cards and keep walking. Most women 'glow' when given these cards. It means more because nothing is expected in return. Of course, if you are a woman and would like to hand one of these cards to a guy that gets your 'wow' – please do!

On the back of each card it says
> *"Something special about you has compelled someone to give you this 'wow'. Pass on this card or keep it to remind yourself that you have been appreciated*
>
> (space below for a personal message)

> *"Remember – the card giver can't talk to you unless you choose to talk to them."*

For more information or to order inexpensive packs of these cards visit www.WowCardz.com

Other books by Roy Sheppard

The refreshingly direct no-tech way to increase your business.

For experienced sales people, or for those who run their own business, practice, agency, firm or consultancy and may 'hate' selling. This book helps you deliver increased sales, higher commissions, more profit, in less time whilst feeling good about yourself.

Do you brighten a room when you walk in - or when you leave? What mistakes do you unwittingly make when meeting and greeting strangers?

This handy book of pocket wisdom offers answers to those questions and many more together with hundreds of practical tips and ideas.

To order these titles and others
visit www.PeoplePortfolio.com
or your preferred bookstore.